OBJECTIVES, OBSTACLES, AND TACTICS IN PRACTICE

Objectives, Obstacles, and Tactics in Practice is the first book that compiles practical approaches of the best practices from a range of practitioners on the subject of working with Stanislavski's "objectives," "obstacles," and "tactics."

The book offers instructors and directors a variety of tools from leading acting teachers, who bring their own individual perspectives to the challenge of working with Stanislavski's principles for today's actors, in one volume. Each essay addresses its own theoretical and practical approach and offers concrete instructions for implementing new explorations both in the classroom and in the rehearsal studio.

An excellent resource for acting and directing instructors at the university level, directing and theatre pedagogy students, high school/secondary theatre teachers, and community theatre leaders, *Objectives, Obstacles, and Tactics in Practice* serves as a resource for lesson planning and exploration, and provides an encyclopedia of the best practices in the field today.

Valerie Clayman Pye is an Assistant Professor of Theatre in the School of Performing Arts at LIU Post, where she teaches Acting, Voice, and Speech, and Shakespeare in Performance. She is the author of *Unearthing Shakespeare: Embodied Performance and the Globe* (Routledge 2017).

Hillary Haft Bucs is an actor/improviser, playwright, and director. She is an Associate Professor of Theatre at Western New England University where she teaches Acting, Improvisational Comedy, and Playwriting.

OBJECTIVES, OBSTACLES, AND TACTICS IN PRACTICE

Perspectives on Activating the Actor

Edited by
Valerie Clayman Pye and
Hillary Haft Bucs

Routledge
Taylor & Francis Group

NEW YORK AND LONDON

First published 2020
by Routledge
52 Vanderbilt Avenue, New York, NY 10017

and by Routledge
2 Park Square, Milton Park, Abingdon, Oxon, OX14 4RN

Routledge is an imprint of the Taylor & Francis Group, an informa business

Library of Congress Cataloging-in-Publication Data
A catalog record for this title has been requested

ISBN: 978-1-138-33593-6 (hbk)
ISBN: 978-1-138-33597-4 (pbk)
ISBN: 978-0-429-44341-1 (ebk)

Typeset in Sabon
by Swales & Willis, Exeter, Devon, UK

To Thomas, Jolie, and Owen: the heart of all of my objectives.
– *Valerie*

To Jeff, Chloe, and Marissa: for your love and support, and for helping me overcome the obstacles during this amazing journey. You all are my North Star.

– *Hillary*

Contents

Acknowledgments

Long before this was a book it was an email thread, born from a conversation between kindred spirits; an excited conversation – the kind that begins as simple small talk, gathers momentum, and keeps calling out to you, demanding to be heard. Together, we were curious about the nuances of how we engage with the core principles of Stanislavski's work with our students. Like Ophelia – "we know what we are, but know not what we may be" – we knew well how we were currently teaching these principles, but knew not how else we *could be* teaching them.

For years, both at the annual conference of the Association of Theatre in Higher Education (ATHE) where we first met, and throughout the academic years that followed, we returned to this excited conversation. Each new group of students brought new challenges, and our collaboration was built from late-night conversations and a mutual desire not only to be stronger, more dynamic artists, but also to be inspiring and effective teachers. We are grateful to see this discourse develop into a resource that will spark new conversations about how we do what we do. We are grateful to ATHE, and particularly to the Acting Focus Group, for providing us – and so many others – the opportunity to share ideas and the scholarship of our practice on a regular basis, and for the community that we've found there.

We are incredibly grateful to Stacey Walker and Lucia Accorsi from Routledge for their belief in this project and their ongoing support. It has been our absolute pleasure to work on this under their steadfast guidance. We extend our deepest appreciation to Rose Bonczek for her feedback during the writing of this book. We also wish to acknowledge our contributors, who have enlivened this conversation in ways we couldn't have possibly imagined when we first began.

Valerie would like to thank her students for keeping her constantly curious; her colleagues at LIU Post, especially Dr. Cara Gargano, Chair of the Department of Theatre, Dance, and Arts Management; Jon

Fraser, David Hugo, and Maria Porter for all of their support. A special thanks to Rose Bonczek for her friendship over the years and for inspiring so much of her teaching. Valerie is grateful to her husband, Thomas, and her children Jolie and Owen for sharing it all (and for letting this book clutter up the dining room table on a daily basis). Many thanks to her very special extended family: it really does take a village! Finally, thanks to Hillary for her keen eye, for being a wonderful collaborator, and for her willingness to debate every detail (ad nauseam!).

Hillary would like to thank all of her Western New England University Theatre students (especially in the 2018–2019 Acting I classes), the actors in *Footloose* and *Hello, Dolly*, the members of the *WNE Stageless Players*, and *Improv on the Rocks* for the joyful exploration that inspired her work, and for their curiosity and eagerness to play. Hillary is grateful for their passion and inspiration, for letting her experiment with the exercises, and for cheering her on during the writing of this book. Hillary would like to thank her colleagues at Western New England University, especially Dr. Saeed Ghahramani, Dean of Arts and Sciences; Dr. Anita Dancs, the Chair of the Department of Arts and Humanities; Dr. Jennifer Bieneke and the Committee on Release Time; and Dean Maureen Hart Keizer, Associate Dean of Students for their support over the years and in the writing of this book. Thank you to Robert Barton, Professor Emeritus of the University of Oregon, for his willingness to support the development of "Improvised Fantasies" based on his "Rehearsed Futures" exercise. Hillary would like to express her gratitude to Dr. Kiki Gounaridou, Smith College Theatre Department; and Dr. Harley Erdman, Chair of the University of Massachusetts Department of Theatre for their friendship and mentorship over the years and for inspiring her writing and teaching. Hillary is grateful to her husband Jeff, and her daughters Chloe and Marissa for all of their support and cheering on. Many thanks to her family: Susan Worth, Herbert Haft, Gary Worth, Jennifer Nelkin, and Elaine and Roger Bucs for their love and support (and for letting her finish this book at their home during the family vacation). A very special thank you to her co-editor, Valerie, for her partnership, expertise, amazing editing prowess, and for always saying, "Yes, and …"

Introduction

It's not hyperbole to say that traces of Stanislavski's legacy can be found in nearly all forms of text-based actor training in the Western world. There are countless books dedicated to the history, practice, and study of Stanislavski's system, and this volume does not aim to add – nor compete – with those. Instead, *Objectives, Obstacles, and Tactics in Practice: Perspectives on Activating the Actor* aims to offer a sampling of the best practices of how to engage Stanislavski's key principles with students of all levels, from beginner to advanced. This volume serves as a complement to those other books – one that practitioners and teachers of practice can reach for that will help to infuse their teaching and their rehearsals with fresh, new perspectives.

We've focused this volume around the three key principles that serve as the backbone for the actor's process – particularly for the actor-in-training. What we have no intention of doing is to attempt to prescribe a particular methodology or to advocate for a particular way of doing something; quite the contrary. This volume serves as a celebration of the very different ways that *objectives*, *obstacles*, and *tactics* are explored through practice. We fully expect that readers will already have their own ways of engaging with these principles; perhaps ways that they are not willing to give up. What we have found over the course of compiling these essays, is that there are so many complimentary approaches that can be adopted – both one-time explorations as well as lasting implementation.

We will categorize this volume around the three key principles of objectives, obstacles, and tactics, although we fully recognize that each of these three is so intricately dependent upon the other two that this division is – to some extent – a forced and a false one. However, although these three are so intertwined, we've organized them according to each exercise's primary focus. We foresee that you will be able to read this volume either in a linear fashion, or you can choose to dip

1

into each of the essays at random, according to your needs and interests. Although these essays can stand independently, we have found that the dialogues that have emerged between and amongst them have been especially compelling. Themes surrounding actor training and Stanislavski's teaching have encompassed areas from play and spontaneity, to improvisation; the evocative use of imagery, the use of technology as a tool that ignites the actor's process, and also the holistic integration of the body-instrument across specialization in actor training – the desiloization of disciplines, if you will – where "acting" engages fully with "voice"/"movement" disciplines not as discrete units of study, but as a cohesive whole that moves together towards a unified expression of a given text.

Simultaneously, these essays also serve as a snapshot of the myriad ways that other key practitioners – such as Michael Chekhov, Moshé Feldenkrais, Keith Johnstone, Rudolf Laban, Arthur Lessac, Sandford Meisner, and Viola Spolin – along with game theory and the psychologist Mihalyi Csíkszentmihályi's theory of the flow state, all interface with Stanislavski's system. The amalgamation and integration of these influences expands how we think about the current landscape of actor training pedagogy. How do we teach what we teach? How do we engage with Stanislavski's principles *today*? How are *we* able to activate Stanislavski's teachings in ways that our predecessors couldn't?

The training of actors has long been an oral tradition. Before Stanislavski documented his approach, the mechanics of actor training remained the work of tradesman, passed down through experiential learning and research through practice. While the advent of formalized actor training programs and the proliferation of MFA Acting and Theatre Pedagogy programs indicate that this may no longer be the case, much of the work we do as actors and as acting teachers remains steeped in the oral tradition. The essays featured here have all been adapted or adopted – co-opted, if you will – from work that was introduced through practice. Each author has endeavored to trace their work to its origins, but that lineage has not always been elucidated clearly. At times, we could be caught in a "chicken and egg" conundrum: an author's work has paralleled the work of others even when there was no distinct relationship between the two. In these cases, we have tried to illuminate those parallels, even if the exercise was not directly derived from that particular source.

We'll begin with objectives, since without objectives, it is difficult – if not impossible – to address obstacles or tactics. First, we'd like to begin by addressing that the objective, which Stanislavski referred to as the "task" or the "problem" (*zadacha*) has been translated to mean different things. David Hugo's chapter (which doesn't fall in the objectives section, but in the one dedicated to obstacles) addresses the ways in which Sharon Carnicke unpacks the influence that Elizabeth Reynolds Hapgood's translations of the term has had on actors' understanding of the "problem." The actor's approach begins with an understanding of what the task is – the central "problem" that needs to be solved; the goal one wishes to achieve, the "task" to undertake. As the actor strives to achieve these goals, to undertake the task at hand, they[1] are met with resistance – obstacles – that impedes their ability to achieve their desired result. Like David Hugo's, Kevin Hoffmann's chapter holds that resistance at the core of the actor's pursuit – so much so that it is incorporated directly into the articulation of the goal itself. In all cases, as the actor encounters opposition (both subtle and deliberate), they respond to that resistance with a change in the manner of their pursuit; they shift tactics.

When talking about objectives, it is important to acknowledge that there is not just one way to phrase an objective statement, though each of us may think that our way is the "right" way. There are different schools of thought about which objective statement is the most playable, or even the most accessible to students. Our collaborators come from different schools of thought on how to phrase the objective, and only a handful of chapters actual specify their methodology for how to craft the statement. As a reader, know that your way of crafting the objective statement can work with all of our exercises, and you may even have fun trying a different method. For instance, many of us were trained to formulate the statement like this: I want/need + powerful playable verb + other character + desired result. For instance, such a formula would look like this, using the play *Proof* (that is referenced in Jeanne Leep's chapter): I want to force Hal to give me his backpack. Why do you need to force Hal to give up his backpack? You can add the desired result to your phrase as well (so that/in order to): I need to force Hal to give up his backpack so that I know the truth. Another possible phrasing places the result you want to achieve from your partner in the foreground; the statement leads with the effect you want to have on your partner. In this case, the phrase could be: I want/need to get Hal to give me his backpack. An Essential Action format (Practical Aesthetics) could be: to make someone do the right thing. When the obstacle is built into the phrasing, the statement could look like this: I want to force Hal to hand me his backpack, but I am also attracted to him or he is preventing me from grabbing it. Kim Shively's chapter on Point of View draws upon Meisner's work, and in this instance, the phrasing is based on a character's personal lens. In this instance, the example could be phrased: to get a foe to give me the truth (or to hand over his backpack).

Since this volume aims to offer perspectives on activating the actor, there is perhaps no better place to shift our focus than to obstacles – those resisting forces that drive us to change our course in pursuit of that thing that we absolutely need. The perfectly phrased objective statement means nothing if it lacks resistance. Our chapters on resistance engage multiple facets – from Janet Hayatshahi's physical exploration of the principle to Davida Bloom's real-world application, which introduces the concept to beginning actors through circumstances familiar to us all. While it's easy to mistake resistance as a negative force to be overcome, Fabio Polanco and Diane Bonfiglio identify how obstacles can lead to the highly coveted flow state (Csíkszentmihályi).

As the actor is met with opposition and resistance, they must adjust and respond to how they aim to achieve their objective. These shifts in tactics also serve to galvanize the actor. Along with objectives and obstacles, this trinity serves as the North Star of the actor's process. Each time the actor shifts and strategizes, the objective ignites and the resistance is challenged. This makes for dynamic performances. Our chapters on tactics range from what appears to be child's play – a game of tag, in the case of Lynn Deboeck's essay, to more serious play: improvisation (Nathan Stith), game theory (Jeanne Leep), and Johnstone's status work (Jean Dobie Giebel).

We can also see how a tactic shift differs from a beat change, in the exercise "Hunter Hunted" (Valerie Clayman Pye), which illustrates how tactics shift organically within a beat, and how the whole trinity shifts once there is an event. It's not unusual for actors in training to find it difficult to discern the differences between beats and tactic shifts, for change is often experienced intuitively. All of the essays featured in this volume are designed to place the actor at the moment of discovery, and they do so in innovative ways.

Across all three of these key components, there are chapters that investigate how Stanislavski's work is enhanced and enlivened by the work of his successors – those both directly and indirectly related to the primary teaching. Anjalee Deshpande Hutchinson explores Michael Chekhov's work with psychological gesture as it relates to objectives. Dennis Schebetta draws on his experience as a Meisner teacher to use Meisner's connection to spontaneity play freely. Conrad Alexandrowicz illustrates exciting ways to use Rudolf Laban's work to activate tactics. Caroline Good explores tactics through explorations with Arthur Lessac's NRGs, while Lesley-Ann Timlick applies work from Moshé Feldenkrais in her investigations. Deric McNish combines work from both Viola Spolin and Louis Colaianni in his explorations.

As we are training actors, we are also helping to develop and expand actors' imaginations. Maria Porter taps into the use of images as a way of helping actors to connect to heightened text in Greek drama, scoring the "un-scorable." Hillary Haft Bucs's exploration of "Rehearsed Futures" uses improvisation to help actors to see what is at stake when it comes to overcoming their obstacles. Big, bold choices come into play in John Kaufmann's exercise, which culminates in an actual competition that requires both commitment and a sense of humor. Timothy Johnson shares an imaginative exercise that is perfect for the first day of class, at any level.

Several of our chapters look to the changing topography in actor training, as technology shifts the possibilities of what we can accomplish in our classrooms. Rebecca Covey and Aaron Alpern incorporate text messages into an exploration of tactics that enables students to respond in real time. In "Creating a Physical Score in a Snap ..." Tom Pacio leverages students' social media skills to help them curate scores as part of their character analysis and development. Finally, Welker White identifies simple, yet incredibly effective ways to use the camera we carry in our pockets as a diagnostic tool for assessing objectives, obstacles, and tactics in practice.

We hope that you will find in our volume not only potential solutions to some of your classroom challenges, but also inspiration to develop your own new and exciting ways to solve the pedagogical puzzle of the actor's craft.

Notes

1 Throughout this volume, we will use the inclusive pronoun "they" as it corresponds to the actor, rather than limiting actors to binary gender pronouns.

PART I
PLAYING OBJECTIVES

ONE

Money in Your Pocket

Meisner, Objectives, and the First Six Lines

Dennis Schebetta

As a Meisner teacher, I often saw students struggle to connect the improvisational elements of the technique to their scene work. After weeks and weeks of students moving from the simple Repetition game into more advanced elements of independent activities and "the knock on the door,"[1] they would come alive with spontaneity and truthful moments, but as soon as students were handed a scripted text, they would revert to old habits, displaying preconceived ideas and falling into clichéd line readings. Also, the exercises in the Meisner sequence felt physically static, with little movement in the space. This work greatly benefits when supported by outside movement and voice work. When movement is not incorporated in some way, all physical inhibitions return as soon as actors are up on their feet. This, in turn, stifles the inner impulses, and the core of Meisner's work is connecting to those honest impulses. "The First Six Lines" came out of a need to create an easier transition, both mentally and physically, for students from improvisation to scene work – so that they could realize that the scene should feel as spontaneous as the Repetition game and they should respond in the same way – truthfully and off their partner's behavior.

Much has been written about Sanford Meisner's technique and the foundation of "the reality of doing."[2] Most are familiar with the early exercise, the Repetition game (i.e. an actor makes a statement and the other actor immediately repeats exactly what they hear and so on).[3] Not all are aware, however, that Repetition develops into a complex improvisatory exercise that conditions the actor's instrument; building listening and concentration skills, developing the imagination, heightening awareness of truthful impulses, and honing an actor's point of view. (If you are unfamiliar with Meisner's technique and the Repetition game, I would recommend reading any of the books in the bibliography).

Unlike a traditional Meisner teacher, I modify the Repetition game so that students are standing and then incorporate movement exercises. This keeps students present and connected, not just to each other but also to their bodies. I use plush indoor snowballs which are soft but have some weight (juggling bean bags work just as well) to add a sense of play, which is a variation of an exercise developed by John Basil (who had worked long ago with Grotowski). Not only is it fun, but also gets them to physicalize the text and add meaning, even if they don't know the context or given circumstances of a scene. The snowball fight also gives a specific objective ("to win"), even if that objective is not necessarily the one they may end up using in the scene.

In the Meisner technique, the objective is introduced well into the sequence. Students have been working with the Repetition game for several weeks, adding independent activities, relationships, and the "knock at the door." At this point, there is less and less actual repetition and the exercise feels more like an improvisation, which is our goal: to eventually drop the Repetition game completely once it has served its purpose. The objective is introduced as a simple and specific imaginary justification to start the exercise (a reason to knock on the door of their scene partner who is in the room working with an independent activity). For example, you loaned your scene partner 100 dollars and now you need it back so you can take your girlfriend out to dinner for your anniversary. It may never even come up in the exercise as the interactions of the actors take priority over "trying to make a scene." At this point, I have observed students fall into the trap of ferociously latching onto their objective, forgetting about working off their partner. The First Six Lines addresses this problem, as a reminder that characters are not always direct, that there is subtext. As actors, we need to trust that our objective is there underneath and driving our actions. As William Esper states,

> A good objective is like having money in your pocket. Let's say you leave your apartment one morning with eighteen twenty-five. You put the money in your front pocket and you forget that it's there. You don't walk around the streets of New York City saying over and over: 'I have eighteen twenty-five in my pocket! I must remember …'.[4]

In other words, objectives are not something you can act. They exist as part of the work, but actions (or tactics) are the specific building blocks of behavior upon which you achieve (or don't achieve) your objective.

The First Six Lines

The First Six Lines is a variation on how students in a traditional Meisner sequence would work with text on their first scene. Typically, students are handed an entire scene and asked to memorize it by rote, without reading the entire play or crafting a character other than themselves. Students work on the scene as an exercise in moment-to-moment work, letting memorized text replace the repetition, but with the same spontaneity. I concentrated on the first moments as a way to prepare them to work on the rest of the scene, as handing out a whole scene to an undergraduate to be memorized immediately can be an overwhelming task for them.

Although The First Six Lines grew out of my work with the Meisner sequence, it could easily be modified as a way to introduce a scene regardless of the techniques you are using to train your actors. As a teacher working in any scene class, I find my attention focusing extensively on the beginning of scenes because if the actor missed that first moment taking in their partner, or didn't know their objective, point of view, or relationship, then it really didn't matter what else they did later on.

In the Meisner technique, the first scene should have a simple conflict between two characters, each with their own distinct point of view. Scenes should mirror the earlier exercises, with one character knocking on the door or entering and another character in the room doing an independent activity. Although some Meisner teachers choose scripts from the early 20th century, I tend to choose contemporary plays by recent playwrights. Contemporary plays have accessible language and offer greater diversity. I also encourage students to work on unfamiliar scenes in order to discover new material and make fresh choices.

Prior to this exercise, partners should be assigned and roles cast, but students should not know what play or scene they are doing yet. It is important to frame this as an exercise, not as a scene, so that the stress and pressure of putting on a performance won't seep into these early stages. Print the lines out in a large, easily readable font (14 or 16 pt.) and remove the title and characters' names, as well as any stage directions (especially if there are any adverbial acting directions). The character's names can be replaced with A and B, as if it were an open scene.

For example:

                    A
        It didn't work.

                    B
        You're not doing it right.

                    A
        I'm following instructions.

                    B
        You always do this.

What You Will Need

- A copy for each student of the first six lines of their scene as described above.
- A copy of the full scene as excerpted from the playscript.

- A secondary handout for each scene which gives simple details of the given circumstances, including the characters' relationships to each other. These details should include time, location, space, relationship, and any incidents that may affect the action in the scene. For example, one character has recently learned that the other character may be having an affair with her husband.
- A small plush or foam ball. I'm a big fan of indoor snowballs but you can also use juggling bean bags. I'd avoid using tennis balls or other bouncing balls so students aren't spending more time chasing balls than working on their text.

Physical Setup

You will need ample room for your students to move around the space so it is best to clear the room of chairs or black boxes.

Directions

Preparation

Assign partners as A and B based on how you have cast the scene. Give the handout with the first six lines and inform the students that they must memorize the words by rote for next class. (You may want to demonstrate to them what "by rote" means – mechanical or flat, no intonation or "acting." Have two actors stand up and read through the lines and guide them to do less.) Treat this as though it was a self-contained exercise, without telling them it's the first six lines of their scene.

Exercise

Have the students pair up with their partners and ask them if they have memorized their lines exactly. Most students will be comfortable with the words, but have them review the lines anyway. Then have them put the paper down and do a speed-through, until they can do the lines without hesitation or mistakes. Next, have the students walk around the space as they say their lines, walking alongside their partner, careful not to bump into anyone. Again, aim for no hesitations or mistakes (though there will be both once they start moving). After that, have each partner face each other, a few yards away. Give each pair an indoor snowball. Have the students first throw the ball back and forth underhand until they find a consistent rhythm that is mutually agreed upon, without discussion. Once they feel they have a good rhythm of throwing the ball, tell them to once again go through their lines, with the objective of keeping that same rhythm. Many of the students will drop some lines (and balls), which may provide some laughter and chatter. If the students seem confident, then modify it by having them once again walk around alongside their partner in the space, but adding the throwing of the ball as they walk. For a more

advanced variation, you can have them separate as pairs so that each is
wandering the space in various areas as they throw the ball, and try to
listen for their lines over the cacophony of other actors shouting lines.

Collect and set aside the snowballs. At this point you can ask questions
about the difference between responding to their partner in the Repetition
game and responding with memorized text. What are the challenges?
Most will talk about getting in their head or anticipating what will be
said. You may throw out the question: How does one keep an improvisational feel of spontaneity when an actor knows what's coming next?

Bring up two students as an example. Ask them to say their lines –
again, with no "acting," simply flat. Emphasize that these are merely
words without any meaning yet. It's their job as the actor to give them
meaning, which we will work on in this exercise. If you are working
within the Meisner sequence, review the concepts such as the reality of
doing and "living in imaginary circumstances." Their goal is to listen
and be present with their partner, reacting off of their behavior. The
challenge, of course, is that with repetition it is clearly all improvised,
so of course everything feels spontaneous.

Ask them to use the text as if it were a repetition. This means that
the text will no longer be "flat" and without emotion. They should be
achieving a more "conversational reality." It should seem like two
people actually talking and interacting with each other. The students
need to work off the other partner and what is being given in terms of
behavior. For example:

```
                    A
          It didn't work.

                    B
          It didn't work?

                    A
          It didn't work.

                    B
          It didn't work.

                    A
          It didn't work!

                    B
          You're not doing it right!

                    A
          I'm not doing it right?

                    B
          You're not doing it right.
```

Some students may try to "act" the scene, reverting to habits that
may have inhibited them in some of the repetition work, but remind
them to work off their partner, not play a scene. You haven't added

any imaginary circumstances, relationships, or an objective yet. You may want to tell them what Meisner said: "The text is like a canoe and the river on which it sits is the emotion."[5] This is not to say that emoting is acting, but emotion can and often is a residual of the behavior and the actions you see on stage. The aim is to avoid a cliché in reading the lines. If the line is "I love you," one may think that this line should be spoken in a romantic way, but if two characters are in a fight, it may come out quite differently, depending on what is happening in the scene. Context is key, not just from the given circumstances, but from the behavior of our scene partner.

When the students are ready, add the snowballs and tell them they are going to say their lines while they have a snowball fight. Have each student line up across from each other and tell them to use as much as the space as possible. Their objective is simple – to win the snowball fight. The other students can cheer for who they want as the snowball game commences. If a student drops a line, tell them they can always use the repetition. (Alternatively, another student can be on-book.) You will notice the lines come out differently and the students will find different meanings in them. A snowball fight inherently has an objective (to win!) as well as an obstacle (the other person). At this point, you may want to have a small discussion about what changed in the language and how it sounded. It's important to note that the "line readings" were not forced or felt like "how they were supposed to be read."

The final step is to give the students a few details about their specific scene to help them craft the imaginary circumstances. Give the students the second handout with the given circumstances. It's best to work just with the pair that has been doing the snowball fight as an example for other students to observe first before giving the second handout to other groups. (You may want to remind the students about how the circumstances affect the scene, especially in regard to environment and relationships.) Also, ensure that you relay any important information or incident that may have happened immediately before the scene. You don't need to give too many details. Keep it simple and specific. Relate it to the circumstances they have already been working on in their crafting of the exercises from the Meisner sequence. Remind them that the aim is spontaneity, so that it feels like improvisation, just like the Repetition game. Have the students work with the text and side-coach as they play the scene. Ask the students watching about what they observe in the scene and how the actors are now relating to each other. Have the actors work through the scene again.

With the entire class, discuss what objectives they think might be present for each character. Not from the context of the words, but what they saw in terms of behavior and how the actors interacted. Once you have talked about the objectives, discuss how actions have come out of that objective and relationship observed in the behavior.

What actions did they see in the scene? For example, how did these actors treat each other? What were they doing to each other?

Tell the students that this is how they should work on this first scene together, not as a scene, but as an improvisation with text. Everything the students were doing in the Meisner exercises should be present in this exercise as well. The difference here, as Esper says, "is that instead of catching the impulse and responding with Repetition – or whatever comes to you in the moment – you let the line of text bounce out of you on the impulse created by the other person."[6]

Have the students work in their own groups and give a presentation at the end of class. Then discuss the objectives and actions in each scene.

Homework

At the end of class, hand out the full scenes to your students and instruct them to work on their scenes in this way – memorize the lines by rote and then improvise with the text. After they have worked this way, then have them write down their objective and their actions.

Post-exercise Reflections

Here are some discussion questions you may want to pose as you work through this exercise:

- How did the objective of winning the snowball fight affect the scene?
- Given the behavior you've seen, what objectives do you see in the scene?
- Given the relationship between these two characters and the given circumstances, how do you think that would affect the opening moments?
- Are there any independent activities your character could be doing in this scene?
- If you enter in this scene, what is a simple and specific reason to knock on the door? This could be related directly or indirectly to the given circumstances.
- One of Meisner's principles is "Don't do anything unless the other person does something to make you do it."[7] How does this apply to your objective and/or the actions you play?

Going Forward

The First Six Lines is a useful tool to prepare students to work on their entire scene without making any preconceived ideas. It is important to treat this first scene as an exercise and therefore I don't require the students read the entire play, create a character, or do any text analysis (all that comes later). The focus is for them to remain spontaneous and work truthfully off their partner in imaginary circumstances, all while having their objective resting "in their pocket." Once students realize they don't have to "show" they're trying to achieve an objective and can just perform their actions moment-to-moment, they begin to really have fun and play.

Notes

1 The Meisner Technique begins with the simple Repetition game and progresses into more complicated improvisational work, including adding physical activities while participating in repetition, as well as being "at the door," which includes knocking and entering as the other scene partner is working on an activity. Text is added as scenes learned by rote in order to work moment to moment. A concise overview of the Meisner two-year sequence can be found in "The Meisner Technique" by Victoria Hart in *Training of the American Actor* edited by Bartow, Arthur, 51–96, published by TCG, 2006.
2 Meisner, Sanford, and Dennis Longwell, *Sanford Meisner on Acting*. Vintage, 1987, 16.
3 The following is an over-simplified explanation of the Repetition game. The game requires listening and repeating exactly what you hear. You could even go so far as to tell your students that this is their objective – to put all their attention on the other person and listen as closely as possible ("To listen" is a very playable action). Two actors face each other. One actor begins by making a factual physical observation such as "You have glasses." The other actor repeats exactly what they hear, but instead of saying "You have glasses," she must remain truthful, changing the pronoun to "I have glasses." Then the first actor repeats. The dialogue may look like this:

                    A
            You have glasses.

                    B
            I have glasses.

                    A
            You have glasses.

                    B
            I have glasses.

It is important that students answer without any pause before speaking. In that one-second pause, the brain filters the behavior and inhibits the impulse. We want actors to act before thinking, to achieve spontaneity. In the early work, this is particularly tricky. The beauty of this game is that actors don't have to think of a line, they only repeat. There are no rules for how many times to repeat, but the repetition can change when actors become aware of an impulse, when something happens, such as a smile or a laugh. If an actor sees it and reacts, they make that new observation. Then that becomes the repetition. Another wonderful aspect of the game is that there are no mistakes. If you mishear or blurt out gibberish, then that becomes the new repetition. The rules are simple – we want to keep all our attention on our partner, be truthful in our response, but also keep the observations about them and in the present tense. Everything is about the moment happening now. Not two seconds ago. Not in the future. Avoid chit chat like the weather or what they had for breakfast. There is no pressure to be interesting, to be funny, or to make a scene. If something happens you think is funny and makes you laugh, then you laugh. If you get annoyed, or bored, then that is also valid.

An important point to remember is that this Repetition game is a wonderful tool, but we are not yet doing any acting by Meisner's definition ("living truthfully under imaginary circumstances"). The game evolves as the students evolve, and we add the independent activity, entrances, relationships, and emotional preparation. Once we add the idea of "imaginary circumstances," then we enter the wonderful world of acting. If you are unfamiliar, I'd recommend looking at Esper, William, and Damon DiMarco, *The Actor's Art and Craft*, Anchor, 2008, 33–46.

4 Esper, William, and Damon DiMarco, *The Actor's Art and Craft*, Anchor, 2008, 131–132.
5 *Sanford Meisner on Acting*, 115.
6 *The Actor's Art and Craft*, 163.
7 *Sanford Meisner on Acting*, 34.

References

Esper, William, and Damon DiMarco. *The Actor's Art and Craft*. Anchor, 2008.

Meisner, Sanford, and Dennis Longwell. *Sanford Meisner on Acting*. Vintage, 1987.

Silverberg, Larry. *The Sanford Meisner Approach: An Actor's Workbook*. Smith & Kraus, 1994.

TWO

Psychological Gesture

Michael Chekhov Exercises on Physicalizing the Objective

Anjalee Deshpande Hutchinson

Introduction

Acting for a grade can be very confusing. Acting classes housed in academic settings, such as undergraduate programs, set up a supposition that acting is like many academic situations in which there are singular right and wrong answers, a system that students have been conditioned to accept since kindergarten. The pressure to find the "correct" answer engages the actor's mental capacities in such a way that it often takes over the process of creation. Yet as most acting teachers know, the mental capacities are only one component of what is needed when undertaking the process of creation. And in the initial phase, intellect alone fails to inspire. When asking student performers to articulate their acting choices, students often squirm, uneasy about the "correctness" of their answers. Character objectives when identified purely by thought process, analyzing the given circumstances of a play, are seldom gleaned from a place of inspiration. More often they are "figured out" by making a first attempt at an answer, an answer to an academic question rather than an experiment in response to a creative impulse.

So how do we as educators and artists, within an academic setting, train performers to engage their full imaginations and playfully follow their creative "hunches" before allowing their mental capacities to refine and polish their choices? How do we clarify for students that grades are based on the creative quality of their choices in relation to the given circumstances without paralyzing them with fear? The way we do it is by giving them the tools to circumvent the intellect and glean creative inspiration from a multitude of different access points to their imaginative capacities. One of the most effective tools for doing just that is Michael Chekhov's Psychological Gesture.

As his student, Chekhov's understanding and approach to Stanislavski's work was always from a playful point of view rather than from memory, a strict commitment to authenticity or an intellectual understanding of narrative. Chekhov's work strayed even further away from intellectual approaches after a spiritual reawakening mid-career when, after a breakdown, Stanislavski supported Chekhov's return to health by introducing him to hypnosis, Eastern spirituality, and the work of Rudolph Steiner which in turn introduced Chekhov to anthroposophy. Anthroposophy, as defined by Steiner, is a philosophy which "postulated the existence of a spiritual world comprehensible to pure thought"[1] but fully accessible to humans through the development of consciousness and spiritual perception.

Towards that end, Chekhov's approach to objectives, obstacles, and tactics embodies a playful, spiritual point of view. This approach asserts that performers can draw down visceral corporeal imagery from a Jungian type of creative unconscious, housed in the actor as well as in all of humanity. This takes the pressure off the actor to deduce the "correct" objective for her character and instead invites the performer to pursue multiple creative possibilities for her character objective through the exploration of imagery and physicality.

Within this powerful method is one of Chekhov's most useful tools: Psychological Gesture. This tool not only engages the physicality through vivid imagery, it does so through intuitive kinesthetic response. Psychological Gesture asks the actor to play with physical archetypes in multiple creative ways. Actors experimenting with character physicality and movement are offered the opportunity to see what choices resonate deeply. In this way performers used to working with traditionally analytical methodologies are asked to enter the pursuit of finding an objective backwards, allowing them to first intuit what characters need rather than deciding intellectually what they *should* need. Once the main Archetypal Gesture is unearthed, the actor then takes the next step and colors it with the emotional qualities the actor associates with the character. This takes the focus from the deeply rooted archetypal metaphor to the specific character psychology. Only after the archetype (which symbolizes primal desire) and character psychology (which clarifies emotional need) are both discovered through physical explorations, do we allow the actor to then analyze the objective through an intellectual lens. This end component of analysis, rooted in the intellect, completes the comprehensive process of character development but circumvents the learned behavior of starting with intellect first. Once all three components of the character objective are revealed through a distinct physical manifestation, actors can continue to explore by establishing a gestural character vocabulary. These gestures are produced by continuing the physical investigations into character through the same means that the original Psychological Gesture (the physicalization of what is commonly referred to as the Super Objective) was first discovered. Through these investigations, artists identify several gestures (spiritual, habitual, emphatic, occupational, etc.) that reflect traditional character analysis, including meaningful understandings of obstacles, fears, tactics, and even character biography. This vocabulary becomes metaphoric shorthand for the character that can offer any number of physical variations resulting in a nuanced but consistent performance as the character grows and changes throughout the course of a play. These tools can also be used exclusively as internal tools, offering tangible creative ways to access the inner life of the character throughout the play.

Exercise: Introduction to Psychological Gesture

*Adapted with permission from *Acting Exercises for Non-Traditional Staging; Michael Chekhov Re-Imagined*, by Anjalee Deshpande Hutchinson.[2]

1. The PG Warm-up
2. Archetypal Gesture
3. Psychological Gesture
4. Using the Psychological Gesture (PG)
5. Creatively using the intellect to serve the imagination.

Exercise Goals

*   To access creative impulses and find ways to manifest them in performance.
*   To circumvent the intellect as the first stop in finding acting choices.
*   To explore Character Objective through the Physical Imagination.

What You Will Need

*   Open space to move (ideally a studio space or theatre).
*   Students dressed to move.
*   1–3 hours depending on time available, best suited to 8–16 students at a time; best practice would be two 1 and ½ hour class sessions or one 3-hour rehearsal. If splitting into two classes, consider stopping after teaching the full PG exercise (#3) which defines the tool fully before allowing for the creative use of the tool in character work for the second class.
*   Optional: Have everyone read a play together (before class) that you can reference easily during the work. If you decide to use a play, have them select and memorize a few lines from one particular character you want the whole class to focus on.

Physical Setup

*   Chairs moved out of the way or preferably out of the space.
*   Jackets, coats, and backpacks and other personal items moved out of the way or preferably out of the space.

- Students begin anywhere in the room, eventually (although not from the start) they will need to be arms-length apart from each other and be able to see you.
- Teacher/Facilitator can move through students or be off to one side.

Directions

Part 1: The PG Warm-Up

A good way to begin working with gesture is to have the ensemble move around the space and call out some archetypal personae (examples below) and ask them to find a gesture for these personae as soon as they hear the prompt. If a person takes too long reacting to the prompt, point out to them that they may be trying to think about a solution to the prompt instead of reacting to it kinesthetically. This is a symptom of "looking for the right answer." Ask them to instead fulfill the first gesture that comes to their body (not their mind.) It doesn't matter if it makes sense to anyone else or even to them. Sample archetypal personae:

- King
- Servant
- Hero
- Queen
- Mother
- Lover
- Villain
- Seducer (or Cad if they know the word)
- Temptress (allow gender to be specific so that actors try on both)
- Orphan
- Father
- Mad Man
- Crazy Lady
- Witch
- Monster
- Feel free to add more!

Once they begin, encourage them to make full body gestures in tableau. I encourage this by prompting actors to extend the gesture through the whole body. The first gestures help actors to think in terms of archetypes free of positive or negative connotations, so encourage them to examine the choices they make. For example:

Did you give us a gentle mother – are all mothers gentle? Can you give us a mother that may or may not be gentle but is still mother?

Ask the actors to go from one extreme to the other in the gesture, starting at the opposite extreme to begin. If your gesture is a gesture that unfolds, start at the most folded, contracted place your body can be and then transition before reaching the end. Then ask the actor to sustain the end a few beats.

Ask them not to rush, to have a clear beginning, middle, and end. Ask actors to add some resistance to the movement but at the same time to notice and release any unnecessary tension in the body.

Have half the actors sit where they are and watch the other half. Run through a few more archetypal gestures (AGs). Then switch. Once both sets of actors have run through a series of archetypal personae (APs), discuss with them which archetypes looked similar on all the actors and which didn't. Then ask how this may correspond to the Jungian idea of universal unconscious (the idea that the human unconscious is filled with archetypes that have been created by the whole of humanity and/or society, not by the individual.) Note also the very unique interpretations and how that is okay too – giving rise to the instinctual kinesthetic response.

Then ask if they gave their APs a value judgment (unintended quality). Good or bad. Note that you didn't give them a quality, and if they applied one, that this is not archetypal. A hero who kills one person to save others is not completely good. An evil dictator who cares about their children is not completely bad. These are exciting and complex descriptions of multifaceted characters, but we are not there yet. We are only looking for the archetypal form of the person before we layer story, either good or bad, onto them. If there were any AP that everyone had trouble keeping neutral, ask them to go back and try some of those APs again. Ask them to work to remain neutral in terms of a value judgment, but to give them a full gesture in tableau that extends through their whole body. When they have run through them, ask them what has changed.

Part 2: Archetypal Gesture

With your ensemble, take one session to work through all of the following archetypal gestures. If you have not worked with gestures before, allow the group to go slow and make sure the participants work hard but do not hurt themselves.

There should be resistance: "You get out of this what you put in!" but ask them to avoid strain in regards to their own body. Every actor must be aware of the limits of their own personal capabilities, and if they have an injury they should modify the exercise to allow for the greatest range of motion without further injury. If you do not have *"To the Actor"* by Michael Chekhov (the main reference for Archetypal and Psychological Gesture), it is okay to have them improvise each gesture: "Give me the biggest possible push" so long as they are being mindful of their own limitations and what their body can do.

Ask them to:

- Start from a place of stillness.
- Find the one full body gesture that embodies this Archetypal Gesture.
- Let go of judgment, there should be no value judgment to the gesture, it is neither good nor bad, it just is.
- Have a clear beginning middle and end. Beginning and end should be physical opposites (left to right or up to down, etc.). An equivalent would be the preparation for the action, the action and the aftermath (sustained release). The sustained release should last for a few beats at least.
- Have a sense of form (an attention to the whole body in space).
- Have a feeling of ease (a focus on the movement as satisfying/gratifying to perform in some way).
- Have a feeling of beauty (an attention trying different ways until that one that strikes you as most interesting/captivates the imagination is found – and then a sustained ending point).

Then have actors repeat the movement for 3–5 minutes until they feel it is the strongest representation of the gesture. With each gesture, when actors become comfortable with the physical movement, ask them to incorporate first their breath (inhale should begin the prep, exhale should be middle and end) and then their voices (with sound not words) as an extension of the body. Ask them to use their deep diaphragmatic voices emanating from their abdomens and groins. Urge them to sustain the last moment (just like the sustained release of the physicality) instead of abruptly ending in a glottal shock.

Gestures[3]:

1. Push
2. Pull
3. Throw
4. Drag
5. Smash
6. Lift
7. Gather
8. Tear
9. Penetrate
10. Reach
11. Expand
12. Contract
13. Wring.

Part 3: Psychological Gesture

Once you have worked through all of the Archetypal Gestures, have one to five actors stand and demonstrate one of the Archetypal gestures for you. They can all show at the same time. Then ask for a descriptive "quality" from the other actors. They can be more abstract at first. Give them some examples:

- Cold
- Hot
- Damp
- Sticky
- Swishy
- Dry
- Hollow
- Etc. – feel free to add your own!

Ask the five actors to add each quality to the physicality as they once again fulfill their Archetypal Gesture. A cold push. A hot pull. A damp tear. A sticky gather, etc.

Then have everyone play with abstract qualities attached to the AGs they were already playing with. As they play with the abstract qualities and AGs, add tempo – or as Chekhov refers to them, the quality of *staccato* or *legato*. What happens when the movement becomes slower and rounder? What about quicker and sharper?

After experimenting for a while, introduce one character from the play you are working on if you are working on a play in class or performance. If you are not, often times a fairy tale character that everyone is familiar with works well. Everyone can work on the same character to start. Ask the actors to list some emotional qualities of that character. Examples could include:

- Honest
- Grieving
- Heroic
- Whiny
- Arrogant
- Cruel
- Etc. – add more of your own as you see fit.

Once you have gathered enough emotional qualities about one character, ask all the actors to experiment with these emotional qualities added to the AG they have explored. You can call out each of the qualities and give them time to attach them to their AG. The cruel lift. The grieving throw. The heroic smash. Etc.

Ask them to consider their characters and then ask them all to get up on their feet and move around the room (stopping when they want to work on a PG) and play with at least three different archetypes that may fit their characters, and three different emotional qualities for each archetype. Recommend that as they start with AGs, they try polar opposite AGs to give them new information. If one AG seems right, try the polar opposite gesture to see what you find. Push/Pull, Smash/Lift, Expand/Contract. Once they find a few archetypes they like, they should then work on attaching a few different qualities they like to each of the AGs until they find some particularly interesting PGs. Ask them, what are these PGs to their characters? The greatest desires? The deepest fears? Their internal/external struggles? Moment to moment struggles in a particular scene?

Part 4: Using the Psychological Gesture

Once they have been introduced to AGs and PGs and have found their unique character PG that resonates, ask the ensemble to begin moving around the space working with the PGs. Imagine that there is a scale of 1–7 on how much your character reveals (consciously or unconsciously) about the inner sensation of the PG. Level 7 is large and abstract, the biggest possible physicality of what is going on in regards to the sensations of the PG. Level 7 is abstract and full body. Level 1 is the same internal energy of Level 7, just contained, beneath the surface – but radiating out energetically all around. Michael Chekhov referred to this tool as "Veiling."

Tell your actors to plant and give the full PG when you call out. Call out a few times and then ask them to keep experimenting while moving about the space. This movement could mean stopping and planting to work an AG at full 7 in terms of energy and abstract movement, or using the PG in a more concentrated way at a 1 or 2 while continuing to move. You can be flexible with moving and/or stillness, they don't have to adhere to a rule in the exploration.

Coach your actors:

- Reveal what's beneath the surface at a 2
- At a 6
- At a 3
- At a 1
- At a 7
- Etc.

Coach your actors to:

Expand and make your movements as big as they can possibly be while still maintaining the PG. This largest expression is the gesture at a 7 (out of 7). It can be abstract, grotesque, or cartoonish but the PG must still have all the beginning, middle, and end components in it. It must also be full body.

Now ask them to take their PG to a 5, so less abstract and more realistic on the surface than a gesture at a 7 but more abstract than a gesture at a 2.

Now ask them to take their PG to a 3 and a 1 etc. One should be hardly perceivable. It is not an outward PG but rather one that is happening continually on the inside. Or is communicated perhaps with a glance or a breath. A helpful catch phrase is "Have the gesture just up and underneath everything you are doing" or "Just behind the eyes. Smash with your breath. Gather with your gaze." Etc. Chekhov used the useful word "simmer" – have the PG simmering just below the surface.

Coach them not to ignore their legs and the bottom half of their body! The energy should be up and underneath but "low" and underneath as well: full body movement even when it is completely veiled. When actors are in "simmer mode" – be sure to make them aware that the energy is simmering up and underneath their whole body, not just their face, eyes, torso. Have them practice the "whole body simmer."

If there is time, it is nice to allow half the ensemble to watch the other half during this exercise and then switch. This will allow your actors to see how the large abstract movements still emerge in the veiled expression of them.

When you are ready to move on, ask actors to perform the PG internally at full 7 but externally explore stillness. This is asking the actors to feel the gesture inside but to *try not to show us* the gesture (per se) in movement (although some small movement/expression/ breath may surface.) For example, if the actor's PG is a painful tear (ripping, not crying), have them imagine they feel a painful tearing within them, but in this moment they must remain still. It is often engaging to demonstrate this with one or two actors who may have particularly resonant PGs for the whole class. Then have all the actors explore moving around the room. Or sitting down, standing, etc. Then have a few actors with different PGs moving about the same room with the full resonation of their PGs underneath (internally). And then have one of the actors add a line of text with the PG attached (or have them improvise fairy tale character text). Have all the actors run lines with the PGs attached. Tell them to feel a full 7 underneath but only reveal at a 1. Maybe have them drop into their gesture at a full 7 physically before saying the line again with the PG up and underneath.

Split the group and run the exploration of the internal/external PG again. Ask the actors onstage to end with a point of stillness or a pause and send what they are experiencing out into the audience. Hold them there for at least 3 seconds and then release. Ask what the actors in the audience saw or felt when actors were radiating out into the audience without moving. Most likely your audience members will affirm that the radiation of what is beneath the surface is a very powerful tool in communicating to spectators what the character is feeling and/or going through without the actor having to physically "show" a thing. This is the power of a strong PG. It never has to make it onstage; it lives up and underneath – simmering vibrantly below the surface creating an energetic performance experience for everyone.

The PG is most often used as an internal handle on the character, a way for the actor to understand and manifest the character onstage. It is generally not a visible gesture in performance, although some actors find that the contained gesture, deeply veiled is very exciting when it "appears" in the exploration of a scene. An internal smash can manifest in the tapping of nails on a desk. An internal lift can appear in a smile or a lifted spine. A PG attached to a line becomes supported physically as well as vocally and can take on a whole new meaning.

Chekhov refers to these discoveries as "improvisational jewelry," explorations that result in exciting physical texture in performance. Texture that is decidedly not created through the intellectual answer to questions such as "what are the character's habitual gestures?"

Part 5: Creatively Using the Intellect to Serve the Imagination

(Post-exercise reflections for new leaders to consider as the discussion points.)

As you walk around observing the work, pick one or two actors who have created something resonant. Have the other actors stop and ask them to watch those specific actors you selected. Ask actors in the audience if they perceived an image or metaphor in what they have seen.

Give them examples of other kinds of metaphors that have come out of PG work:

- She was tearing her heart out and throwing it away.
- He was happy to destroy – smashing something joyfully.
- She was lifting something to watch it fall.
- Etc. – add more as you find them in your work or that of your ensemble.

Ask them to consider (and share) the metaphors that could be interpreted from their own character PGs in relation to the role of their character within the play. Ask how their PG metaphors could be revealed throughout the play and how the metaphors of each actor's objectives play out over and over in different ways, like a refrain or the chorus of a song throughout the story. Psychological gesture is an Archetypal Gesture that has a quality (or more than one) added to it.

This gesture is the physical manifestation of what many generally call "the Super Objective." Ask actors how their PGs reveal their character's greatest desire?

Then ask the actors to engage the intellect to complete the PG work. This can be explored through discussion or in writing assignments.

Ask:

- Did any other AGs and PGs resonate in your exploration?
- Can PGs change for characters in a play?
- Is one PG an overarching PG and then are other PGs revealed within the original PG?
- Could other resonant PGs actually be scene PGs or monologue PGs?
- Do they change?
- Are there conflicting desires?
- Could your character's greatest disappointment be revealed through a PG? Maybe a PG that is the opposite of one you were playing with or maybe one that resonated differently?
- How can a PG be an obstacle that your character constantly strives against?

This process asks actors to connect a character's primal AG desire (the "Will" sphere as Chekhov calls it), to the character's emotional qualities (the "Feeling" sphere) becoming the PG. The last section then asks actors to creatively engage in text analysis (the "Thinking" sphere) to further flesh out possibilities for obstacles and tactics from a similar place of instinctual kinesthetic response. Once those discoveries are made, the intellect is utilized to house these gestures (whether externally or internally) in specific sections of the story from which all of these revelations were inspired.

Instead of looking for the objective through the intellect, we find it through the body. These modes of exploration allow the actors to "play with" different kinds of objectives, landing on the ones that resonate most deeply with them in the physical exploration process. This practice of engaging the "Thinking Sphere" last allows intellect to be in service of the imagination, asking ultimately for metaphors that connect the physical Psychological Gesture to the given circumstances of the character and the play.

Although Mark Monday writes in his excellent Chekhov textbook *Directing with the Michael Chekhov Technique* that the PG consists of only two parts; the form and quality of action,[4] I believe adding this final component, the intellect, back into the formula to complete the full interpretation is most satisfying to the student actor. The intellect is used as a tool to articulate the creative and physical discoveries in an artistically engaging way. This gives the actor full access to her/his creative capacities. This ownership yields a pride in the work that resonates with a fully embodied performance. It also places the character within the greater arc of the play.

Physicality on its own cannot continually ignite the actor's imagination to its fullest potential, regardless of how creative that physicality is. Creative physicality must be paired with metaphor and story that awaken the desire in the artist to pursue. Kids jumping on a trampoline will do it for a while, but they are bored easily. Kids imagining that they are trying to touch the sun, that they are Icarus flying, become inspired. The inspiration continues when they continue the story, imagining themselves touching the sun and then falling from the heavens to earth, which in turn awakens a continued desire to pursue. It also launches a desire to imagine what both the flight and the fall would look and feel like and how the transformation occurs. The intellect gives the physicality home and direction within the story.

Conclusion

Psychological gesture is an ideal tool for revealing character objective through the physical imagination: a combination of kinesthetic response and the fertile creative capacity held in the unconscious. By experimenting with character need through gesture and then continuing the exploration with detailed emotional imagery that saturates the gesture, we allow actors to "play with" different kinds of physical objectives, landing on the ones that resonate most deeply with them in the exploration process. Only after they have landed on particularly interesting movements that are exciting to embody are they asked to interpret this movement and how it connects to the play. Intellect is utilized in service of the imagination, asking for a metaphor that connects the physical Psychological Gesture to the given circumstances of the character and the play.

Given the tools of physicality and imagination as entry points, and the encouragement to explore central questions about the world of the play and its people through these entry points, we allow our actors to create beautiful renderings of complex humans that reflect deeply engaging embodied understandings of character. It is not enough to have students answer the question, "What is your character's Super Objective?" We want students to show us. And when they get comfortable with their own hunches as well as embracing creative ways to physicalize those hunches, then we get students less squirmy about "getting it right" and more excited about showing us exactly what they imagined, discovered, and created today.

Notes

1 "Anthroposophy." *Merriam-Webster*, www.merriam-webster.com/dictionary/anthroposophy.
2 Hutchinson, Anjalee Deshpande. *Acting Exercises for Non-Traditional Staging: Michael Chekhov Reimagined*. Routledge, 2018. Exercises 3.3, 6.1, 6.2, 6.3: The Rapture/Veiling and Refrain/PG.
3 Chekhov originally had only seven gestures[1] but The National Michael Chekhov Association (NMCA) offers additional gestures, which have been

employed by many actors. I include them here because they are very useful in practice. Mark Monday, Artistic Director of the Great Lakes Michael Chekhov Consortium includes "Opening and Closing" to the list[2], which NMCA houses under a separate category of exercise. Sarah Kane of the The Michael Chekhov Centre UK has developed a whole series of exciting additional Vocal AGs that expand on Chekhov's gestures and the work of Rudolph Steiner. She describes merging the work as integral, and that "Chekhov work is anthroposophy in practice."[3] Expanding or contracting this list to suit your lesson plan is optional.

[1] Chekhov, Michael. *To the Actor*. Routledge, 2005.

[2] Monday, Mark. *Directing with the Michael Chekhov Technique: A Workbook with Video for Directors, Teachers and Actors*. Bloomsbury Publishing Plc, 2017.

[3] "Notes on Contributors." *Theatre, Dance and Performance Training* 4.3 (2013): 437–439. doi:10.1080/19443927.2013.858902.

4 Monday, Mark. *Directing with the Michael Chekhov Technique: A Workbook with Video for Directors, Teachers and Actors*. Bloomsbury Publishing Plc, 2017.

THREE

Making Sport of Objectives

Teaching through Student-Developed Physical Competition

John Kaufmann

"Make sure they *really* do it," my graduate school mentor emphasized as I prepared for my first semester of teaching at the University of Iowa. He suggested an assignment where students perform a simple act, like tying their shoes, in front of the class. This assignment helped me realize the importance of giving students opportunities to focus on real physical tasks in their acting.

That year, the Iowa Hawkeyes had a remarkable football season, coming from behind to win game after game in the fourth quarter. I had several of the players in my class, and sports became a helpful metaphor for the actor's job. The trappings and pageantry of a football game are inherently theatrical, yet students comprehend that athletes do not *perform* playing football; they simply pursue their physical objectives with abandon. Acting on stage is inherently physical, but beginning students often focus primarily on the imaginative and performative aspects of the work.

To connect the investment of an athlete to the imagined circumstances of the actor, I expanded on the assignment my mentor had taught me. I developed the "Real Action Scene," a dramatic scene that culminates in an actual physical competition between actors. Students create their own characters and context, with scenes that reflect the diversity of students' interests and experiences. Empowered to create personal and physical content, students become less self-conscious and really "go for it" during performances. Audience members are invested as well, aware that they are watching genuine human struggles with palpable stakes. The assignment connects well with Stanislavski's teachings, specifically objectives, tactics and the "magic if." It engages students of varying skill levels and offers objective criteria for feedback. I use this assignment fairly early in the semester, after students have gotten to know each other through collaborative play and they understand the idea of playing tactics to achieve a goal.

Real Action Scene Assignment Goals

After developing, performing, and reflecting on their Real Action Scene, students will be able to:

- Identify and pursue a strong *objective*.
- Understand that objectives have a clear *measure of success* that can be realized in the framework of the scene.
- Employ a variety of *tactics* to achieve their objective.
- Recognize that actors *fully commit* to, rather than indicate, tactics.
- Identify clear, high *stakes* to help actors (and audience) invest in the scene.
- Create *physical and invested* performance.

Assignment Overview

Students will develop and perform an original 4–7 minute scene in which two characters compete in an actual physical contest. The Real Action Scene contains the following elements:

- An established scene context and a challenge to compete.
- Clearly defined rules for the competition, with clear criteria and measure of success.
- A robust pre-contest ritual.
- A clear start to the competition.
- High stakes established and respected throughout scene.
- Meaningful consequences experienced by the players at the end of the scene (an actual reward or consequence).

Step One: Read and Discuss an Example of a Real Action Scene

The class reads a sample scene outline to explore one way the assignment might be realized. Use my example below, or create your own.

Real Action Scene Example Outline: "Joining the Village through the Maabna Challenge"

Characters: Gwikon and Elzdor

Context: Gwikon wishes to join the Maabna Village. To achieve this, Gwikon challenges Elzdor (the local champion) to the "Maabna Challenge." If Gwikon is victorious, Gwikon is welcomed into the village.

Sample Dialogue

```
                    Gwikon
Elzdor, great champion, hear me! I challenge you to
the Maabna Challenge, in order to join you and your
villagers as a full member!

                    Elzdor
Gwikon, you are a filthy intruder! You are not one of
us! I accept your challenge, and I will destroy
you. If you are defeated, you will be marked with
the indelible mud of the outcast! Do you accept
this fate?

                    Gwikon
I accept, champion Elzdor. But if I am victorious,
I receive a plot of land, a pot of gold, and you
yourself will wash my feet in the bucket of
welcomeness.

                    Elzdor
Ha! We shall see, pathetic wanderer. The first to find
three spheres of glory and hold them together off
the ground will be the victor. The time has come!
```

Pre-contest Ritual: Both actors participate in a choreographed dance and chant about the greatness of the village and how all residents must prove their mettle. Then, the players' hands and feet are ceremoniously bound (classmates can be recruited for this). They are blindfolded. They are spun around and placed on the ground. Five "spheres of glory" are hidden around the playing field.

Rules: The first player to find three "spheres of glory" (large rubber balls hidden throughout the space by classmates) and hold them all together in the air is the victor.

Clear Beginning of Game: The village elder [a recruited classmate] blows a trumpet to officially start the context.

Clear Measure of Success: The first contestant to find three "spheres of glory" and hold them in the air is the victor.

Meaningful Consequence

- If Elzdor wins, Elzdor rubs actual mud on Gwikon's face, neck, and arms. Scene ends with Gwikon being "banished" and leaving the room.
- If Gwikon wins, Elzdor washes Gwikon's feet and welcomes Gwikon to the village. They may even embrace.

Class Discussion of Sample Scene: Instructor leads a discussion that identifies key aspects of the scene and prepares students to create their own scenes.

- Note how characters, context, competition rules, and stakes are communicated clearly to the audience through exposition.
- Ask students what purpose the pre-game (contest) ritual serves. Identify that it prepares the audience, puts performers "in sync," raises the stakes of the scene and transitions us to the field of battle.
- Ask if they think that the competition described is fair in that most students would have the potential to win. They will need to consider this when they develop their own contests.
- Note how the competition is inherently physical and dramatic. Ask if students think they would enjoy seeing this competition played out with their classmates. Would they be able to clearly track who was winning and losing? Identify the specific moment of victory?
- Emphasize that the scene and ritual should be well-rehearsed by the actors, although the competition's outcome should not be planned.
- Explain that the competition should be "play-tested," rather than rehearsed. Test-play should reveal safety and logistical issues, so that both players can put 100 percent effort into winning the contest when they present for the class. For example, the elder (a peer referee) may need to have a signal to keep players safe if they get too close to the audience, etc.
- Note that the stakes are real for the actors as well as the characters. We would really see the mud rubbed onto the body of the actor playing Gwikon, or see a student washing another student's feet. Stakes should be chosen carefully to be truly desirable or unpleasant without doing real long-term physical or emotional harm.
- This is also a time to discuss/review personal boundaries and intimacy guidelines in scene development, rehearsal, and performance. Would they be comfortable performing in the sample scene? If not, how might it be adjusted? If so, what might be an example of something that might push them out of their comfort zone. Emphasize that the assignment should involve risk, but they should advocate for their own boundaries. Competitions and consequences should be physical and meaningful to the actors, but they need not involve physical contact or pain.

Step Two: Assign the Scene Template

After reading and discussing the sample scene, students have a sense of where they are going, and are primed for the journey. Students are assigned a scene template to complete. I have each student complete their own template before assigning partners. After completing a template on their own, students work with partners to create a shared template for their scene and performance. The shared template may draw more from one partner's ideas, be a combination of the two drafts, or evolve into something different. The final draft is turned in for instructor feedback.

Real Action Scene Template (Shared with All Students)

- Who are the *two characters* in the scene?
- What is the *context* for the scene? (Where are we? What is going on in this world/environment?)
- Write out the *dialogue* that sets up scene for the audience (exposition). Dialogue should establish scene, characters, competition and *high stakes*.
- What is the *pre-competition ritual?*
- What are the *specific rules* of the game/conflict/battle? How/when are these communicated to the audience?
- What is the *clear start* of game/conflict/battle? (Note that this is different than the beginning of the scene itself.)
- What is the clear *measure of success* for the game/conflict/battle? (The clear indication that one has won/lost?)
- What are the *meaningful consequences* for the winner and/or loser?
- What marks the *clear end* of the scene?

Step Three: Instructor/Peer Feedback on Performance Outline

Instructor feedback on the templates is critical. Guidance here can keep students on track and set them up for success. I find the process satisfying because the structure invites clear and objective feedback. It becomes easy to catch pitfalls and redirect scenes toward clear storytelling and invested competitions. Comments should focus on:

- Are the rules clear for the players/competition? If so, are they clearly communicated to the audience within the scene?
- Does the game feel derivative? Does it fit the chosen context? It may be ridiculous, involve props, or be inspired by other games, but encourage students to make it their own.
- Is there a clear start to the competition? A mushy start muddies the drama.
- Could either player potentially win? Games should consider the specific players' ability levels.
- Is the scoring objective rather than subjective? This is a challenging concept for some students, and a common pitfall in scenes. Avoid a contest where "the better artist wins." Push them toward clear criteria in such cases. For instance, a classmate can judge who has drawn more circles

on a page, or even which drawing is more colorful, but not which is more beautiful. A single judge works better than a large group, etc.

- Is the scene or competition potentially dangerous (physically or emotionally)? Have students address any possible dangers in their scene or game structure. Students can only fully invest if they are confident that the scene structure and game rules protect their physical and emotional safety.

- Do players genuinely care about the stakes/consequences? It is vital to the scene that the stakes are played out as part of the scene (actor A hands actor B the homemade cookies, or actor B kneels down and kisses actor A's shoes, etc.). There is a direct corollary in this assignment between meaningful, tangible stakes and a scene that engages the actors and audience.

- Are the final consequences potentially harmful (physically or emotionally)? This can be somewhat subjective. High stakes are important, but it is healthy to consider their impact on the actor. Rather than physical pain (a shoulder punch) or verbal abuse (shouting "I'm a big loser!"), I steer actors toward silly but visceral stakes (the loser drinking a teaspoon of vinegar or singing praises of the victor, etc.). Whatever the choice, it is best to discuss options in the planning stages and make sure actors are comfortable with what they might experience in performance.

Step Four: Rehearsal

Once students have their performance drafts approved, it's time to rehearse. A thoughtful outline points students toward a successful scene, but here are some suggestions to keep students on track as they rehearse.

- Students may try to avoid rehearsal to keep the scene or competition "fresh." While the outcome of the game should not be fixed, the setup and pre-game ritual should be memorized and well-rehearsed.

- The competition should be thoroughly play-tested. They'll catch things that aren't revealed in the written plan. Are the rules clear? Can both players put 100% effort into winning from start to finish? Is it all over in ten seconds? Might it take an hour? Do the rules allow a sneaky cheat? Is victory clear and objective? Test, play, and adjust accordingly.

- Is the game safe when both players give 100 percent? Play-testing is the time to say "time out!" and adjust any safety issues. Nobody should be harmed in the playing of the game!

- Do actors have all the props that they need for the competition? Nothing should be mimed during the game – that would be as strange as having a basketball player mime shooting and expecting to get two points!

- Are players truly invested in the established stakes? The audience will sense if the stakes are a cop out. Prizes and punishments for stakes should be real as well. If the winner gets a dozen donuts, we don't want a promise, we want to see the actual donuts!
- Do actors "crack up" during the scene/game? If so, then the actors are underprepared, the rules are not clear or the stakes are not high enough.
- Note: performers can recruit classmates to be judges/timekeepers, etc. If they do so, assigned jobs should be objective rather than subjective. It's better to have volunteers lined up ahead of time, rather than right before the performance.

Step Five: Class Performances

Performances may take several classes, depending on class length and size. I tend not to debrief after every scene, other than making one or two points as the next group sets up ("They had a well-rehearsed pre-game ritual!" or "Nice, high stakes – we could really feel them," etc.). I may also videotape the scenes and post them online for students to review.

Scenes are consistently enjoyable to watch, and offer opportunities for strong choices, even for less experienced actors. I have had students create fantasy/science fiction contexts (similar to my sample scene), or more realistic scenarios (like passing an initiation to join a campus club). Pre-game rituals might be a complex handshake, getting dramatically "geared up" or a choreographed dance. Invested rituals serve to focus the performers and prime the audience. Competitions might be sport-oriented (getting objects into a goal), adapted party/childhood games (tag, hide and seek or hopscotch can be riveting if the stakes are high enough), timed or dexterity challenges (building the tallest card house or restaurant-worthy sandwich) or artistic (drawing, writing, or acting with objective criteria). If the rules are clear and the stakes are high, any idea can work. I remember a duo who created a maze of crisscrossing ribbons protecting a treasure, like those red lasers revealed by mist in a spy movie. They raced to be the first to the treasure without touching a ribbon. A memorable consequence was when the loser of a competition had to take off her socks and shoes and walk through the snow for thirty seconds. The class was delighted to watch and laugh as these physical stakes played out. If actors invest in physical objectives and high stakes, the audience becomes invested as well.

Step Six: Assessment

The established parameters and vocabulary of the assignment invite objective assessment of the final performance. The criteria below can be used by the instructor, or audience members can take a moment after each scene to anonymously rank each item on a scale of 1–10.

Rankings are usually consistent and give performers a sense of what peers saw as strengths and challenge areas. I also videotape the scenes and have students assess themselves on the same criteria (before seeing feedback from peers or instructor). High scores are less important than students recognizing their own strengths and challenges.

Criteria for Real Action Presentations

- Scene has clear characters and context.
- High stakes and physical/in-the-moment reward/punishment established.
- Scene and pre-game ritual are well-rehearsed.
- There is a clear signal to mark the beginning to the game.
- There is a clear "measure of success" for victory.
- Audience understands the rules and can clearly follow the action.
- The game is one that either player could theoretically win.
- Both players put 100% effort into winning from start to finish.
- Nothing is faked or mimed during the game.
- Reward/punishments clearly have meaning to the *actors* as well as the characters.

The Real Action Scene offers clear examples of when actors are zoned in and when they are letting themselves off the hook. I reference the project as they move to more traditional scene work, challenging them to find the same focus and stakes that they demonstrated in their staged competition. If a student is self-conscious or cracking up in a scene, the objective needs to be clarified and the stakes need to be raised. Even when the final outcome is scripted, one can play one's tactics to score new tangible points in the battle ("I got her to look into my eyes!" or "I got him to take a step backward!"). For the engaged actor, these mini-battles will play out differently every night. Experience with a Real Action Scene reminds students that they need the focus of an athlete along with the imagination of an artist. They need to identify high stakes and a clear goal, connect success to affecting the other player(s), and really do their physical actions. When they do these things, any scene can be a Real Action Scene!

FOUR

Structured Improvised Scenes

Timothy Johnson

When I enter a studio on the first day of an acting class, the tension in the air is so pervasive that at any moment I suspect the students may run out the door to protect their pride from any eventual scrutiny. This particular assembly of students is often a first for them; the same is true for me. Other than having read their names on my class roster, this is the first time that I can put a name to a face and begin to learn about the personality and process of each student. What if soon after the syllabus is read, I get them on their feet? How about I give them something to do that will innately awaken the child within them that plays freely without judgment? To achieve this objective, what if I devise an improvisational exercise? I'll include some structure to readily activate their practice of playing with an objective and using tactics to contend with obstacles. "Structured Improvised Scenes" incorporates the use of opposing objectives, given circumstances, and foundational acting tools This very same exercise also ignites the use of their imagination, instinct, and intellect to play onstage.

I use this exercise with students of all levels of experience, from beginning to advanced, during our first four class sessions, giving each of them two to three opportunities to explore it. For my beginning-level students, it introduces them to practical things they can do, as they are confronted with conflict in pursuit of achieving an objective. With my more advanced students, it entices them to reignite their previous training. The structure of this improvisational exercise offers all levels a means to experience playful ownership of their spoken text and the actions that motivate it.

Structured Improvised Scenes

Exercise Goals

- To provide a structure in which playing an objective, contending with obstacles, and devising tactics can be playful.
- To invite the spontaneous usage of one's imagination, instinct, and intellect.
- To illuminate the necessity of activating conflict in scene work.
- To engage students in the application of *Foundational Acting Tools* (as defined below).
  - *Beginning, middle, end*: the three parts of a story (exposition, rising action, conclusion).
  - *The three Is* (a term I created): imagination, instinct, and intellect.
  - *The rule of improvisation*: "Yes, and ...".
  - *Given circumstances*: the facts in the text.
  - *Backstory*: a character's off-stage history, both mentioned in the text and imagined by the actor, based upon what the text tells you.
  - *Objective*: what you want yourself or the other character(s) to do, to think, to feel, or to understand.
  - *Tactic*: something you do to help you achieve your objective.
  - *Obstacle*: something that stands in the way of you achieving your objective.
  - *Drama*: conflict.
  - *Talking and listening*: to really listen to what your scene partner says and to respond in-the-moment to what you hear as naturally as you would in real life.
  - *Stanisklavski's "magic if"*: to respond and react as if an imaginary scenario was really happening to you, moment-to-moment, thought-to-thought.
  - *Authentic voice*: use of one's natural, unaffected, conversational speaking voice.

What You Will Need

- A bag or hat containing scene setups which are slips of paper revealing objective, relationship, scene location, and things to think about.
- Use the four examples of a scene setup as inspiration to write additional ones yourself, inclusive of more dramatically challenging subject matter for round two of the exercise (see example four).
- I suggest writing a total of no less than 20 different scene setups. Make sure the objectives for Actor A and Actor B are in opposition, to more readily activate conflict in the students' work.

Physical Setup

Have the working actors create their set using what's available in the classroom. The construction should be based upon the scene location indicated on their scene setup. When class time is limited, I will have the students assist me in creating a general set that everyone will use, such as a living room, even if it means altering their stated scene location.

Directions

- I teach them the exercise by asking the class questions, along with directly informing them how to do it.
  - *What is a Structured Improvised Scene?* (A made-up scene onstage that incorporates the use of opposing objectives, given circumstances, and foundational acting tools.)
- Introduce and/or review the foundational acting tools that they are expected to use during this exercise. Have the students write down the definitions in their required acting class notebook.
- Read aloud the contents of a scene setup and instruct the students of the expectation that they apply its stated specifics during the exercise.
- Request two volunteers to work. If no students volunteer then you'll have to choose them. I always say to the class that eventually everyone will do the exercise.
- Select one of the actors to randomly pull a scene setup from a bag or hat. Only you and the two working actors get to read it.
- Determine which student is Actor A and Actor B. I always choose the first student to volunteer to pull the scene setup and to be Actor A.
- Inform them that as a general rule Actor A will be the first one to improvise spoken text after you say "Lights up!"
- After the working actors have had a few minutes to read the scene setup, have them collaborate on constructing their set using what's available in the classroom boxes, chairs, tables. I prefer that they not mime props. Ask them if they have any personal items such as pens, notebooks, books, backpack, cellphone, lap top, clothes, etc. that they can use as props.
- Before they begin their work, give them a "Places" call followed a few moments later with "Lights up!" Instruct them that when they hear "Places" they can go wherever their instinct leads them to go on their set to begin their scene work. After you say "Lights up!" the scene should begin with Actor A improvising the first line.
- Inform the students that you might side-coach. (Teach the definition: to offer actors suggestions of things they can do to further activate their work, while they are in the midst of doing it.) I tell my students to think of side-coaching as someone whispering supportive tips in your ear, yet you can hear them out loud.

- After two to three minutes have the actors bring the scene to a close. When you sense that the actors have reached some resolution in their scene say "Black out."
- Ask the working actors if they have any scene setup and/or other procedural questions.
- Instruct their classmates that they are expected to observe and take notes on the following for a post-performance discussion: What was each actor's objective? What were the obstacles for each actor? What were the tactics each actor used? What was their relationship? What was their backstory? I tell the students to phrase objectives as what they determined each actor wanted to achieve. The obstacles should be phrased as identifying the conflict standing in the way of them achieving their objective. Tactics should be phrased as what was done to assist the actors to achieve their objectives.
- Once you are assured that the working actors are ready to proceed, say "Places." A few moments after they've arrived at "Places" say "Lights up!"
- The entire Structured Improvised Scene should last no longer than three-and-a-half minutes per student.

Inspiration

My students have taught me that a desire to be perfect often consumes their approach to acting. Consequently, this "want" leads them to have a preconceived idea of what they think is the "right" way to play the scene, which thereby stifles their impulses to respond to their partners. Yet they each possess unlimited possibility for play. I wanted to create an exercise for the first day of class that would offer my acting students a procedure to participate in the creation of a playful two-person scene. I initially thought to have them do open scenes. Then I was vividly reminded of my godson, Eric. When he was younger than five years old and playing alone, I observed how he would miraculously weave a world of active thought into being. He would spontaneously voice each character, giving them names, relationships, and captivating conflict that was colored with an inspired active journey whose end would always surprise me. It was this recollection of my godson that led me to summon my creative juices to devise an exercise that might arouse the child inside my students to come out and play. To play like a child that had yet to be taught what is right or wrong to think; one that is free-thinking and non-judgmental, with their imagination ever sparking sensational, active play. Immediately I knew that this exercise would need the students to give it voice. The eventual text would be improvised by them. I then built its structure with just enough specifics to lessen their ever-present need to "get it right" in favor of playing with foundational acting tools as they bounce off one another's responses, thereby provoking a duel of opposing thoughts, using tactics to attempt to swat away the obstacles. This exercise has been highly beneficial in sparking their senses, leading them to acknowledge the vast difference between when their work is limited by preconception or self-judgment, rather than when they are freely doing something in-the-moment.

Scene Setup

Example One

OBJECTIVE

Actor A: To convince your best friend to apply them self and not fail another college course.
Actor B: To get your best friend to mind their own business.

RELATIONSHIP

- Best friends.
- Your parents are also best friends.
- You were born a day apart and have been an active presence in each other's lives since infancy.

SCENE LOCATION

- Hanging out in Actor B's Dorm Room.
- A fall weekend in early October.

THINGS TO THINK ABOUT

- What collegiate year are you both in?
- Was there something in particular that happened (or a series of things), which could have led to your friend's lack of commitment to do their school work?
- What would happen to your friendship – and that of your parents – if your friend flunks out and you're left alone?

Example Two

OBJECTIVE

Actor A: To convince your friend that they spend far too much time on social media.
Actor B: To convince your friend that they are jealous that you have hundreds more social media "friends/followers" than them.

RELATIONSHIP

- Close friends since third grade; they have shared personal highs and lows together.
- They are in their senior year of High School.

SCENE LOCATION

- At Actor B's house in their bedroom after school, working on their history mid-term project, in which they've been assigned as partners.

THINGS TO THINK ABOUT

- How long has Actor B been "addicted" to social media? Is there an underlying reason why Actor B spends so much time on it?
- Why, at this particular time, has Actor A brought up their concern about Actor B's "addiction" to social media?
- What, particularly, would lead Actor B to think that Actor A is jealous of Actor B's apparent popularity on social media?

Example Three

OBJECTIVE

Actor A: To get your sibling to admit that they read your journal without your permission.
Actor B: To convince your sibling that you did not read it.

RELATIONSHIP

- Siblings; Actor A is two years older than Actor B.

SCENE LOCATION

- In Actor B's Bedroom.
- The month of December.

THINGS TO THINK ABOUT

- Has Actor B used Actor A's personal property in the past without permission? What is the significance of the journal to Actor A?
- Is there something Actor B could have read in Actor A's journal that spoke directly about Actor B or that revealed a secret Actor A would not want anyone to know?

Example Four

OBJECTIVE

Actor A: To convince your friend that their partner is not good enough
for them.
Actor B: To convince your friend to mind their own business.

RELATIONSHIP

- Close friends since kindergarten; they are the same age.

SCENE LOCATION

- In actor B's living room.

THINGS TO THINK ABOUT

- Is Actor A single? How long has Actor B been with their partner?
- What specifically is it about Actor B's relationship with their partner that is the foundation of Actor A's concern?
- When was the last time that Actor B and Actor A spent time
  together? Why?

Reflection

- After you say "Black out" take some time to reflect with the work-
  ing actors and the class about the work.
- Have each actor stand on either side of you, facing their
  classmates.
- Ask the class the following questions related to what they observed:
- What was each actor's objective?
- What were the obstacles for each actor?
- What were some tactics used by each actor?
- What was their relationship?
- What was their backstory?
- Ask the working actors about their experience doing the exercise.
- Offer the working actors specific praise for what they did well.
- Give the working actors notes on things they need be mindful of,
  as in foundational acting tools they did not use or could further
  employ the next time they do the exercise.

The post-performance discussion teaches the class how to identify
objectives, obstacles, and tactics. I make them describe, in active terms,
the specifics they witnessed being used. For my beginning students, it is
their introduction to the importance of designating verbs for objectives,
obstacles, and tactics. With my advanced students, I challenge them to

use more varied and personally stimulating actions, as opposed to settling for ones that are general in their outcome.

The previous training and experience of my advanced students doesn't necessarily make them better at doing this exercise than my beginning students. I can recall many beginning students having more success with it then some advanced students. This exercise is an equalizer in that it requires the actor *to want* to play. The understandable lack of training and experience of my beginning students is not an obstacle for them when doing this exercise, for they haven't as yet solidified what it means to technically get it "right." Once their initial fear begins to fade, they welcome an opportunity to play. If an advanced student is caught up in controlling their work in the exercise with their technique, rather than using its structure to spontaneously play, their work will be limited.

Witnessing students of every level do this exercise will lead you to address their ability to play; you can then assist them to determine specific things they can do to replace whatever thoughts are preventing them from allowing the child inside to play without judgment.

Expect moments during the exercise when the actors may be stalled. Be prepared to side-coach, to offer them *foundational acting tools* they can then use to get their work recharged.

I've also learned that this exercise reveals various aspects of where each student stands with regards to their understanding and application of foundational acting technique. Structured Improvised Scenes provide an opportunity to identify to the student what their work revealed, to then clarify what more they can do to effectively play with objectives, obstacles, and tactics.

Because the desire to be "perfect" to "get it right" is tucked into the minds of many of my students, I find that I, repeatedly, need to remind all levels that acting is process work. I believe it is an ongoing series of things one can come to think to ask, to answer, to do, to experience, that will lead them *to learn of other things* they can then come to think to ask, to then answer, to then do, to then experience.

Each student's goal should be to commit to the process, not to an end result. Yes, there is work required that they need do throughout the process. If that work is liberated by their *willingness to play*, then the process will continue to evolve, affording them unimagined growth and joy.

FIVE

Scoring the Un-Scorable

Maria Porter

When I learned how to score a script – and when I began to teach scoring – I operated under the assumption that the basic methodology of breaking a text into objectives, obstacles, and actions could be applicable across genres. But what happens when it isn't, or when it isn't obvious? I ran into consistent trouble when I coached the classical Greeks, in part because I didn't truly believe these kinds of texts could be scored within the paradigm of objective, obstacle, and action. I set out to create a way to deal with all texts, even the ones that didn't seem to conform, so the student actor could have a common vocabulary applicable across genres, and that would remain consistent, or recognizable, as they traveled from teacher to teacher, building one skill upon another.

This is an original system of scoring that eventually translates into objectives and actions. I have found it particularly useful with texts that are heightened, declamatory, or rhetorical; texts lacking subtext. The goal is to help the students activate this kind of language, and to find the humanity and personal connection to the heightened context and characters.

Inspiration

I was playing the role of Hecuba in *Trojan Women*, and I was having difficulty scoring Hecuba's opening monologue, in part because she was speaking to herself. I began as I usually do by finding beats, objectives, actions, etc. but I could neither fully activate the text, nor find a meaningful connection to my intention. I managed to get immediate objectives and actions on paper, but they did not excite me. I began again and asked myself – "what is she literally saying?" I wasn't trying to paraphrase, but to look at the subject matter in each beat, or chunk of text. Then I took a Post-it note and labeled that chunk with a short phrase. The text read:

> Lift my head! I will lift my head!
> This is not the beautiful city I have known.
> This is not the city whose every corner is part of me.
> This is not my home.[1]

I wrote: GET UP! on the Post-it note. Then I fleshed out the label, using colloquial language that was authentic to my personal way of speaking. A short phrase that summarized what the language in that beat was about, but phrased in a way that activated me. I ended up with, "Wake up and smell the coffee." I went through the entire monologue this way and, eventually, further into the rehearsal process than I was accustomed to, found a way to turn the labels into immediate objectives. I was freed up by allowing myself to be more general in the first pass of scoring, and also delighted by the language I allowed myself to use.

In my Advanced Acting curriculum, we focus on heightened language texts. The class combines scene and monologue work with a physical training sourced in the Suzuki method. When we start with the Greeks, I invite them to toss out the vocabulary of immediate objectives and actions or tactics they'd been using for their work in psychological realism, and to replace it with the terminology I developed after my experiment in *Trojan Women*. Previously, I'd found that students were applying the methodology they'd learned in Basic Acting to these texts in a cursory way, and it held no meaning for them. Even if they managed to activate the texts, they lacked a personal connection to the characters and contexts. I speculated that this was because the combination of heightened context and rhetorical language overwhelmed their ability to connect to the given circumstances and the character. My system combines a cognitive means of text analysis with a physical one: the activated body, in conjunction with language true to the individual, gives the actor a personal and specific understanding of what the character wants, and how they hope to achieve it.

Setup: Glossary

We're going to replace some common vocabulary associated with the Stanislavski method with other terminology. Here's a glossary of the new terms, and the vocabulary they loosely replace (in parentheses).

Chunks (Beats):
Chunks are sequential sections of text that are talking about the same thing. In text that appears to be inactive, this way of thinking about

beats is useful, because it frees students from the onus of having to consider the text through the lens of what am I trying to get, or do in this section.

Documentation (The Score):

Students will read the play from which their scene or monologue is taken, and if using the Greeks, will research any myths that feature the character. The myth research will provide them with a larger context in which the character appears in literature, and provide them with additional given circumstances that will supplement those found in the plays. The student is now ready to develop a score, and create that documentation. The paper score should have one side on which the text is laid, and a blank page opposite, with columns associated with the various steps of the process. (See Table 5.1.)

Drama-mapping (Paraphrasing):

A label that explains what the chunk of text is about, written from the actor's point of view, not the character's. Before discovering what the "Post-it phrase" is, the student assigns a basic "dramaturgy label" to the chunk of text. This step happens in tandem with breaking the scene down into chunks.

Label (Immediate Objective):

A short phrase that both encompasses what is being said in that chunk of text, and the character's point of view about it. It is phrased in colloquial language that is relatable to the individual actor. It can develop from a title-like phrase: "You stink" to a longer phrase: "I can't stand the stink of you." The use of language that is personal to the individual actor is important, because it plants the seeds of her connection to character, context, and intention.

Personal Metaphor (Spine/Super Objective/Scenic Objective):

An archetypal statement that addresses both the driving overall intention of the character through the play, and the overall obstacle inherent in the character's journey. An expression of character and context that motivates you as a person, and gives you a stake and a personal connection to the character and the context. The metaphor uses the first person, and can begin with a statement that reflects the overarching statement regarding a primary motivator of the character: "I always get what I want." But the metaphor needs to encompass the entirety of the narrative of the scene or monologue, so I might suggest that the actor add on something like, "… and you are no exception."

Directions

Step One: Drama-mapping

It is time to break the text down into "chunks" by drama-mapping the score. It is helpful to direct the student to think in broader subject groupings. The language of the drama-mapping is quite simple, as you can see in the sample score. To teach this step, I will distribute a monologue from a play that all the students are familiar with. I break them up into smaller groups, and task them with first finding the subject groupings, delineating them with horizontal lines, and then finding simple language that describes what each chunk is about. The students then do this on their own, outside of class, for their own texts. The sample I use, and that is featured in the sample score, is an excerpt from one of Clytemnestra's monologues from Ted Hughes's adaptation of *The Oresteia*, in *Agamemnon*.

Step Two: Finding the Personal Metaphor

At the same time, the student will begin to develop a personal metaphor, culled from the research they've done on the script. I will give some guidelines, as well as the working definition, so the student can begin this work outside of class. The student will return in the next class session with several samples of potential metaphors, and we will work out the verbiage as a class. The example given in the glossary, "I always get what I want, and you are no exception" would be a good starting place for the student, because the phrase suggests a potential interaction or engagement with another character – sowing the seeds of action and intention. Contradictions that are embedded into this phrase are also useful, as they suggest an obstacle that must be overcome. An example might be, "I am moving on, but I'm stuck here with you." The second clause allows the sense of engagement with an image, or another character, and the conjunction "but" suggests that there will be obstacles to overcome in order for the character to "move on." When the student finds a personal metaphor that resonates with them, they have achieved something crucial: a personal way into extraordinary circumstances.

When the student has arrived at a statement to which they feel a connection, we work on how to physicalize it. In the case of Clytemnestra, featured in the sample score, a potential personal metaphor might be: "He took it all, but now I have everything." (referring to Agamemnon). The actor will physicalize this personal metaphor – creating one action or gesture for the first clause, and another action for the second. The student might create an action for the first part of the phrase that embodies a sense of being bereft, or empty; and the second action might be celebratory in nature. The student will then say the first part of the phrase as they make the first action, and then shift to the second as they execute the next one, and they will repeat this five or six times, to engrave the sensibility into the body. Extended actions here are more useful – if the body is too quotidian, it becomes difficult for the student to experience the heightened nature of the context. So, if the action is small, or only incorporates the upper body, I will suggest that they extend the gesture more into the space – or travel through the room, doing the actions. Typically, developing the phrasing for the personal metaphor will take up a good portion of one class session, with a brief instruction on how to physicalize it to send them into their studio time outside of class. When they return, I'll look at how they have developed the physicality of the metaphor, and coach them individually. Often the student has changed the phrasing, or has found many iterations of the metaphor while working on her own. I encourage this, because I want them to understand that the score is malleable, and will shift as their understanding of character and context deepens.

Step Three: Finding the Label

The next step is for the student to find the label for each chunk. Again, we are trying to find the "real speak" for the individual student. Working back and forth from the drama-mapping label, the knowledge the student has about the character and context, and the work she's done on developing the personal metaphor, the student will come up with labels that speak to what the character is saying, and that express the character's opinion. In class, I will use the example from the script that we've "drama-mapped" together. In the next session, the students bring their work to class and say each label out loud. The rest of the class is allowed to comment whether or not the choice seems like that person's "real speak." For instance, if the student comes up with a label that says: "Revenge is mine" and the class feels that language is artificial, we encourage them to find language that is more daily, and more personal – that connects them to the sensibility that is present in the text. An alternative might be: "I'm gonna get you, m*(*&^^r f&^ %$%r!)." This example of a label synthesizes what the text is about in the chunk (getting revenge), and also expresses the character's opinion about the object of that revenge. The test is in the individual student; language that works for one might not work for another. It's helpful to have students in the class who have worked closely together over time as barometers of the authenticity of the phrasing, but having worked with this technique over time I can fairly well gauge a student's immediate connection to the label, especially when we get to the next step.

Step Four: Physicalizing the Label

After the "real speak" version is established, it's time to physicalize the label. Depending on how quickly the students have found their "authentic" label, we can start this in the same class session. The student will say the label out loud and, as they are saying it, I ask them to find a gesture that helps them find a visceral connection to what they are saying. This gesture can be quite quotidian: a hand that brushes through the hair, or a finger pointing, but just as in the work with the personal metaphor, I coach the student into extending the gesture through the repetition of the action and the label. It's important that the repetition not be mechanical – in other words, they are not executing the gesture and saying the label the same way each time. The point is not to codify the gesture and the label, but to give the student a sense of the distinct sensibility of the chunk. Through the physical work, the student embodies their understanding of the nature of that chunk. After several repetitions, I'll ask the student to articulate what each label is about. She might reply, "this chunk is accusing, and the next one is about celebrating." By doing this, the student is inadvertently beginning to assign objectives and actions to the beats. This is done with each label, until the student has assembled a very loose physical score, beginning with the articulation (and physicalizing) of the personal metaphor, and the subsequent labels, each of which has a distinct physical sensibility. After this session, the students will work on their own to physicalize each chunk in this manner.

As you can see in the next step, the student will document the physical action associated with the label in a very simple way – so they can remember what was discovered either in class, or in their personal studio time. In the sample score that follows, the documentation of the action can include yet another label that helps the actor remember the quality of the action that is unique to her sensibility.

Step Five: Translating into Objectives and Tactics

For the next class, I will ask students to memorize a line or two from a chunk. I'll ask a student to go up and begin the repetition of the label and the action. I will stop them and ask the class, "what is x doing?." I am asking them to "read the body" of the student and interpret the sensibility of what is going on with them. I might get responses like – she's sad, or angry, or violent, that describe the quality of what she is doing. My prompt is then, "but what is she doing physically?", which might elicit responses like – she's threatening, or pleading. Then I will check in with the actor and ask them if they connect to any of the offers and if not, encourage them to find a word that is meaningful. More often than not, the class gives a variety of options, and the actor chooses one, or tweaks one of the offerings. Then, I will ask a student to put their attention on the chosen verb and continue to repeat the action, while still repeating the label. Then I ask them to shift to text, while still doing the action. (Remember the action is not an illustration of the verb that they've just been given – it was derived from the label.) The text has then been activated through the articulation of what the body was doing as it was embodying the label.

Sometimes the immediate objective is found before the actions, and it can be found in the same way as detailed above: I might get a response that refers to what the students think they are reading in the actor's intention: "she wants to get him away from her – I see her pushing something away." I could also ask the actor – why are you doing that action? She could then respond – "I want him out of my sight", or "to get him away from me." In which case I would coach her to rephrase the label she had chosen, in this case perhaps "you're disgusting" with "get away from me." I would then ask the students – "what is she doing to get him away from her?" We could then come up with a variety of actions that would work with that immediate objective, derived from the student's physical expression of the label, and subsequent immediate objective. Once I've worked with a couple of students in this way with one chunk, I will send the students off on their own to work on the rest of their scores. When they return to the next class, with more text off-book, I will look at their practical work as I look at their documentation, and make sure that they've activated and scored the text in a way that is meaningful to them while still honoring the dramaturgy of the script.

I have typically instructed our students to find the immediate and scenic objectives first, and then tactics. But in loosening the vocabulary, I have found that allowing the various parts of the score to arrive as they do, much like filling in a crossword, better frees them up to score the script thoroughly and specifically. Once I have introduced this approach with the first scene in the semester, they use it on their own with the second scene. In this second round of scene work, I might ask that the first showing be a physical label exploration, while saying the labels out loud through the progression. This approach allows for a fast turnaround from assigning a scene to getting it on its feet, as the first staging does not require text memorization.

Scenes

This technique works in the same way with scenes. Each person in the scene completes the process in the order detailed above, however after the individual actors have created their loose physical scores, I put the scene partners together, and they repeat their labels back and forth with the actions, again not mechanically – but finding the escalation or development of the label through the chunk. I will prompt them to move onto the new label, when I feel like they've found an "arc" through the beat. Translating these into immediate objectives is much easier, because they have each other as feedback for what they are either doing to one another, or wanting from one another.

Obstacles

I haven't addressed the scoring of obstacles here, because I have found that physical obstacles are embedded in the quality of the physical work. This is in part because the students are trained in a form of the Suzuki method that teaches that resistance and physical obstacle are always present in the body, and as a result, present in these kinds of physical explorations. In the absence of this kind of physical preparation, I would suggest that the students ground themselves in a low center of gravity, and work with extending physical gesture out into the space. Working with a sense of heightened resistance, present in the quality of the air around them, has also proven useful. For example, the student might imagine that they are performing these actions in a room filled with a thick substance like mud, or wet cement. These elements can transform a quotidian gesture into something more physically engaging. Repeating these actions and accelerating the tempo of the repetitions is also useful. Another way to engage the student in physical obstacle is to have another student push or pull them while they are repeating the action and verbiage of the label. Obstacles are generally the last element to be scored, after the student has translated the labels, and has a better sense of the transactional nature of the text.

Post-Exercise Reflections

When I codified this method, I only used it in acting classes that focused on heightened texts. However, through anecdotal data from students about how this process differs from a more cognitive approach to scoring a script, I have found that students experience such a release from worrying if they'd found the "right" objectives or actions, that they use the method on contemporary texts with heightened language and given circumstances. Examples of playwrights that lend themselves to this way of scoring are Suzan Lori Parks, Chuck Mee, Will Eno, and José Rivera, to name a few. I attribute this to several elements in the approach: the use of casual, often colloquial language in creating the "label", and a lack of preoccupation with having to immediately translate this language into actions and objectives. The communal approach: having the class observe each actor physicalizing the label, and then contributing suggestions about how they can transform it into the language of objective and action, also relieves the students of having to work this out on their own. The observers can see what is happening to the actor, even if the actor cannot name it herself, because of the visceral nature of the approach. They know what is happening in terms of objective or tactic because they can see it. The actor, when given various suggestions from the observers, knows which action or objective strikes a chord in them, because they've embodied it, even if they couldn't name it initially. It's important to remind students that the score is a living, organic document that develops over time, and is ultimately a map, or a skeleton of the character's journey through the play. The goal is to activate text, to make specific choices, and to imbue these choices with a personal understanding that will allow the actor to live truthfully in given circumstances, even within text that is seemingly inactive. This approach supports others methods of text analysis and character development by creating a foundation of understanding based in the individual's embodied understanding of character and context.

Documentation

Table 5.1 P.M. He took it all, but now I'm the boss

	Drama map	Label	Physical actions	Objectives	Actions
You heard me pronounce the words required by the moment. The moment has passed. Those words are meaningless. How else could I have killed this man – my deadliest enemy? Lies and embraces were simply my method. The knots in the net that enmeshed them.	She admits she was lying.	I was lying the whole time.	"Whatever" – push away w/arms – wriggle fingers.	To "come clean."	To toss off. To dismiss.
I pondered this for a long time. And when the moment for action came I made no mistake. See, my work perfected. I don't disown it. Every possibility of error I wrapped in a great net – not a fish could have slipped from the shoal. His struggles merely tightened the tangle.	She thought of everything.	I got it all covered.	"I got this" – wrists flip up/extend and flex arms at elbows.	To prove to them that I really did it.	To reveal. To brag.
Then, at my leisure, choosing the best places on his helpless body, I pushed the blade into him. Once, twice. Twice he screamed. You heard him. Then his eyes started elsewhere. His body arched like a bow being strung, every muscle straining for life. I placed the point for a third and final time and drove the blade clean through him.	This is what happened.	I nailed him.	"Putting the nail in the coffin" –right arm moves downwards in twisting, screwing motion.	To get them to relive it with me.	To relish. To delight. To nail.
This was my thanks to God for fulfilling my prayers. I offered this murder up to God – protector of the dead.	She did it for God.	I did it for Him.	"Praise be" – arms up, fully extended, palms facing each other.	To make sacred.	To sanctify.
Then the blood belched from him with a strange barking sound. A foaming jet that showered the walls and showered me, like a warm spring rain that makes the new-sown corn swell with joy and the buds split into blossom. I felt my whole body exult. So there it is old me of Argos. Applaud or weep, as you please. I exult.	This is what it looked like and felt like to her.	It felt fabulous.	"Calgon take me away" – arms swooping motion up and over body.	To make intimate.	To savor. To gloat. To celebrate. To shock. To flip off.

Hughes, Ted. *The Oresteia of Aeschylus*. London: Farrar Straus & Giroux. 1999.

Notes

1 Kennelly, Brendan. *Euripides' the Trojan Women, a New Version.* Bloodaxe Books, Ltd., 1993, 12.

SIX

Creating a Physical Score in a Snap
Using Social Media to Appeal to the Smartphone Generation

Tom Pacio

It is fair to say that social media and technology have forever changed modern communication and culture. Much in the same way that the telephone changed how people connected over large distances, the television changed the living room, and the personal computer blurred the lines between working at the office and working at home, the smartphone has impacted the daily lives of those of us who keep them in our hands and pockets at all times.

While the perceived value of these handheld phones/computers/jukeboxes/televisions is uncontested, they bring with them newly created obstacles – especially in the classroom. It is impossible to ignore the smartphones in the hands of students, and perhaps unwise to disregard how they have changed the way students experience the world. These changes force faculty to adjust; many course syllabi across disciplines outline rules for the presence and use of smartphones in class. While I believe that these guidelines are important, it is my strongly held opinion that the best training must recognize such cultural developments as smartphones, and we, as educators, should embrace and use them to reach students in new and creative ways.

Theatre has always been home to storytellers. As acting teachers, we shape future storytellers, providing them with paths to awareness and tools to unlock honest choices based on text, impulse, and behavior. As an acting teacher, I am interested in how I can directly connect student experiences with technique. Our job as educators is to bring to students our enthusiasm and our innovation as we approach the challenges of training, play analysis, and all of the exciting circumstances involved therein. We must seek opportunities to pay attention to the ways in which students see the world so we can effectively bring the work to them and bring them to the work.

First, we must recognize how smartphones have changed storytelling. Look at how they are being used by students to communicate with peers and loved ones. The emergence of the "story" as a form of narrative expression in social media has evolved social sharing into something more intimate, casual, and ubiquitously frequent than traditional communication forms such as letters, handwritten notes passed in class, or even talking on the phone. According to their website, Snapchat defines a story as "a select collection of your Snaps that play in the order you took them. Your friends can see your 'story' for 24 hours, so they can see your day unfold."[1] From personal experience it is not unusual to see my high school-aged nieces swiping quickly through the stories of their friends to do just this: watch their days unfold.

Snapchat, Instagram, and Facebook stories provide us with a new type of narrative. What was once casual and free-form is now curated, labeled, and contextualized to give others a personalized view of an ephemeral event or day in our lives; a narrative that invites and challenges our senses and sensibilities to consider (marvel at/engage within/ creatively explore) new forms of storytelling. The popularity and cultural shift towards social media stories has affected other creative fields. Consider how journalist, Neil Shea, navigated how to adapt his craft accordingly:

> I came to understand the Instagram experience, with its constant flow of images and text boxes, presented an alternative story geometry that demanded from me new things. Shorter stories, sure, but also the app asks for a deeper consideration of photographs and the rich, nuanced ways that words and pictures work together. Over time I realized that beneath the selfie surface, Instagram provided a powerful, unexpected, and mostly underutilized storytelling tool.[2]

Shea's comments present a version of storytelling that is not only more quickly digestible, but also multi-sensorial, "an alternative story geometry." A new geometry invites a different balance of the language of imagery to the images themselves. This can challenge the way we ask student actors to use their imaginations to unlock the imagery of dramatic texts, specifically those written in heightened language. How married are we to the relationships between written imagery and embodiment? Is there any room for considering new ways these elements might work together?

Concerns that these devices might be harmful to the imagination and collaborative energy necessary to become a successfully trained actor are abundant. It is not surprising that acting teachers are resistant to smartphones in ways that reach beyond their being a distraction in a classroom. In the recent book *Turn That Thing Off!*[3] Rose Burnett Bonczek, Roger Manix, and David Storck lead a detailed exploration of the impacts excessive use of smartphones can have on student creativity and collaboration. While they are clear to recognize the value of these devices as professional tools, they state a resounding "However ... " to highlight the potential obstacles they create in the study of human experience: from how smartphones have affected awareness and spontaneity to the overall collaborative process, going as far as to identify an "empathy gap." Taking their observations and concerns into account, as well as the evident truth of continued social adoption of smartphone technology as a foundation of daily life, we envision the next relevant question. Given the assumption that smartphones are here to stay, how might we use these new communication tools to our advantage? Are there opportunities to step into the lens, the geometry of storytelling, that are ingrained in today's "digital natives," and use them as a way to reach students? Might we inspire imagination, introduce key elements of script analysis, and forge new understanding of how smartphone stories can inform dramatic ones?

My first encounter with a social media story in an acting class was within the context of an exercise similar to Uta Hagen's Basic Object Exercise, which asks students to create two minutes of solitary behavior to present to an audience. One student incorporated taking a "Snap" into her solitary work, which seemed to break the rules of the assignment: the guidelines clearly prohibit scene partners, including phone calls. After careful consideration, I realized that within the daily life of this student, creating a record of herself in a private moment to then share with friends and family was common practice. With this in mind, I newly considered this behavior appropriate to the exercise. This generation sees and interacts differently with the world around them, even in their solitary moments, because of social media. To younger smartphone-users, private moments can (and to a certain degree, *must*) be outwardly shared.

When the student was asked to repeat the exercise, to see whether the presentation had been rehearsed as instructed, or merely improvised, it was repeated faithfully, demonstrating its rehearsed nature. Remarkably, the performance of taking the "Snap" itself was faithfully reproduced: the taking of the picture, getting the angle just right, and adding the filter to make it perfect before posting were all distinct actions. This in-depth study of behavior was exactly what the exercise called for – it had logic, and steps, and it was repeatable. Before addressing larger issues about potential obstacles smartphones may present to student actors, we need to first accept that the very definition of *private moments in public spaces* has been forever changed.

So, if storytelling and privacy have been changed drastically by this technology, how do we, as teachers of performance, engage our students accordingly? The answer to this question is twofold. First, we must make the connection between these new forms of media and how they affect how our students see the world; secondly, we must find ways to capitalize on these perspectives to make effective links to pedagogies and vocabularies for successful actor training. The study of repeatable human behavior is just one part of actor training. While the Basic Object Exercise gives us a new way to think about private behavior in this new era, it is the intersection of social media, storytelling, and script analysis that provides us with additional opportunities for connection.

One of the first basic steps in script analysis work is creating a list, or chain of important events. In his book, *Script Analysis for Actors, Directors, and Designers*, James Thomas says, "The easiest and most accessible way to come to terms with a play is through the events of the plot. Action analysis starts by identifying the play's major events and then builds on this foundation."[4] Once a play's major events are identified, we can begin to break them down into their smaller parts (units and objectives) to be embodied in performance by actors.

The skill of breaking down something large into smaller parts is what connects script analysis to social media stories. The way in which a student's day on Snapchat or Instagram is divided into a series of "Snaps" is parallel to a student studying any play (or scene within a play) and breaking it down into smaller parts or units (of action). What are the most important parts of a scene? What are the major events? The process for deciding this is similar to what students do when deciding if they want to put one of their selfies into a story for all to see. It is important to keep in mind that not every "Snap" or "Insta" post becomes part of a social media story. Snapchat and Instagram stories are not a 24-hour feed, but rather a curated collection of images the student has chosen to be important to the narrative of their day. "So, an actor must proceed, not by a multitude of details, but by those important units, which like signals, mark his channel and keep him in the right creative line."[5] Acknowledging their personal control of the narrative can help them understand how to extract the most important information from a script. The next step in the process is activating these units from the page to the stage (or rehearsal room).

Social Media Stories and the Physical Score

The "Physical Score," as introduced in *Acting is Believing* by Charles McGaw, recommends a list of actions that will become the score of a scene.[6] Much like a piece of music is to a musician, the physical score becomes a record of the scene through all stages, from script analysis, to the rehearsal studio and experimentation, to finally becoming a source for a repeatable performance. In addition to recording units of action, McGaw recommends naming each unit, as "each of the units has been given a name suggestive of the essential quality and the basic reason for the series of actions. Choosing an appropriate name for each part of the structure is an extremely helpful technique ...."[7] The naming of units helps create the map of the scene to guide work sessions in and outside of class time.

Social media stories offer an opportunity here in two different ways: first by asking students to use an image instead of a name, and secondly by offering the option of adding a hashtag to the series of units. This allows the students to curate the action of a scene in the same way they do their social media story. My favorite example is from John Patrick Shanley's *A Lonely Impulse of Delight*[8] at the moment when the character Walter confesses his love for Sally the Mermaid, to his best friend in the play, Jim. One of my students named this moment #mermaidlove.

In addition to providing some contemporary context for the importance of scoring objectives and units of action, when students choose images instead of words to divide the scene, they can also utilize these images during in-class work sessions as an alternative exploration of the action of the scene. In the case of the Shanley play, I asked students to embody their hashtags as images, using their own bodies and those of their classmates to imagine visually what they had created. This was my attempt to create a "Snap" in real life. What resulted was a series of tableaus that told the whole story of the scene. The students were able to do this with ease and creativity, two words I would not use if I were to explain my own experience with tableau work. There is something about the ability to create image-based narrative that allows for more sophisticated work, even without any instruction in what tableau work might be. While the Shanley play allowed for a strong connection between social media and storytelling in the context of a semester-long acting class (the same class as my Basic Object "Snapper") it was clear there was more investigating to do about the potential application of these connections to the physical score. What would it look like to design a workshop that could be dropped into any acting or scene study class?

Application

I believe there are many ways in which an instructor could take different parts of the example above and use them in a classroom environment. That said, when applying an increased respect and understanding of smartphone and social media to the performance classroom, it is important to recognize a few things from the very start. The first is that hashtags are not "new." Let me say that again: hashtags are not new – they were first applied to social media by Google designer, Chris Messina, in 2007[9] – the same year the iPhone debuted![10] With these exercises we are not trying to dazzle students with our ability to be cool or current: we are applying an existing language in which they are proficient in the hopes of capturing their attention and activating their imaginations. Hashtags offer an effective way to employ the score labeling McGaw asks of us. In addition, the humor and levity of using this language get students laughing and collaborating – it is both accessible to them and a productive application of performance pedagogy.

When designing an exercise using social media stories, select a scene that is rich in subtext and, when possible, style. While this exercise will work with most contemporary drama, there is far more imagery present in heightened language and more opportunities to "break the rules" with period-style pieces. When looking at material, seek out scenes that have clear objectives, subtext, and rich, broadly drawn characters. I want to be clear, choosing a style scene does not mean you are teaching style or any skills beyond that of an introductory performance class, the same text can be used for basic skill building.

Once you have your scene (or scenes) chosen, be sure to instruct the students that they should bring their phones to class and that they will be using them. Something to consider is that some students may not have Snapchat accounts, or any social media – this is fine as it is only important for this exercise that their smartphone has a camera. If you have students who do not have smartphones, check to see if you can access some digital cameras, which will give those students the majority of the experience.

Directions for Facilitating a "Snap" Exercise: Day of Workshop

Step One

- Separate the class into teams, with half playing one character and half the other, giving you multiple sets of pairs.
- Next, ask each pair to divide the scene up into a beginning, middle, and end.
- Once that is done, together they will further dissect the scene into units of action and beats.
- At this point they should name the beginning, middle, and end of the scene with a hashtag, using the same process as McGaw suggests.
- Have students choose to name smaller beats in the scene as a pair or on their own, also with hashtags.
- You can stop the exercise here and have a conversation about the process each group used for creating their hashtags and how those choices relate to the beginnings of a physical score.

Step Two: Ask Students to Use Their Writing to Produce an Image

- Unlike Shea, who uses the image to inform his writing, the result will be the same: an integration that depends equally on image and text.
- Please note: the "text" should be the hashtag created in this step.

- Once they have explored each moment/unit of action from their previous work, task them to keep only those that are important to the story. This is where you will see the curatorial skills students develop using social media.

Step Three: Physicalizing the Work

- Now that each pair has a scene that has been mapped out with hashtags, ask each group to physicalize this work, creating each hashtag into a tableau and taking a photo with their phone. This will result in a "Snap" version of the physical score that you can ask the students to share out with the rest of the class.

Step Four: Fusing Script Work and Personalization

- The last step in the process is to ask each actor to consider the "Snap" journey they have built from the perspective of their character in the scene. It is in this final step where the work fuses script analysis and personalization and does so using the technology we so often ask students to put away so they can work.

A Very #Wilde Score

In the summer of 2018 I taught a workshop in the context of the Vassar College and New York Stage and Film's Powerhouse Theater program which explored in a more intentional way this relationship between social media and the physical score. In the workshop, I split the students up into seven pairs and gave each group the "tea scene" from *The Importance of Being Earnest* by Oscar Wilde. Participating students can be seen in Figures 6.1 and 6.3.

After choosing a character (Cecily or Gwendolen) each pair followed the steps from above. The results of this were both very funny and also telling about how the students saw the structure of the scene. Three groups chose "#firstimpressions" for the beginning of the scene, two groups created "#saywhat" in the middle, while another two used "#notyourman." Potentially even more interesting than these repetitions were the hashtags that fused words or ideas together, namely "#peanutbutterandjealous" and "#sabotogary" (to be read *sabotage-ary*). See Figure 6.2 for more examples of hashtags.

The next step in the process was to ask each actor to look specifically at their character's journey through the scene. The power of a social media story is that it is shot from the perspective of the narrator/taker/storyteller. So, with this in mind, what might the scene look like from the perspective of Cecily versus that of Gwendolen?

Figure 6.1 *The Importance of Being Earnest* with Chloe Catoya and Hannah Franklin

List ten (10) #hashtags for the scene:

Beginning	Middle	End
#firstimpressions 3	#saywhat 2	#frenemies
#newfriend or #bff 4	#notyourman 2	#sabotogary
#wishuwasugly	#theboyismine	#GTeaFO
	#peanutbutterandjealous	

Figure 6.2 Hashtags created by workshop participants at the Powerhouse Theater Training Program, Vassar College 2018

In ways that I could not imagine, this part of the workshop took off. Each of the seven groups set out to take the important events of the scene (identified by their ten hashtags) and began creating "Snaps" of these moments from the perspective of their character. They carefully crafted photos of arms outreached to greet the other, of the spoiled tea, of a private moment outside of the view of the other character where they could share their true thoughts. When these were shared it became clear that the "Snap" story could be a record of subtext for the scene. One could argue there are few better scenes to study subtext than the tea scene and for this reason the results were dynamic and whimsical.

Borrowing a little from Shea's earlier quote, I began to see the "nuanced ways that words and pictures work together," as I explored

Figure 6.3 *The Importance of Being Earnest* with Jason Zhang

this new geometry. One unexpected result from the exercise was to underscore the use of emojis. Students used the different special "filters" that Snapchat offers in ways that further illustrated their points of view. Students put butterflies over their heads in "Snaps" to signal vanity or typed the line "I'm so fond of being looked at" over the photo. Additional text and emojis were added as needed, and even the drawing tools were used to circle other characters in the scene (one group had a Merriman stand-in), as well as the use of another tool of the platform to cross out or redact the more private material in Cecily's journal where she recorded Ernest's proposal.

When sharing out the work, students physicalized the "Snaps" in the same tableau format. While I think this is an important step for their embodiment of the work, I would highly recommend having the necessary technology available for each student to share their "Snaps" on a screen or projector *in addition* to their bodies. This allows them to share the various tools and filters otherwise absent from this work. Regardless, it was thrilling to see the different versions of the scenes, the enthusiasm of the actors, and to highlight how many of the scenes had similar events they were emulating in their "Snaps," just as they had done with the hashtag portion of the workshop.

This work is fun, it encourages collaboration and laughter, and it invites students to synthesize seemingly divergent methods of storytelling they may experience in their lives and training. That said, exercises like this are an "on-ramp" to the more complicated roads of technique and training; their potential lies in the opportunity to capture the attention of the non-major, the novice storyteller, as well as the aspiring actor. I am not suggesting that by capitalizing the connection between image and text in social media that we begin reducing full scripts to a series of emoji and training into apps, I am suggesting we can use it to cast a wider net to find more storytellers by meeting them where they are: on their phones.

Smartphones are not going anywhere anytime soon; technology will grow and change and shape generations to come. Performers have always been storytellers, long before the printing press and the daisy-wheel typewriter, and we will continue to be so long after we are all cyborgs who order pizza by thinking about it. Our craft, our training, our ability to pass on the traditions we hold so dear depends on our ability to adapt, to search for new connections that meet our students where they are so we can then take them on a journey. Once we have done that, we can task them to find ways to further integrate any technologies into their creative process and to discover the line when they are no longer useful; we can also challenge them to seek out alternative moments that inspire them put down their phones, to watch a play, and to collaborate with others in ways we may consider analog. Perhaps this is a way to close the gap, or at least bring storytellers to the table who before may not have looked up from their smartphones long enough to consider the invitation.

Notes

1 Snapchat support, www.support.snapchat.com/en-US/a/my-story-friends.
2 Shea, N. (2015). *How to Tell Powerful Narratives on Instagram*. [Online] Niemanstoryboard.org. Available at: http://niemanstoryboard.org/stories/how-to-tell-powerful-narratives-on-instagram.
3 Bonczek, Rose Burnett, Roger Manix, and David Storck. *Turn That Thing Off! Collaboration and Technology in 21st-Century Actor Training*. Routledge, 2018.
4 Thomas, James. *Script Analysis for Actors, Directors, and Designers*. Routledge, 2015.
5 Stanislavsky, Konstantin, and Elizabeth R. Hapgood. *An Actor Prepares*. Bloomsbury, 2014.
6 Stilson, Kenneth L, Larry D. Clark, and Charles McGaw. *Acting Is Believing*. Cengage Learning, 2015.
7 Ibid.
8 Shanley, John P. *A Lonely Impulse of Delight*. In *Welcome to the Moon and Other Plays*. Dramatists Play Service, Inc, 1985.
9 Edwards, Jim. "The Inventor Of The Twitter Hashtag Explains Why He Didn't Patent It." *Business Insider*, 21 November 2013. [Online] www.businessinsider.com/chris-messina-talks-about-inventing-the-hashtag-on-twitter-2013-11.
10 "2007's Memorable Pop Culture Moments." EW.com [Online] www.ew.com/article/2007/12/21/2007s-memorable-pop-culture-moments.

PART II
OVERCOMING OBSTACLES

SEVEN

Engaging Obstacles

Kevin Hoffmann

Obstacles are simple to define: that which prevents or complicates the pursuit of an objective. This definition reveals how one affects the other. Students are frequently asked to identify obstacles as a part of their process, perhaps in a scoring, but what is commonly underestimated is just how effective obstacles are at connecting an actor to the other aspects of their technique. When we employ strong, relevant obstacles we are more deeply rooted in the given circumstances, more strongly connected to our objective and raise the stakes of our scene.[1]

Stanislavski uses the word "obstacle" in *An Actor's Work*[2] and describes "counter-action"[3] in relation to main action (the actor's pursuit of objective). Like a swimmer walking into the ocean, there is one force (the swimmer's legs) encountering an opposing force (the ocean pushing against them). An opposing force complicates the scenario, creating conflict. The swimmer's circumstance would be completely different without resistance.

Stanislavski refers further to obstacles in describing his concept of "adaptation,"[4] where the actor must change their actions or behavior in response to complications that arise in the moment. These complications (obstacles) – whether large or small – alter the forward action by justifying adaptation on the part of the actor. In short, obstacles spur or prompt adaptation.[5] Without them, the forward action of the play would be a straight line with no deviation. Obstacles enrich the action for both actor and audience and provoke dynamic behavior.

But not all obstacles are equally useful to actors. We must find strong obstacles that are truly oppositional to our objectives. Like a track runner jumping hurdles, we must address obstacles that are directly in our path. Additionally, once we've identified strong obstacles they must be incorporated into our performance so that they are experienced in a physical, visceral sense, beyond the intellectual comprehension of the script.

Students readily grasp obstacles and objectives on an intellectual level, but understanding their effect on the actor's performance requires deeper investigation. This principle can be elusive to fully employ and embody in practice and, as educators, the challenge lies in finding ways to help our students experience these concepts in their own work.

Let's begin with a simple exercise that has served me well for years and consistently works like gangbusters. I use it when students first comprehend the concepts of objective and obstacles, but have yet to experience them in their bodies. Even after the fact, the game remains a great warm-up activity for any studio class.

Exercise: Angels and Demons

Goals

To experience, physically and psychologically, the effect of having a strong objective and obstacles to counter it.

What You Will Need

8+ students (the game is more fun when played with a full class).

Physical Setup

A studio classroom with plenty of open floor space to move around.

Directions

- Have students begin walking briskly through the open space in the room. Encourage them to use the entire space to avoid falling into a predictable movement pattern. Touching other players, or talking, during the exercise is not permitted.
- As students are walking, tell them they must privately select another student in the class to become their *angel*. Once this selection has been made, they should keep that knowledge to themselves.
- When you say "Go," tell the students that their objective is to get as close to their *angel* as possible, because their *angel* makes them feel safe.
- Say, "Go."

   a. The students will inevitably run around the space, making adjustments that usually end with all of them in a clump or two. Give some time for the movement to conclude before moving on.

- Ask the students to resume walking through the space, remembering who their *angel* was.

- Next, the students select another person to become their *demon*. As before, they should keep their selection to themselves.
- When you say, "Go," tell the students that their objective is to get as far away from their *demon* as possible, because their *demon* threatens them.
- Say, "Go."

  a. As before, the students will run around, adjust, and usually end up against the walls. Give some time for the movement to conclude before moving on.

- Ask the students to resume walking through the space, remembering who their *demon* was.
- When you say, "Go" a final time, tell the students that their objective is to continually keep their *angel* between themselves and their *demon*, using their *angel* to shield themselves from their *demon*.
- Say, "Go."

  a. The game intensifies as the students constantly adjust to achieve their objective while confronting obstacles. This part of the game also has the highest stakes, so the running and giggles increase.
  b. If the students start to grab one another to hold someone in place, remind them that they may not touch another student.
  c. Let them play long enough that they become out of breath. If the game continues to be played to its full conclusion, the students will create a straight line across the space that allows them to fulfill their objective without having to move.

- Conclude the game with a discussion.

Inspiration: This game was introduced to me by James Haffner, Associate Professor of Opera at the University of the Pacific and Artistic Director of the Great Lakes Michael Chekhov Consortium. I still teach the game as it was originally taught to me.[6]

Post-Exercise Reflections

- In the final part of the game, what were you trying to accomplish and what was in your way?
- Were your obstacles static or constantly changing?
- Did the stakes increase or decrease as the game progressed? Why?

Sourcing Obstacles

With a better understanding of obstacles and their relation to objectives, let's consider three sources where obstacles are found. As a reminder, we're looking for strong obstacles that are truly opposidional to the objective.

1. **Given Circumstances**
   Obstacles are inherent in the world of the play provided by the playwright. The who, where, when, why, and what provide context that governs and informs the actor's pursuit of their objective. The investigation of obstacles should be a part of thorough script analysis and many students relish the detective work involved. As the actor works through the text, their goal is to uncover obstacles that will have the greatest impact on their objective and require the most adaptation. These obstacles affect the "how" of the scene.

2. **Spontaneous Givens**
   Obstacles may arise in rehearsal or performance as the scene is being played. Discovered spontaneously, these become givens incorporated into the truth of the performance. For example, if my scene partner has just yelled at me, I must adapt accordingly or risk violating the truth of the moment.[7]

   Spontaneous givens differ with each performance and require the actor to adapt anew. Actors must acknowledge each other's behavior or actions as a source of obstacles that alter the forward action.

3. **Imagined Obstacles**
   Obstacles can be constructed by the actor's imagination. Based on the givens provided by the playwright, these obstacles are created by the individual actor to augment, specify, and trigger them in performance. For instance, an actor may make a strong choice, not implicitly stated in the script, like being secretly in love with another. As a result, this imagined detail introduces a host of new obstacles into the scene. The ability of the actor to invent, imagine, or craft obstacles to serve is a concept of great importance.

Quality of Obstacles

As discussed earlier, not all obstacles are equally useful. It's important to find strong obstacles that will truly alter your pursuit of an objective, just like the runner jumping hurdles in their path.

Students commonly make the mistake of choosing weak obstacles that have little effect on their chosen objective. Understandably, we are programmed to avoid obstacles in our own personal lives. But as I tell my students, "Obstacles in real life are bad, but obstacles for actors are good!" I want my students to not only look for, but to make full use of the barriers they uncover.

To help students learn what a strong obstacle is, I differentiate between two types: *true* and *kinda obstacles. Kinda obstacles* are the ones students most frequently identify. While technically obstacles, *kinda obstacles* are weak, vague, and do little to affect an objective.

True obstacles are those which are clear, strong, and have a compelling effect on an objective. When identifying an obstacle, ask yourself, "Is this *truly* in my way, or *kinda* in my way?"

Exercise: True vs. Kinda

Goals

To identify and experience the difference between strong and weak obstacles.

What You Will Need

8+ students.

Physical Setup

One student acts as the primary participant, the others stand facing them.

Directions

1. Have two students stand and face each other about 10 feet apart. Choose one student to be the primary participant. This student is given the objective of touching the opposing wall by walking in a straight line with as little deviation as possible. The other student stands in silent opposition and cannot move or touch their opponent. On the word "Go" the primary student will pursue their objective.
2. Say, "Go."

   a. The primary participant walks toward their opponent as they move to touch the opposing wall, veering slightly off course in avoidance, when necessary.
   b. While technically an obstacle, the opposing student represents a *kinda obstacle* scarcely altering the path of the primary student.

3. Reset the exercise but now add 6+ additional students to the opposing student's side, creating a wall of bodies blocking the primary student. On the word "Go" the primary student will pursue their same objective.
4. Say, "Go."

   a. The primary participant now encounters a much larger obstacle and may no longer veer slightly off course. As they near the wall of students they begin to look for new ways to move through or past their obstacle.
   b. Let the primary student reach a point where they must decide how to adapt, such as trying to squeeze under someone's legs, moving someone in the wall, etc. Conclude the exercise once the point is made.

c. This time a whole wall of students made for a *true obstacle* that definitively alters the path of the primary student, forcing them to make a significant adjustment.

Post-Exercise Reflections

- What was the difference in the level of effort between the two variations of the game? How did this impact the stakes and actions of the primary student?
- What happened when the primary student reached the wall of students and had to make a change?
- Which version of the game did you find more interesting to watch?
- To the primary student: What did each feel like to you? How were they different?

Experiencing Obstacles

Now that we understand where obstacles are found and what makes some superior to others, we will focus on practical application. The following exercise will help students experience obstacles in the body in relation to an objective.

Exercise: Talk to the Hand

Goals

To feel obstacles at work and experience how they strengthen connection to an objective.

What You Will Need

Two students, one small ball or hacky sack.

Physical Setup

Students face one another, about 5 feet apart. Student A has the ball, Student B does not. Usually I do this exercise with the entire class at once, divided into pairs.

Directions

1. Have the two students stand facing each other about 5 feet apart. They will remain in this position until directed otherwise and will not move closer to one another. Student A holds the ball out to their partner, showing it in their hand. This student's objective is to keep the ball away from their partner.

2. Student B focuses solely on the ball their partner holds. Their objective it to get the ball from their partner. They *want* the ball, they *need* the ball. Feed this actor side-coaching to enhance their desire for the ball.

   a. Examples of side-coaching might include: "Lock your gaze on the ball," "Imagine how marvelous it will feel to finally hold it in your hands," "Think of all the fun you could have with this ball!," "Are you really going to let this person keep you from getting what you want and deserve?"
   b. Have them put a hand on their belly as you side-coach and suggest they can feel their need for the ball growing in their gut, like butterflies in their stomach. Throughout the exercise, prompt this student with reminders that they need the ball and can feel that need in their gut, perhaps even asking them to say aloud, "I *want* the ball. I *need* that ball."

3. Now Student A raises the ball above their head, at arm's length, out of reach of their partner, like a big kid playing "keep away" from a smaller kid. Student B still focuses on the ball, but now they have an enhanced obstacle.

   a. Ask Student B, "How does this make you feel? How does this affect your need or want for the ball? Any change happening physically in the pit of your stomach?" Ask the questions but don't stop to discuss, just let the questions guide their observations.

4. Now Student A, keeping the ball above their head, raises their other hand so that the palm is facing their partner's face in a "talk-to-the-hand" gesture. Have them get closer so that their hand is about 6 inches away from their partner's face.

   a. Again, ask Student B, "How does this make you feel? How does this affect your need or want for the ball? Any change happening physically in the pit of your stomach? What did it feel like to have your partner move their hand closer to your face?" Don't stop to discuss.

5. Tell both students that when you say "Go," Student B is free to go after the ball by any means they wish. Student A must continue to keep the ball away from their partner.

6. Then slowly count off in a dramatic fashion to build tension, "On your mark ... Get Ready ... Get Set ... Aaand ..." Stop right there. Do **not** say "Go." Instead, end the standoff and tell them to relax. Usually, they feel a bit cheated as the produced tension begins to dissipate without the conflict coming to fruition.

7. Switch partners and repeat the game, but tweak it slightly, such as having the partner with the ball slowly walk away while holding it

above them, or giving a mocking or taunting look to their partner to make the experience fresh for the other student.

8. Near the end of the exercise with the second student, tell them that unlike the last time, you'll absolutely let them complete the exercise and go after the ball. As before, count down dramatically to raise the tension between them, but again do **not** actually say "Go."

9. Have the students relax and breathe.

Post-Exercise Reflections

- What was the obstacle and how did it register in your body? What did it feel like?
- Was there an increase in tension as the countdown began? Why?
- What did your objective feel like? Was that feeling altered at all as you connected more to the obstacle or as the obstacle intensified?
- Did any emotions come up for you as a result of the exercise? If so, why?
- Did you find yourself inventing a story about yourself, your partner, and the ball?

Kinds of Obstacles

In addition to what we have previously discussed, we must also consider that there are two different kinds of obstacles[8]:

1. **External** – Obstacles that exist outside of the actor.
   - Examples: a door, furniture, time, they're not looking at you, you're in public, it's begun to rain.

2. **Internal** – How one's internal conflict or emotions can act as an obstacle, including many obstacles pertaining to interpersonal relationships. They could arise from the given circumstances or be imagined by the actor.
   - Examples: fear, anxiety, obsession, love.

While mining the text and the given circumstances for obstacles that are compelling, it's best to consider both internal and external obstacles. The external may be the most apparent but not necessarily the richest (remember: *true* vs. *kinda*). It's important to urge students to delve deeply in analysis and rehearsal so that they don't stop at the first thing they find. When students are asked to score their script on a particular project, such as a scene or monologue, I ask them to identify one of each kind of obstacle for each beat.

Connecting Obstacles and Objectives: the Magic "but"[9]

Relating obstacles to objectives is something I have students do from the beginning. Using the analogy of driving a car is particularly apt to explain how this works. When driving, there is a constant negotiation of acceleration and braking as you move towards your destination. This holds true for the actor as well; the objective acts as the "gas" and the obstacle acts as the "brake."

On their scores, students include obstacles with their written objective. By putting the two next to one another, we are able to determine if the obstacle is truly relevant (*true* vs. *kinda*), whether it effectively

Table 7.1 Attaching obstacles to objectives

OBJECTIVE ONLY	OBJECTIVE + OBSTACLE
You and your husband have been having some relationship problems and are trying to sort things out. It is morning and your partner is finally communicative, opening up and trying to tell you something. Objective = I want him to tell me what's wrong.	You are running behind and are already late for work. You know that today there's a meeting with a big client and you're in charge of the whole thing. (Objective) I want him to tell me what's wrong **but** (External obstacle) I'm late for work and have to keep getting ready.
Your teenage daughter has just come home from the movies and has entered the house noisily. You're in the nursery and have just put the baby to sleep. Objective = I want her to make less noise.	The baby is extremely fussy, waking at the slightest noise, and you spent hours trying to get her down. (Objective) I want her to make less noise **but** (External Obstacle) I have to communicate to her quietly so that I don't wake the baby.
You've been put in charge of delivering a key presentation at work. Your boss is in attendance and you want to impress her. Objective = I want her to smile and nod.	You're terrified of public speaking, didn't have enough time to prepare your presentation and have been harboring a crush on your boss for months. (Objective) I want her to smile and nod **but** (Internal Obstacle) I'm distracted by what she thinks of me.
You have finally worked up the courage to ask out a friend of a friend. You think there's been a positive vibe but you're not completely sure. Objective = I want them to say "yes."	You have a history of bad relationships and you're worried it's always been your fault. (Objective) I want them to say yes **but** (Internal Obstacle) I'm afraid of being rejected.

heightens the objective and whether it prompts adaptation. In essence, this adds the element of conflict to the actor's objective.

Students attach obstacles to their written objectives by adding the word "but." For example, "I want **objective** *but* **obstacle**." This formula works best with internal obstacles. Table 7.1 contains some examples, with a brief set of givens, describing an objective and its obstacle:

In the examples above, you'll notice I used the word "but" to set my obstacles in relation to my objective. I teach students this format to inextricably link obstacles to objectives. The format provides a target for your need and a barrier for that target.

It's also important to note that obstacles that are grounded in your other (partner or listener) will impact you the most and have the greatest effect on your objective. Identifying obstacles that exist in the external world is important but connecting those obstacles to your other will bear the most fruit.

Using Imagery with Obstacles

How we articulate an objective and obstacle can be just as important as the objective and obstacle itself. When teaching these concepts, we provide guidelines characterizing the good from the bad and students endeavor to comply in their written work. Even if they succeed in meeting these guidelines, they may never take what they've articulated into practice. They remain words on a page. One of the factors that can prevent incorporation is how they write their objectives and obstacles as statements.

Actors respond strongly to imagery. We frequently integrate imagery into our teaching of tactics or actions, but imagery can also be employed in other ways. As a final step, I ask students to translate their objective and obstacle into a detailed and evocative image to bridge the gap between the analytical and the practical. The aim is to craft an image, encapsulated in a simple sentence, which allows them to connect on a visceral level. The image contains aspects of the objective and obstacle and is based in the actor's analysis, scoring, and rehearsals.

It's important to note that there's no right or wrong here. Finding an image that serves the artist is subjective, but the image must be sufficiently detailed, specific, and evocative for the individual. Our goal is to create a metaphor that allows us to connect to our objective and obstacle simultaneously. Table 7.2 contains a few examples.

Each of the examples with imagery contains an element of objective and obstacle, and is based in specifics that were identified in a student's analysis of a scene. As of yet, there's no specific formula for translating your objective and obstacle into imagery. It's up to the individual artist to craft something that serves and pinches them artistically.

Table 7.2 Integrating imagery into objectives and obstacles

WITHOUT IMAGERY	WITH IMAGERY
I want Blanche to take my hand, **but** she's scared and suspicious (*A Streetcar Named Desire*).	I want to get the scared kitten to come out from underneath the couch.
I want Mary to sit down next to me, **but** she's moving about the room, lost in her drug-induced imaginary world (*Long Day's Journey Into Night*).	I want to catch the butterfly flitting through the room without hurting her.

Final Thoughts

Moving forward, it should be noted that actors need to rehearse with all of these elements to put them into practice. It is up to the actor to find the best obstacles as a part of analysis and rehearsal. Suggest rehearsing with different obstacles to determine what feels best in opposition to the objective. In playing the scene, encourage actors to run headlong into their obstacles, to train themselves to become more responsive and sensitive to them.

The means by which we employ obstacles can reap big rewards for the actor. By focusing on their connection to other aspects of the actor's technique and looking at new ways to use obstacles, students can more effectively take the concept from page to stage.

Notes

1 For the sake of this writing, while I may refer to the actor's work as their "scene", it should be noted that the concepts and explorations below pertain to their work as a whole, including monologues or the entirety of a role within a play.

2 The need for opposition to one's objectives is described in Chapter 7, "Bits and Tasks", "Life, people, circumstance and we ourselves endlessly set up a whole series of obstacles one after the other and we fight our way through them, as through bushes. Each of these obstacles creates a Task and the action to overcome it." *An Actor's Work* by Konstantin Stanislavski. Routledge, 2008, p. 143.

3 "Every action meets a counter-action and the second evokes and strengthens the first. So, in every play, parallel to the Throughaction, there is an opposing counter-Throughaction coming from the opposite direction to meet it." *An Actor's Work* by Konstantin Stanislavski. Routledge, 2008, p. 318.

4 "This word, Adaptation, is the one we shall use in future to designate the ingenuity, both mental and physical, people use to adjust their behavior and so influence other people, their object." *An Actor's Work* by Konstantin Stanislavski. Routledge, 2008, p. 259.

5 "Every new circumstance in life, in our surroundings, place and time produce corresponding changes in our Adaptations." *An Actor's Work* by Konstantin Stanislavski. Routledge, 2008, p. 260.

6 James learned this game from Anastasia Coon at the Pasadena Playhouse Director's Lab, who in turn cites Anne Bogarts's Viewpoints as the original source for this exercise. *The Viewpoints Book: A Practical Guide to Viewpoints and Composition* by Anne Bogart and Tina Landau. Theatre Communications Group, 2005.

7 "Every moment onstage must be endorsed by belief in the truth of the feelings being experienced and in the truth of the action taking place." *An Actor's Work* by Konstantin Stanislavski. Routledge, 2008, p. 154.

8 This concept was first taught to me by Rick Seer, former Program Director and Head of Acting at The Old Globe/USD MFA Acting Program.

9 This concept was first taught to me by Rick Seer, former Program Director and Head of Acting at The Old Globe/USD MFA Acting Program.

EIGHT

Active Obstacle Image Scoring

David Hugo

How often do we find ourselves preparing for an audition, rehearsing a song or monologue without a scene partner? When working on a monologue or song alone, how can we play an objective without a scene partner to react to? The issue of rehearsing alone is often times overlooked in basic scene study and acting classes; yet in order to find work rehearsing monologues and songs alone is perhaps the first stumbling block to an actor's success, since the first call of an audition is most often presenting a monologue or song in a room alone.

In my early years of training at a prominent university I was taught to focus on my objective and to picture the person's face to whom I was speaking while performing a song or monologue; I took this somewhat vague direction from my professors and pictured my invisible scene partner's face like a photograph: my image was stagnant, one-dimensional, and far from active. I never really imagined that the image could be an active image. Maybe a simple adjustment to an actor's analysis that emphasizes not the objective, but the image as the obstacle, is a positive step towards working solo on a monologue or song?

During my professional acting career, I began to work with active images in songs and monologues unconsciously without any thought as to why it was working. I didn't know then that the songs and monologues that I had performed well, the songs and monologues that helped me get repeated callbacks, were the audition selections where I was connected to images not only emotionally *but actively*. I consciously began developing these ideas into a process of acting when a student of mine, Jamie Boswell, presented a song in class that he had been struggling with. In prior classes he had been stuck playing emotion and not objective, but in this class he nailed the song. The song was extremely active; he was fighting for his objective with a wealth of psychological verbs, which kept him from falling into an emotional trap as before. That day I asked to see his written score and noticed that the personal source imagery he was working with was not just any old image of his invisible scene partner, but the image of his scene partner doing something actively against his objective, which served as an obstacle to his needs. The given circumstance of the song was that he was once in love with his scene partner who had hurt him deeply by ending their relationship. His images were of his scene partner actively hurting him. For example, in the first image his invisible scene partner was laughing at him as he was asking him to come back into the relationship, and in the second image his scene partner was actively deflecting him as they walked out the door. He had made his invisible scene partner just as active as he was. I ran back home that night, opened up my old journals, and saw in my own written scores that the songs where I had gotten repeated callbacks were the songs that had images that were active, much like Jamie's. While in the songs that never seemed to work, those scores had images that were only emotionally loaded and not active. This discovery inspired me to create this process.

My first understanding of how important an active image can be for an actor came from working with Jason Moore, a prominent director of film, television, and Broadway theatre. I worked with Jason when he was the resident director of the Broadway production of Les Misérables . Jason said he cast actors who made him want to turn around in the room to see to whom they were speaking. I must point out that the song I auditioned for Les Misérables with, the song which also got me cast in the Broadway National Tour of Jekyll and Hyde, was a song which I used active images to act.[1]

Why Work with Active Obstacle Images?

In the essential book, Stanislavky in Focus, Sharon Carnicke explains how the Russian word zadacha was translated by Elizabeth Reynolds Hapgood as "objective," but it's more accurately defined as "problem" or "task," i.e., what the character is trying to fix, solve, or achieve. If this translation is precise, then American actors may have been looking at objective (as a goal) in a different way than Stanislavki intended.[2] If the Russian word zadacha really means "a problem to solve," maybe Stanislavski was concentrating on both emotion and action simultaneously, since obstacle leads to an emotional need while simultaneously producing something to overcome with action. It also produces a much more organic and ephemeral way to respond and attempt to achieve an objective, leading the actor to solve a riddle in the actual moment of performance, which in turn prompts the actor to make natural organic discoveries along the way.

To make my point further about how the actor responds and thinks truthfully in the moment, let's take the simple (hypothetical) given circumstance that my girlfriend and I are breaking up and I want her to forgive me and take me back after I have cheated on her. The image in front of me is emotionally charged because I am in love with my girlfriend of ten years, I want to marry her and I think of her as my soul mate and will do anything to keep her in my life. The images of her: belittling me, laughing at me, trying to leave the room, actively throwing things at me, and threatening our relationship are the emotional connection and stakes of this particular moment in time. They are the active obstacles which are emotionally charged and produce an urgency to achieve my objective. When I work, these specific images proceed in front of me like a movie, which in turn makes me active and cause me to react in a specific way based on the circumstances. I act because there is a problem: she is actively threatening to leave me; only then do I decide to fight urgently for her to forgive me by begging, pleading, demanding, and guilting her back into my life. I become active and choose psychological verbs organically based on the "Active Obstacle Image" of her leaving, which is emotionally charged and active simultaneously.

The Ability to Work Alone

One of the greatest advantages of Active Obstacle Image Scoring is that it gives the actor the ability to work alone and yet find organic reactions. How often do we leave acting classes and find that it is difficult to work because we don't have a scene partner? I often came across this issue when preparing for auditions in the professional world of musical theatre. Auditions for musical theatre typically start with the actor singing a song alone in a room before "sides" are introduced. I use this process to prepare students for musical theatre auditions, monologues, and "sides" as well as the preparation for a performance. In my class, the students work alone on each step and present each step of the work before moving on to the next. It is important that the students are secure in each step before moving on to the next step in order to have the greatest impact on playing action. This is especially important in the final two steps before adding music.

The Nine-Step Process

The following are the nine steps used to create physical compositions using Active Obstacle Image Scoring for both monologues or songs.

Step One: State What the Problem Is

One of the most basic steps for trained actors is stating their objective, and this can be solved quickly by understanding what the "problem" is. Have the actor research the given circumstances of the musical and work to understand why their character sings the lyrics that they sing in order to understand what their character wants. In the scenario above, the problem is that my girlfriend is leaving me, leading me to the objective: I want her back! Notice how the objective is stated in one simple sentence and starts with the first two words: "I want ..." Many of my students find that their objective changes and becomes much more specific by the end of this process, so it's good to remind them to not be so determined to stick to their first choices.

Step Two: Break the Text into Complete Thoughts

The actor then breaks their text into complete sentences. A song sometimes seems more difficult to break into complete sentences because it is poetry and also is composed of musical phrasing. Try not to allow the music to dictate the phrase. A phrase for this exercise is one complete thought.

Step Three: Find an Active Image for Each Complete Thought

The actor now finds one image for each complete thought. Since the actor understands what the problem is and they have an idea of their character's objective, have them make specific choices as to what their invisible scene partner is doing that serves as an obstacle specifically to each phrase of text. In a soliloquy-style song, the students may respond by saying, "But there is no one in the room at the moment." However, there are the memories of the person they are singing about connected to the need for them to change. Any active image connected to the person you are speaking to or about is acceptable as long as it is emotionally connected to the obstacle and an urgent need to change the situation. For example, the first image in the scenario above might be the image of my girlfriend walking out the door. Notice that the image is of her actively threatening to leave.

Step Four: Choose Archetypal Gestures Based on Images

Once the actor finds their images, they begin to choose an archetypal gesture from the following list for each phrase of text. An "archetypal gesture" is a term created by Michael Chekhov. They are codified movements derived from natural gestures that either contract or expand energy. I use them to help my students to actively speak and sing text. To decide on an archetypal gesture, the actor first stands in the room visualizing the active image in the space in front of them. As the actor watches the image play out before them, they look for an impulse from their center to move their body either forward, backwards, or up and down first. Then they start to play with the different archetypal gestures that move in the same direction until they find the appropriate gesture. The gesture should be a reaction to the image in an effort to change it, not to indicate what the actual image is. I can't over-emphasize the difference between the two ways of working. Reacting in order to change the image will be active, while attempting to indicate what the image is will lead to an emotional connection and/ or indication, and will not lead the actor to actively fight to change the obstacle.

Archetypal Gestures

I find the following gestures, taken from Michael Chekhov's training, work well with actors who do not have a great deal of movement training; however, the actor can use gestures from many sources. The most important aspect of performing the gesture is that the action begins at one polarity and moves to the exact opposite polarity, forcing the actor to shift their weight and use their entire body. A simple gesture that only engages the arms will not engage the voice in the later steps. The action must be a fully embodied experience to get the most out of the gesture; what Maria Porter defines as a "real" action.[3]

I use the following archetypal gestures:

Push
Pull
Penetrate
Smash
Lift
Grasp
Throw
Rip/Tear
Embrace
Drag
Smash
Gather
Grab
Wring

Step Five: Define the Quality of Movement[4]

The actor then further defines the gesture with a specific quality of movement for each archetypal gesture based on the image. Each quality should be extremely specific in order to make the actions unique and interesting. This will keep the actor from playing the same quality of action over and over again, or what I would call "the one-arm puncher:" *the actor who has found only one action to get what he wants.*

I use many qualities of movement from several different practitioners. The following are some of the qualities that I feel my students relate to best.

Chekov – floating, flying, radiating, molding.
Lecoq – earth, water, air, fire.
Laban – flick, dab, mold.

All of these qualities help to maintain and specify the physical archetypal gesture (verb) while moving to the next step of integrating voice and body while speaking the text. I can't emphasize enough how important it is to work to specify these qualities – especially for the young actor who will tend to cling to one quality that they emotionally connect to if they are not pushed to take their time in step five.

Step Six: Link the Images and Gestures into One Composition

Once they have selected a gesture for each image, the actor can begin to connect each image with the gesture and string them together into a physical score. This is the moment when the actor will begin to link the images together like a movie. My students like the idea of the images being like a music video because music videos usually jump from circumstance to circumstance. Music videos work better in their minds because sometimes an active image is an external image of the invisible scene partner doing something while at other times it's an internal memory.

For example, in the scenario above an external image is my girlfriend leaving and the internal image may be the girl I cheated on her with, or maybe even the first time my girlfriend and I met.

Step Seven: Adding the Text to the Composition

In order to make this process work it is essential that the actor finds the psychological action based on the physical gesture and image, not on their interpretation of the text. This is probably one of the most crucial steps in allowing the voice to become active. Be careful not to let the archetypal gesture change in quality. It is common for the actor to want to take on a new quality of movement that represents the text and not the action. For example, if the text was the simple statement, "I love you," the actor may fall into the vulnerable, open way of pronouncing "I love you" to penetrate another's heart, leading them to a softer, flowy quality. However, if the obstacle image is an active image of their scene partner running out the door to get away from them, they might find the urgency and need to smash with a quality of aggressive fire. It is essential that they stick with the initial quality that was the impulse taken from their image. Realize that as the actor adds text their score will need to be flexible. At some moments they will find the need to repeat a gesture or elongate it, which should always further specify the quality of action that was defined above based on the image. The actor will do this by staying focused on the image and perform the archetypal gesture based on their reaction to the image. This allows the actor to find action in the voice based on the physical action and quality of the gesture taken from the image. It is important to state that there is no need to make the text sound natural at this moment.

Step Eight: Start Singing with the Composition

Adding the music can present the same issues as the text does, except now the actor begins to alter the composition based on the musical phrasing. Again, have the actor cling to the choices found while creating the composition and don't let them fall back to shifting the composition to fit the vocal quality.

Step Nine: Drop the Composition

Now that the actor has found the action in the text, it's time to begin to drop the physical composition. The actor then begins to veil the gestures. Veiling the gestures is a process of making the gestures smaller, allowing them to become natural everyday gestures while still keeping the vocal energy and actions found via the archetypal gestures. For example, a veiled smash might translate into the actor shifting their body up and down with the same quality of movement, but without the hands; whereas a pull could be a simple step back with intention. The actor should also allow some of the gestures to remain or at least the physical need to move. If done correctly they will find that they will still have a natural engagement of the body that moves naturally with intentionality.

Taking the time to do these steps in the order suggested is the key to success. Leaving out a step or rushing ahead will only lead to an inactive performance and one-dimensional work. When I teach this process the students present in three steps and they are not allowed to move forward unless the step is solid. The first step is to present the composition with no text, the second is to present the composition with text, and the third is to present the composition while singing. In the final step of presenting the composition with singing I help them strip away the composition and find the natural movement that still embodies the physical action.

Active Obstacle Image Scoring may contain many components and seem rather time-consuming for the actor and teacher; however, after the students have completed the steps the first time the process moves more quickly. As the process becomes habitual the student will begin to naturally create strong active images and choose archetypal gestures quickly. The students will develop the ability to switch actions quickly and specifically to get what they want. They also begin to understand the integration of body and voice and what it means to have a fully embodied experience as an actor.

Notes

1 I am indebted to my colleague Maria Porter with whom I have studied and worked for the last ten years. Please see her contribution to this volume (Chapter 5); some of the following quotes are from forthcoming work by Porter. Her technique uses images drawn from personal sources to create physical scores. She "sources her work from the Suzuki method, but it is enhanced with other physical training techniques borrowed during her many years as an actor and director: specifically work developed by the Odin Teatret, Cristina Castrillo of Teatro delle Radici, and Anne Bogart." The exercise that follows builds on Porter's technique, but is different from Porter's compositional work in that I use active obstacles for the images, Michael Chekhov's Archetypal gestures, and qualities of movement to devise the physical actions.
2 Carnicke, Sharon Marie. *Stanislavksky in Focus*. Harwood Academic, 2003. 226.
3 I would suggest that anyone wanting to use this method take a Chekhov class, research his method in depth, or take an actor's movement class such as Suzuki, Laban, or Lecoq training in order to understand how to truly embody a physical gesture.
4 A quality of movement is the manner in which the gesture is executed. I like to think of this as adding an adverb to the verb. In psychological scoring I might write to viciously attack, "viciously" being the specific way I am attacking, while in physical scoring I can push with the quality to *mold*, pull with the quality to *fly*, smash with a water quality, or throw with a flick or dab quality.

NINE

Resistance

Janet Hayatshahi

How does an actor use foundational tools from a psychological, Stanislavski-based training to feed a more physically engaged body? In other words, how do you get an actor out of their head and into their body in performance?

Many of today's theatre classrooms and rehearsal studios focus predominantly on using *psychological* action as the key to character development. As an actor, director, and professor of theatre I am always investigating new exercises that in some way connect with the foundational acting terminology I used in my own Stanislavski-based actor training but that also, in some way, bring in modes of training from outside that system. I am most curious about finding a more accessible vocabulary to use in my classroom, offering a way to connect with those fundamental training methods I used while I attended conservatory in the 1990s, while using contemporary terms and models of learning to access the work.

My own personal creative work started veering towards a more physical approach to character development once I began thinking about access points towards a more corporeal actor motivation. I was motivated towards finding a system that worked beyond the intellectualized and heavily internalized exercises I had in my wheelhouse. As I churned through the processes I had been taught, I began wondering if working towards *objective* and *action* in a purely psychological sense was enough. Could one little verb at a time provide all the motivation needed for developing a rich character? What systems existed beyond this hyper-psychological one? To this end, I started adding physical work to my process and developed exercises like "Resistance."

In my conservatory and undergraduate BFA training, stillness was a common motif; actors were often rewarded for their ability to stand still and deliver text without any "distracting" movement. In the years since my training, I have found that some of the best ways of accessing

Stanislavski-based acting terminology (such as objective, tactic, or obstacle) have come from directing students/actors towards motivated physical acting choices instead of focusing on the purely psychological ones. To do this, the motivation comes from finding something to be reactive to, instead of focusing purely on action alone. After all, an action would naturally have a reaction, right?

If we think of these two things (action and reaction) in physical terms, we can imagine the physical state of *action* being about moving forward in space and the physical state of *reaction* as the tug that tries to stop us from making that forward motion. The *reaction* is the force that gets in the way of forward momentum. Sometimes that force literally stops us in our tracks, but most of the time, the tug, the pull, the restraint it provides, is just small enough for the two forces to be at odds with one another. When these two are in opposition, then there is tension, and this tension can be riveting to watch. The Resistance exercise looks at actor motivation through a physically charged perspective, focusing not only on *action* but also on *reaction* so that the two terms can be in opposition with one another, using a *push and pull* method to activate the work.

Resistance Excercise

Exercise Goals

To find ways of activating actor motivation through a physical perspective.

This exercise helps to create a duality of intellectual and physical storytelling. It works by exploring physical tension between two bodies in space.

Materials Needed

- A piece of fabric about 5 feet long and between 6–12 inches wide (a long scarf will work).
- Six to ten lines of memorized *active* text from any play (one with a clear conflict).[1]

The Resistance exercise is inspired by Iben Nagel's Green Exercise. Nagel's exercise was primarily focused on investigating the need for tension in relationships and, by using fabric to create this tension between two bodies, gave the actor this framework as a launching pad into their work. My adaptation of the original exercise uses Nagel's wonderful basis for tension with fabric and takes it further by adding components of language, shifts in tempo, use of space, and creating vignettes for further experimentation and articulation of the work.

Physical Setup

This is a partnered exercise.

After choosing a partner, one person (Person A) puts the piece of fabric around the hips of the other person (Person B). Both people face in the same direction. Both people have their feet placed directly under their hips, bending their knees slightly to sit into the pose; the weight of their torso should be directly over their thighs. If the two individuals are drastically different in height, the taller person might need a bit more bend in the knee in order to adjust their height and be as evenly matched with their partner as possible.

Directions

In this exercise, it is important to use *soft focus*. The best way to explain soft focus is to think of it as an opening up of our seeing, where no one object is in ultra-pointed focus, but everything in your line of sight is seen. Think of soft focus in relationship to driving a car – you can see all the cars and the traffic and the people and the street signs around you, but you don't stare at any one of those things; instead you have them all in your vision, in your line of sight. This is soft focus.

Using soft focus, Person A begins moving forward slowly, being careful to keep their weight balanced between both legs so there isn't any swaying back and forth from one hip to the other as they walk forward. Person B walks forward with Person A, giving a small tug on the fabric to provide a bit of resistance as Person A travels forward. Persons A and B should communicate vocally about whether the resistance on the fabric is too little, too much, or just enough. There should be enough resistance for Person A to feel the tug without the pull making it too difficult for them to move forward in a comfortable stride. You do not want this exercise to become about who is stronger than the other, or who can pull or push the hardest. The tension provided by the gentle tug of the fabric allows the two bodies to be in slight opposition to one another, not in a tug-of-war.

Push, Pull, and Motivation

Each actor should choose a strong motivation/objective for their character, focusing on the particular segment of dialogue chosen for the exercise. This objective should be actively part of their thought process as they move through the space. Here is an example of motivation/objective:

Let's look at a story we are all familiar with. In *Romeo and Juliet*, every string of events leads to some other event. Let's say that Juliet's main objective is **to spend the rest of her life with Romeo**. She is motivated to do this because of her intense love for him. This *propels* her forward toward him. But for every motivation, in every situation, there is also something that prevents the character from achieving their objective. This is the *pull* (the figurative tug from behind). Allowing for the existence of tension, or a tug from behind, can be equated to a *push and pull* or an *action and reaction*. If these dichotomies did not exist, and objectives were easy to accomplish, there would be no dramatic tension. In the case of *Romeo and Juliet*, Juliet cannot easily reach her objective because of her family. They *pull* her back. They are her "tug." When she tries to move forward, to be with Romeo, she knows that her family would object, and because she cares deeply for them, she is *pulled* back by the need to be faithful to her family.

In other words, when Romeo and Juliet fall in love (action), they know their families will be against their relationship (reaction). When Juliet professes her love to Romeo, her *action* is to love him, but there is also a dire consequence in her loving him. This consequence is the *reaction* to her *action*. The *reaction* is not coming from Romeo, but from an external force (in this case her family) that in some way pulls at her, affecting her forward momentum. Juliet loves her family and doesn't want to hurt them, but she also loves Romeo, and though she is ultimately willing to betray her family for him, the tug from the family never goes away as she moves forward toward Romeo.

Using Language

Once both Person A and B have found a rhythm to their movement in space, they can then add the memorized lines of dialogue. It is best if this segment of dialogue is lifted from a moment of tension in the play (see example in the endnote), allowing the actors to really play with the concept of *push and pull*. As the actors travel in space, they should be aware of how the resistance in the fabric is helping each of them play with the objectives they have chosen for this segment of the script. They should note how the resistance affects the use of language as well, being mindful to continue to keep the physical tension between them, as they engage with words.

Side-Coaching

Here are some side-coaching questions to consider as your actors play with this exercise and the dialogue:

- How does this pull from behind affect Person A's forward momentum?
- How does the resistance motivate Person B's character as they pull at Person A?
- At which points are each of the actors more willing to fight against what they are receiving in order to achieve what they are pushing toward?

- At what point does the act of pulling shift or affect the stride? Why did this happen?
- In what ways does the resistance affect the use of language?
- When does the resistance from behind help the actor achieve an objective?
- When does the physical resistance work against their goal?
- Is there a way for the two opposing forces to work together?

Switch Places

After you have worked in this way for a few minutes, have the actors switch places and allow the other actor to be in front.

More Side-Coaching (in Addition to the Above)

- What changes in the motivation when the physical placement is reversed?
- Now that the actors know what it's like to pull or to be pulled, what information do they carry in with them as they switch places?
- Does the information hinder the work?
- Does the information help them to move forward?
- What do you notice in your physicality? How has your body been affected by the tension?

Once both people have had an opportunity to be in front, have them drop the fabric and engage in the same physical movement (walking in the space, one person just a few feet behind the other), using the same dialogue and moving forward, this time without the use of the actual physical resistance. When you have completed one round of this with one person in front, make sure to switch places so the other actor is in front.

Further Side-Coaching

- Are you engaging with the same emotional and physical dynamism you felt earlier when the pull of the fabric was providing resistance?
- Tap into the same physical awareness you had just minutes ago when the fabric was part of the structure of the exercise.
- What still remains from the fabric tension? Are there remnants of the feeling of being pulled in the energy you are activating now?
- What's missing? How much did the literal physical pull aid in your connection to motivation?
- How can you use sense memory to keep part of that feeling alive in your body?

- If it is hard to connect with the tension you felt while you were using the fabric, feel free to pick it up and re-engage with the physical tension once again before attempting the exercise without the fabric.

Variations of the Exercise

These variations can help the actor discover new information about the direction of the scene. Use the variations below as side-coaching guideposts to move your actors from one component of the exercise to the next, allowing them to play with multiple articulations of their characters.

Tempo

- Without the need to rush the movement, use tempo (speed) to motivate the energy of your character as you move in space.
- Play with physical tempo:
  - try going from one extreme tempo to another
  - switch the variation of tempo between the actors (i.e. one plays with slow, the other with fast).
- Play with vocal tempo:
  - what happens when you slow down or speed up the language?
- Allow physical tempo and vocal tempo to exist in opposite extremes:
  - i.e. move in a slow tempo, but speak in a fast tempo.
- Another opposition:
  - try moving in the space as quickly as possible while elongating the vowel sounds in your text.

Tempo is such a powerful tool in performance (particularly when driven by objectives), but this tool can easily be misused or overused because it's so delightful to manipulate speed. The trick here is to not lose the connection you had with resistance just because you are playing with physical or vocal tempo. Keep activating the physical work, the feeling of the fabric, and the push/pull you have engaged with as much as possible. Use tempo as a means towards finding ways of incorporating actions that surprise you, actions that were perhaps not your go-to choices, but ones you found while being playful with tempo.

Space

- Work in close proximity to your partner. Get as close as you physically can to one another and speak the text.
- Work with distance – find yourselves as far apart from one another as possible in your space.
- Notice how these extremes in proximity affect the work.

- Place yourselves across the space from one another, at opposite extremes of the room, one person facing away from the other. How can you work with still feeling the resistance of the fabric even when it isn't physically in the space with you and you are far away from your partner?

Vocalization

- Try whispering your text. What does this do to the work?
- Play with volume. How does it affect the quality of resistance?
- Person A speaks as quietly as possible while Person B speaks at full volume. Don't think of this as being yelled at or as yelling. Instead, allow the motivations for being heard come from the different extremes in volume.

Note

These are not variations you should do in one session. Spread these out over several class sessions or rehearsals and really work at making discoveries through playing with each one of them fully.

Once you have spent sufficient time experimenting with all of the variations above, here is another version of the exercise you can try.

Vignettes (Frozen Pictures)

Actors should only spend about 5 minutes creating these vignettes. Don't allow them to take too long to develop these – overthinking will not help. If an actor works too hard to map out their choices (really dictating the precision of each one) as opposed to trying them in the moment, they can get in their own way. It's best to be as spontaneous as possible and see what their initial impulses bring to the process.

Instructions

- Person A and B hold the fabric again.
- Using the fabric to create tension between you and your partner, create five vignettes that represent the physical quality of the scene you are working on. The fabric can be used to create any shape you wish as long as it is taut and allows for tension between the two bodies.
- Each of the vignettes are actual frozen moments and should be treated as such – there should be no movement inside the frozen frames, only movement between each vignette. This does not, however, mean that you are holding your breath. Allow your breath to activate and breathe life into these vignettes.

- You can transition between the frozen frames in any way you would like, using varying tempos or qualities of movement.
- Once you have created the five vignettes, add the language you have been using to these frozen moments. Speak the dialogue as you transition from one moment to another, allowing the language to motivate the action between frozen frames. Perhaps the use of dialogue helps to motivate tempo or the quality of movement in each transition. If using entire sentences doesn't work for you, feel free to use repeated phrases or words from the script. In other words, use as much or as little of the dialogue as you would like as you transition from one vignette to another.

Variations on Vignettes

Space

- Still using the fabric, work in close proximity with one another – how does spatial relationship change the tension of the piece?
- Allow proximity to help dictate your objectives. Being close to or far away from people and our surroundings can speak volumes about what is happening in a given moment. Is it easier to get to your objective when you are close to your partner? How does being close to or far away from your partner shift the perspective of your character? What if you were to put furniture between your bodies? How would that change the perspective of the work? What if you were to use the architecture of the room to help tell the story? Try standing in a doorway, leaning against a window, or lying on a table as you work. How do these variations alter the storytelling? What happens if you play with proximity and distance as you are playing with architecture and furniture in the room?

Tempo

Play with timing.

- Allow yourselves to move from one vignette to the next using varying tempos. How can you play with speed as a motivator? Use varying speeds in your transitions as a way to activate your motivation. Not every active motivation works with fast speed. How can you use other tempos to motivate your needs? For example, try shifting from one frozen picture to another using a hyper-fast tempo in the transition. When you land in the first vignette, find an impulse to move, using a medium tempo, then try a hyper-slow tempo in the next transition, as you switch to the next vignette.

- Allow the moments within the vignettes to exist in varying tempos as well. Discover how variations in speed and pauses affect the resistance of the piece. Can you hold a frozen moment of time for more time than feels comfortable to you before shifting to the next moment? What happens when you let this happen? What new information do you gather when you are dealing with hyper-awareness of time?

Language

- Use the language directly, speaking the exact lines, exactly as written, or play with repetition of phrases/words to give variety to the piece.
- Breathe! Allow breath to live between words or phrases.
- Pause. Pause between words, between lines, between and inside of the thoughts.
- Play with how you speak – focus on over-extending vowels or clipping consonants to highlight moments of text.

Use all of the above to play with variety, keeping in mind that you are always working with resistance, allowing tension and reaction to be part of the investigation.

Post-exercise Discussion

After you have tried the exercise in each of the variations provided, you can engage your actors with questions about how accessing the physical work complimented the psychological work. Here are some questions you can ask them about the process:

- How did working with *resistance* and *tension* help shape a new way of accessing *action* and *reaction*?
- Did the physical work help motivate the psychological objectives?
- In what ways did the two modes (physical and psychological) work together? In what ways were they disparate?
- How do you carry the basic tenets of this exercise with you into the rehearsal room?
- How then will that rehearsal process carry into the performance itself?

My hope is that Resistance work gives actors options towards creating an embodied character. Understanding embodiment as a tool for building character is what we do as actors. Think of this exercise, and its many variations, as a key towards accessing physical options in character development, particularly in ways that work with activating a palpable physical tension between characters' bodies, giving the work on stage a more physically charged and activated sense of motivation.

Notes

1 Active text is a segment of dialogue in which the characters are working with strong immediate motivations, either directly or through subtext. Here is an example of active text, extracted from Act III, scene v of *Romeo and Juliet* by William Shakespeare:

> JULIET
> Wilt thou be gone? It is not yet near day:
> It was the nightingale, and not the lark,
> That pierced the fearful hollow of thine ear;
> Nightly she sings on yon pomegranate-tree:
> Believe me, love, it was the nightingale.
>
> ROMEO
> It was the lark, the herald of the morn,
> No nightingale: look, love, what envious streaks
> Do lace the severing clouds in yonder east:
> Night's candles are burnt out, and jocund day
> Stands tiptoe on the misty mountain tops.
> I must be gone and live, or stay and die.
>
> JULIET
> Yon light is not day-light, I know it, I:
> It is some meteor that the sun exhales,
> To be to thee this night a torch-bearer,
> And light thee on thy way to Mantua:
> Therefore stay yet; thou need'st not to be gone.
>
> ROMEO
> Let me be ta'en, let me be put to death;
> I am content, so thou wilt have it so.
> I'll say yon grey is not the morning's eye,
> 'Tis but the pale reflex of Cynthia's brow;
> Nor that is not the lark, whose notes do beat
> The vaulty heaven so high above our heads:
> I have more care to stay than will to go:
> Come, death, and welcome! Juliet wills it so
> How is't, my soul? let's talk; it is not day.
>
> JULIET
> It is, it is: hie hence, be gone, away!

TEN

Returning the Dress
Demonstrating Objectives, Obstacles, and Tactics
Davida Bloom

When working with beginning actors or students taking Introduction to Theatre classes as part of General Education Programs, it is important to develop entertaining and compelling exercises in order to effectively expose students to the general principles of our craft. This is particularly true for students (like those in my Introduction to Theatre classes) who have never attended live theatre, much less worked on a production. When I initially tried to define the terms objectives, obstacles, and tactics through a simple lecture, the students did not appear to comprehend these important concepts. I developed the "Returning the Dress" exercise to provide an experiential exploration of these basic components of acting.[1] Currently, my students interact with this exercise before I even mention Stanislavki's terms, and their understanding of these concepts has definitely improved.

In addition to the entertaining and compelling aspects of Returning the Dress, the efficacy of this particular activity illuminates the relationship between Stanislavski's techniques and various branches of science. The ease with which students can relate to and execute this exercise is based in part on the fact that the exercise mirrors everyday human behavior. The connections between Stanislavski and science are not surprising as early in his career Stanislavski wrote about creativity, declaring that "laws exist ... in all creative processes. They are indubitable, completely conscious, tried by science and found true."[2] While later in his career Stanislavski may have distanced himself from the linkages between the sciences and his approach to acting, as Jonathan Pitches notes in his book *Science and the Stanislavsky Tradition of Acting*, an analysis of Stanislavski's practice "reveals a startling continuity of ideas, a deep and consistent relationship between science and the System."[3]

Another vivid example of the connection between science and Stanislavski is outlined by Dyer Bilgrave and Robert Deluty, who explore

101

the similarities between control theory (developed by psychologists Charles Carver and Michael Scheier) and Stanislavski's focus on object-ives. When explaining control theory, Carver and Scheier describe human experience as "a continual process of establishing goals and intentions and adjusting current patterns of behavior so as to more closely match these goals."[4] In a similar vein, Stanislavski writes:

> There is only one thing that can lure our creative will and draw it to us and that is an attractive aim, a creative objective. ... Life on the stage, as well as off it, consists of an uninterrupted series of objectives and their attainment.[5]

Both Carver and Scheier's model of control theory and Stanislavski's acting system suggest that "behavior is purposeful and is regulated by goals and objectives."[6] Additionally, the connection between Stani-slavski and control theory is obvious in terms of obstacles, as both con-trol theory and Stanislavski's system "address conflict and obstacles. Both acknowledge that attempts to reduce discrepancies between the current state of affairs and the desired state of affairs are often blocked by circumstances or by others with conflicting agendas."[7]

In her analysis of cognitive neuroscience and acting, Rhonda Blair explains that "the sense of self originally arose as a by-product of an organism's need to anticipate and gauge the actions of another in order to maximize possibilities for survival, and that empathy is an important aspect of this perception-action relationship."[8] When actors/students commit to the exercise goals, they engage in a perception-action rela-tionship, which activates their sense of empathy. This tendency toward empathy is yet another reason why Returning the Dress is effective.

Returning the Dress

Objectives of this exercise:

• To familiarize students with the terms objectives, obstacles, and tactics.
• To give students an opportunity to engage with the concepts.
• To provide an example of a strong playable objective.

What You Will Need

• A new dress – with the price tag still attached – worth at least $500. Don't panic. I simply purchased an inexpensive dress and changed the price on the price tag. No need to actually purchase a $500 dress in order to use this exercise in your classes.

- A shopping bag for the dress.
- Differently colored 3 x 5-inch cards (optional).
- A script or video of the beginning of Marsha Norman's play *'night Mother* – or another play that contains a scene in which a character has a strong objective and employs numerous tactics in order to achieve that objective (optional).

Given Circumstances for the Participants of the Exercise

I begin the Returning the Dress exercise by telling students that acting is about believing in an imaginary situation, believing that something is true, when in fact it isn't. Next I remove the dress from the bag and ask the students to believe, *really believe* that they bought the dress – perhaps for themselves, or a girlfriend, or a relative. And I show them the price on the price tag – $500. They paid $500 for this very special dress.

Once the students accept this imaginary circumstance I ask them to think of a strong compelling reason why they absolutely must return the dress and get a refund, not because they want to party in Florida during Spring Break; something more urgent, for example, their car broke down, or their cat needs an operation. Without mentioning the "O" word (objective), I ask them to create a reason by imagining and personalizing this compelling need.

Then I explain that the store where they purchased the dress has a very firm policy regarding refunds and store credit: if you do not have the actual receipt, you can't get a refund or even store credit. You MUST have the actual receipt. Not a credit card statement showing a charge, not the tags still attached to the dress, you must have the actual receipt from the purchase. And finally, I give them the really bad news: they do not have the receipt. They have looked everywhere, every pocket, every trash can, and they can't find the receipt.

Beginning the Exercise

I ask the students to write down on a piece of paper three different things they would try if they were face-to-face with the store manager, to get them to bend the rules and give them a refund. In other words, I first ask them to imagine an urgent objective that they desperately have to achieve; a situation that mirrors what Stanislavski mandated when he wrote "Whatever happens on the stage must be for a *purpose*."[9] Their list ensures that they have a plan of action in mind, because as Stanislavski argued, "Every objective must carry in itself the germ of action."[10] Returning the Dress sets the stage for students to "act out" their desire to get their money back for the dress.

In *An Actor Prepares*, Stanislavski outlines nine attributes of objectives, including:

> They should be truthful so that you yourself, the actors playing
> with you, and your audience can believe in them ... They should
> have the quality of attracting and moving you ... They should be
> active, to push your role ahead and not let it stagnate.[11]

Returning the Dress contains these attributes.

After explaining the given circumstances of this imaginary event,
I call on two students. I allow the first student to choose to be either
the person that needs to return the dress (Actor A) or the store manager (Actor B). The second student selected plays the other role.
I explain that Actor B is not "officially" allowed to give a refund or
store credit, although they are allowed to bend the rules but only
under *extraordinary circumstances*. However, their job may be in jeop-
ardy if they do so too often; they must be utterly convinced and motivated to bend the rules. Without mentioning the second "O" word
(obstacle), I have created a situation in which Actor A has a strong
objective, and Actor B presents a strong obstacle to the achievement of
that objective. And then the fun begins!

Typically, when the exercise begins, Actor A asks to return the dress
and get a refund, and Actor B asks for the receipt. Actor A explains
that they don't have it and consequently their request is denied.
I remind the students to remember that list of three things I asked
them to write down, things they would try if they were face-to-face
with the store manager. In fact, Actor B becomes the obstacle, and
when Actor A's request is refused that student must move on to the
ideas they previously identified on their list of three. As with "objective" and "obstacle," I do not use the "T" word (tactic) yet. The store
manager's refusal to refund the money causes Actor A to attempt
a variety of strategies to get Actor B to bend the rules. And when consistently denied, the students must be able to adapt and try alternate
strategies. "While the action and the aim [objective] may be determined
beforehand," Sonia Moore explains, "the adaptation [tactic] will
depend on the partner's behavior and on other obstacles that are
encountered ... Adaptations must be sought in the process of executing
an action."[12] Various tactics emerge when the objective is confronted
by an obstacle.

In order to allow as many students as possible to participate in the
exercise, I generally ask students to try only one of their three ideas.
The next student who tries to return the dress (with a new store manager) must select a new choice from their own list of three. Some students succeed in getting a refund and some do not. I do not impose
a time limit for each attempt, but if it seems obvious that Actor B, the
store manager, is not going to bend the rules, I will acknowledge Actor
A's efforts and end the scene. After each student attempts to get their
refund (whether they succeed or fail) I ask the class to describe what
the student actually did to try and obtain the refund and I ask them to

put the activity in the form of a verb, for example: elicit sympathy, threaten, seduce, cajole, bribe, etc. I write this list of verbs on the blackboard. One of the most inventive choices a student made was when she said to the store manager, "If you don't give me back the money for this dress, I will pee all over the floor." I share this with my classes as an example of the extremes someone might go to if their objective is urgent.

In its simplest form, this exercise appears to focus on the person with the objective: the person that returns the dress, while the store manager merely represents the obstacle. In fact, the store manager also has an objective, to keep their job. As previously mentioned, I do allow the student that plays the store manager to "bend the rules" but only *if* they feel *compelled* to do so. Therefore, in order for the student to achieve his or her objective, they must actively engage the store manager and employ a convincing tactic, thereby meeting the third of the three attributes of objectives, to "be active, to push your role ahead and [to] not let it stagnate."[13]

Rhonda Blair connects this neurological response to the premise behind Stanislavski's "magic if." "Imagining oneself in pain activates similar neural mechanisms as actually being in pain – imagining and being are neurally the same in some aspects."[14] As students imagine, and act out the compelling reason why they need to have the money, and the store manager observes this behavior and empathizes with them, the store manager (along with the students observing the exercise) experiences the other student's pain, and sometimes the money is returned. In fact, when Actor A has an urgent need for the money and honestly communicates that need through a strong tactic, I can observe the energy in the room change as the entire class silently (and sometimes not so silently) urges Actor B to go ahead and bend the rules. This demonstrates the power of empathy at work.

Post-Exercise Discussion

The next phase of the exercise is to introduce the students to the terms objective, obstacle, and tactic. In my large classes I give each student three colored 3x5-inch cards (blue, green, and yellow) and, on a PowerPoint slide, display the question, "Which acting term do you think pertains to what the person is doing when they try to return the dress?" I tell them to hold up the blue card if they think the term is objective, the green card if they think the term is obstacle, and the yellow card if they think the term is tactic. Normally, all three colors are displayed by the class. I then ask, "Which acting term do you think pertains to the store manager's refusal to give the refund?" and again I ask them to select the term and hold up the corresponding colored card. Finally, I refer to the list of verbs on the blackboard and I ask, "Which acting term do you think pertains to the things the person did in order to try and get a refund?" Once again, I ask them to select the term and hold up the corresponding colored card for their answer choice. I go through the questions twice and usually by the second time the students have selected the correct answers: objective to represent the person that returns the dress, obstacle to identify the store manager, and tactic to indicate the various things the person did to try and get a refund. At this point we discuss the three terms to clarify any confusion that might exist.

Applications of the Exercise to Text

I use a scene from the beginning of Marsha Norman's play 'night Mother. (Any other text that includes a strong objective and a variety of tactics will work.) Early in the play 'night Mother, Jessie tells her mother that she is going to kill herself that evening. I ask the students what they think Mama's objective would be at that moment, and they agree that Mama would try and prevent Jessie from killing herself. In an acting class I will ask two students to read the short scene and in my Introduction to Theatre classes I show a clip from the movie version of the play. Depending on the class, I will ask students to identify the different tactics that Mama employs in her attempt to get Jessie to change her mind or I will point out the tactics.[15] This allows me to move from the imaginary situation of Returning the Dress, to an actual play and performance.

Returning the Dress has proven to be an engaging and effective exercise to introduce students to the concepts of objective, obstacle, and tactics. I believe one of the reasons this exercise is so compelling for students is because they can easily relate to the situation, thereby meeting the first and second of the three attributes of objectives outlined by Stanislavski: that they "should be truthful so that you yourself, the actors playing with you, and your audience can believe in them" and they "should have the quality of attracting and moving you."[16] Who among us has not had the experience of having to return something without a receipt, or to try and talk the police officer out of giving us a speeding ticket, or convincing the waitress to allow us to return home to get our forgotten wallet? Not only does this exercise closely mirror human behavior in a common real-life situation, it also demonstrates the degree to which our neural paths are, as Rhonda Blair writes, "wired for empathy" and that through our work as theatre practitioners we are "finding ways of being moved that then can be used to move the audience."[17] This simple exercise begins with an imaginary situation which is then filtered through the imagination of the students (those who do the acting and those who observe) and the impact is both educational and emotional.

Notes

1 I developed and began using this exercise in 2000 as a PhD candidate at The University of Colorado.

2 Quoted in Pitches, Jonathan, *Science and the Stanislavsky Tradition of Acting*. New York: Routledge, 2006. 1.

3 Ibid., 2. Pitches illustrates the connections among various scientific theories and modern systems of acting; for example, Isaac Newton's laws of motion and Stanislavski's focus on objectives, obstacles, and tactics in his Introduction and also on pages 17–38.

4 Quoted in Dyer P., Bilgrave, and Deluty, Robert H., "Stanislavski's Acting Method and Control Theory: Commonalities Across Time, Place, and Field." *Social Behavior and Personality* 32. 4 (2004): 329–340. Quote on p. 330.

5 Stanislavski, Constantin, *Creating a Role*, trans. Elizabeth Reynolds Hapgood. New York: Routledge, 1989. 57.

6 Bilgrave and Deluty, "Stanislavski's Acting Method and Control Theory: Commonalities Across Time, Place, and Field," 330.

7 Ibid., 335–336.

8 Blair, Rhonda "Cognitive Neuroscience and Acting: Imagination, Conceptual blending, and Empathy." *The Drama Review* 53.4, Winter 2009: 100.

9 Stanislavski, Constantin, *An Actor Prepares*, trans. Elizabeth Reynolds Hapgood. New York: Routledge, 1989. 37. Italics in original.

10 Ibid., 134.

11 Ibid., 129–130.

12 Moore, Sonia, *The Stanislavski System*. New York: Penguin Books, 1984. 38.

13 Stanislavski, *An Actor Prepares*, 130.

14 Blair, "Cognitive Neuroscience and Acting: Imagination, Conceptual blending, and Empathy," 100–101.

15 I have identified 18 different tactics in this short scene.

16 Stanislavski, *An Actor Prepares*, 129.

17 Ibid., 102.

ELEVEN

Improvised Fantasies

Heightening Objectives and Obstacles in Scene Work

Hillary Haft Bucs

A common problem among novice actors in early scene work is to lose sight of their objective, to have difficulty in the identification of internal obstacles, and to get stuck playing moments the same way. I teach beginning acting and improvisation to a very specific population of students: non-majors and theatre minors. Since these students are often new to Stanislavski's concepts, I have observed that improvisation is an effective tool to help students understand objectives, obstacles, tactics, and to activate their character analysis. I introduce improvisation at the beginning of an acting course, and return to improvisation when students have moved to scripted scene work. To address these issues, I utilize exercises from Viola Spolin and Keith Johnstone for scene study, as well as improvisational exercises from Robert Barton's book, *Acting Onstage and Off* (2016).

I have adapted Robert Barton's Open Futures exercise to help actors respond in the moment to their partners, fight for their objectives, clarify their "magic if," and identify their obstacles. The Open Futures exercise explores Barton's coined concept of Rehearsed Futures, which is rehearsing "our future in our heads, thinking about some moment ahead when our lives will come together or possibly fall apart."[1] The Open Futures exercise directs students to "identify" and write down their characters' *best possible, worst possible,* and *wildest dreams come true* futures.[2] The exercise suggests that the students prepare "two contrasting scenes" as they would with an open scene assignment in which students use the same lines with two different scenarios.[3] Barton's next step is to run the scenes, "keeping yourself open to moments when the character might fantasize about the future."[4] The final step of the exercise is to discuss how the moments of fantasizing immediately impacted the scene. Barton's Open Futures adds both creativity to the "magic if" and renewed energy to the scene. For my adaptation, "Improvised Fantasies," students improvise their characters' hopes and fears as it relates to their objectives for a particular scene. The improvisational exercise brings about two additional and fun discoveries to what "Open Futures" already has to offer: it reminds actors of the urgent stakes of their objective – the desired result, what they want the other scene partner to do, and in so doing, reveals the obstacle: what is in the way of getting what they want.

The beauty of the Improvised Fantasies exercise is to provide experiential clarification of the desired result and internal obstacle through fantasy. By experiencing possible outcomes, and then subsequently running the scene as intended, the stakes of the obstacle are more apparent. Improvising the fear of what will happen if the objective is not obtained both clarifies the desired result and illuminates the danger of the obstacle. Improvising the fear additionally forces the actor who is experiencing the negative fantasy to deploy new tactics to overcome the greater obstacle.

Below are the steps for Improvised Fantasies. I will describe the steps in general, and then provide examples using a scene from *Uncle Vanya*.

Improvised Fantasies Exercise

Exercise Goals

- To activate character analysis.
- To clarify the objective.
- To reinforce the external obstacle: the other character(s)and/or environment.
- To play against the internal obstacle: character's psychological makeup/internal conflict.
- To add vitality to the scene through investment in the moment to moment work.
- To illuminate possible tactics to overcome the obstacle.

What You Need

- A memorized two-person scene.
  - A scene with the potential for a third character entrance or a heightened sense of urgency can provide more opportunities for improvisational surprises.
- All props that are needed for the scene.
- The ability to improvise.
- Before the exercise begins, it is useful to address parameters and rules for both physical and personal safety since exploring fears can be a sensitive issue for some. I personally have not experienced such issues, but I do set up guidelines of behavior and physical parameters at the beginning of the semester, and then provide reminders before specific exercises.

Physical Setup

- Ground plan setup for whatever you have established for your scene.

Description

Improvisation #1 – Improvising the character's hope for the best possible outcome

Have Actor #1 state the following:

- Their objective.
- What they want the other character to do in order to give them the desired result they are looking for. This is the best possible outcome, the fantasy of what they envision if the actor achieves their objective.
- The external and internal obstacle.
- Encourage Actor #2 to feel out when they want to join in to the hopeful fantasy, or take them aside and give them a specific moment in which to begin the improvisation. This way, Actor #1 has no idea when they will experience the fantasy outcome.
- Remove the external obstacle by having Actor #2 play the scene the way the first actor hopes it will go. Actor #2 will use the memorized dialogue until they improvise the positive outcome, and then Actor #1 improvises the response to getting what they want.

Post-Improvisation Feedback and Next Steps

- After the first improvisation is completed, discuss what it was like for Actor #1 to achieve their objective. The experience can create a clear sense of what the actor is fighting for, as well as how the internal obstacle is affected in absence of an external obstacle.
- After the brief discussion, run the scene with the lines intact. Actor #1 will have a more visceral sense of what they are fighting for, and hopefully a stronger reaction to the obstacle – not getting what they want.
- Discuss whether the actors discovered a renewed commitment to the scene.

Improvisation #2 – Improvising the Fears

- This would be a good time to remind students that this work can be sensitive and to review the parameters and rules for physical and personal safety.
- Ask Actor #1 to state what they think the character fears if they cannot get their objective or what they fear is preventing them from pursuing their objective fully. Encourage the actor to identify if they fear letting of go of their internal obstacle.

- Since the fear can include other characters from the play other than the ones in the scene, put another student on notice to be ready to come and improvise that character.
- Take Actor #2 aside and give them ideas of actions they can take to make Actor #1's fears come true. The fear represents the obstacle, what they are trying desperately to prevent from happening.
- The actor will use their lines until either Actor #2 improvises the new scenario or a third actor enters the scene, and then both Actors #1 and #2 improvise the reaction to the third actor entering.

Post-Improvisation Feedback and Next Steps

- Discuss how it felt for Actor #1 to experience their character's fear coming into fruition. It can be an eye-opener to the actor to viscerally and visually experience what they do not want to happen. Seeing what is at stake raises the stakes for the actor.
- After the discussion, have the actors play the scene again with the lines intact. This time, the emphasis will be on committing more fully to the objective and a clearer sense of the obstacle. Allow actors to improvise physically pursuing objectives with higher stakes.
- If timing allows, and the instructor deems necessary, repeat the sequence with the other actor for both fantasy improvisations.

Improvised Fantasies in Action: the Yelena/Astrov Scene in Act III of Anton Chekhov's *Uncle Vanya*

Improvising the Character's Hope for the Best Possible Outcome

The rationale for doing the positive Improvised Fantasy is to make clear what the actor is fighting for; what they want the other character to *do*. The improvisation helps visualize what is possible by removing the external obstacle. Ironically, removing the external obstacle can help clarify the internal obstacle.

In the first scene, Yelena has asked for Astrov in order to ascertain if he has feelings for Sonya. He says he doesn't return Sonya's affections and then interprets Yelena's interrogation as a ruse to set up a tryst outside of the estate. He wants Yelena to agree to meet him and awkwardly tries to seduce her. Yelena wants Astrov to agree to leave the estate if he cannot return Sonya's feelings. Her internal obstacle is that she is completely taken with him, which makes her feel guilty. Below is one hypothetical improvisation from the perspective of Yelena, which removes the obstacle and hence allows the actor (Yelena) to experience their desired result without much effort. It is helpful that the actor playing Yelena does not know when the actual improvisation will take place. The beauty of improvisation is that it forces actors to stay in tune to each other because just like with the characters, they will not know what is going to happen next. I usually take the actor who is the external obstacle, aside, out of earshot of the scene partner, and tell them to give into the objective early in the scene, and to use the scripted lines until the improvised future outcome. I tell Actor #1 (Yelena) to use their lines until Actor #2 begins improvising the fantasy outcome.

The improvised segment in the transcript is italicized.

> YELENA
> No, you don't love her, do you? I can tell by your eyes. But she loves you. And she suffers because of it. You've got to understand what that means … and promise not to come here anymore.

> ASTROV
> Well, I'm a little old for her. I … Look, I haven't got time to … (shrugs) So what do you expect me to do …?

> YELENA
> God, this is unpleasant conversation, having to talk like this! … And you should leave right away.[5]

> ASTROV
> *No need to worry any further. I shall leave momentarily. Let me grab my map, and I will be off.*

> *(Actor #2 (Astrov) takes Yelena's hand, looks in her eyes, bends down to kiss her hand, drops it, grabs the map and runs out.)*

Some improvisations will be shorter than others. That is absolutely fine, and also illuminating. By removing the external obstacle, there are fewer tactics to play, if any, and hence it is a much shorter scene. In terms of the post-improvisation feedback, I may ask Actor #1 (Yelena) what it was like to achieve the objective. Perhaps the actor may say that they were disappointed because they realized how they much enjoyed Astrov's attention. Hence, Actor #1's internal obstacle of wanting to be with Astrov is clarified. Or Actor #1 might offer that they were let off the hook by immediately achieving the objective, and therefore they do not have to confront their own feelings towards Astrov.

Let's try the improvisation again, but a little further into the scene where Yelena is both in conflict with Astrov's advances and in conflict with her own desire to give in to those advances. Yelena still wants Astrov to leave, and stop tempting her.

> ASTROV
> I give in. Come on, take me! Sink your claws into me!

> YELENA
> Have you lost your mind?

ASTROV
And you said you were so shy –

YELENA
You think I'm that cheap? How insulting! I'm not like that!

(Tries to go) [6]

Astrov, giving in to Yelena's best possible outcome, stands in front of her, to block her, and then moves aside to let her pass. He takes a breath, smooths out his jacket or straightens his tie.

ASTROV
Please forgive me. I have forgotten myself. It will not happen again. I am so taken by your beauty. I will leave at once. I respect you too much to put you in any position that would cause you harm.

Astrov goes to the table, rolls up his maps, turns around, walks to Yelena, takes her hand, kisses it, puts it down, and exits.

Actor #1 (Yelena) experiences the lack of resistance without the external obstacle. It may feel odd that there isn't a counter-action, which is similar to the ease of a Tai Chi flow. As a result, the actor may experience a sense of relief. Also, as is the case with the above scene, Actor #1 (Yelena) can tune into their internal conflict, without the external obstacle. Even though Astrov leaves, Yelena's desire to be with him, and the guilt that accompanies that desire, is still present and heightened. I would then ask the actors to try the scene again, with all the dialogue and obstacles intact, and fight for what they want in that moment, now that the objective has become more internalized and physicalized. When running the scene after the improvisation, Actor #1 can have both a sense of what is lost by not achieving the objective, as well as a more pronounced feeling of the obstacle's resistance.

Improvising the Fears

Sometimes, an actor can lose the urgency of overcoming both the external and internal obstacle. To heighten the need to overcome the obstacle for Actor #1, let's try what an improvised worst possible future might look like. The fear improvisations are fun to play because anything can happen. When the script allows, I like to try to incorporate a third actor because the addition of a character who is not included in the memorized portion of the scene truly lends itself to an improvisational atmosphere. For the example below, let's try the Yelena/Astrov scene again. During the setup, ask Actor #1 (Yelena) "What is your worst fear?" If the actor says they fear they will succumb to Astrov's advances, then the external obstacle is Astrov's temptations and the internal obstacle is Yelena's own desire. That improvisation might be different than if Actor #1 says they fear Sonya coming in. If Yelena fears Sonya witnessing both Astrov's advances and her own desire, the external obstacle is still Astrov, and the internal obstacle is fear of discovery and hurting Sonya. In that case, I would ask another actor to play the role of Sonya, and suggest a point, out of earshot, when Sonya could enter the scene.

Let's start the improvisation after Astrov has begun his advances and Yelena has deflected them by declaring and swearing she is better than he thinks. It could happen like this:

>   YELENA
> I swear to God–
>
>   ASTROV
> You don't have to swear. You don't have to say any-
> thing. God, you're beautiful! I love your
> hands … (kisses her hands).
>
>   YELENA
> That's enough, please! Will you please just go away?[7]
>
> *Maybe Yelena lets her hands linger in Astrov's*
> *hands, giving in to the internal obstacle. Then*
> *Sonya enters the scene so that Yelena sees her.*
> *Seeing Sonya, Yelena forcefully pulls her hands away*
> *from Astrov, who turns around and sees Sonya. Yelena*
> *rushes to Sonya to make amends and may improvise dia-*
> *logue relating to how sorry she is and that it is not*
> *what it seems. Perhaps Yelena throws herself at*
> *Sonya's feet. Astrov immediately talks about the*
> *weather the way he does when Vanya surprises them in*
> *the script. Sonya runs off, and Yelena looks at*
> *Astrov and says, "I cannot stay here another moment"*
> *and runs after Sonya.*

After the improvisation, ask Actor #1 what the experience was like to have their worst fears realized. They might say it added urgency to the scene because they had to overcome the obstacle of Astrov's advances, as well as their own attraction towards him, before it was too late.

Let's try a hypothetical example of what part of the scene may look like after the students return to the scene post-improvisation. When Yelena says, "I swear to God – " she resists by pulling her body away. When Astrov continues on with, "God, you're so beautiful" and takes her hands, Yelena may push him away, move to where the table is, keeping the table as a barrier, and thrust the maps into his chest. Maybe Astrov throws down the maps, and comes around the table, and grabs her waist, getting ready to kiss her. Yelena is confronted with her internal obstacle of the intense attraction she has towards him, breathes in his presence, kisses him quickly, and then pushes him away. As a result of the Fear improvisation, Actor #1 (Yelena) may have a greater urgency to achieve the objective so no one comes in to witness the interaction with Astrov. The urgency can manifest itself with an execution of new tactics, or a stronger physical drive to overcome the obstacle.

Improvised Fantasies takes character analysis from the conceptual to the experiential through improvisation, which helps to clarify objectives and obstacles. Using improvisation to discover the best possible outcome, when the partner gives into the desired result without resistance, may lead to the revelation of the internal obstacle. Improvising the worst possible outcome, which is a fantasy of what the character fears can happen if the objective is not achieved, creates a palpable sense of danger of what is at stake. The improvisation may illuminate the possibilities of what can happen when the objective is not achieved, as in the hypothetical improvisation when Sonya finds Yelena and Astrov together. Once an actor has improvised the fantasy outcomes, when she returns to the original scene her objective and obstacles are stronger and she has renewed energy through the sense of urgency. Improvised Fantasies helps actors discover what's at stake, and builds upon the foundation introduced earlier in the semester: that the fun they discovered through improvisational play is a valuable part of an actor's toolkit.

Notes

1 Barton, 151.
2 Ibid., 344 Appendix E, Exercise 5.15.
3 For more information on Robert Barton's Open Scene exercises, see Chapter 4 in the Barton, 2016, 7th edition, pp. 118–29.
4 Ibid., 344, Appendix E, Exercise 5.15.
5 Chekhov 236–7, Schmidt translation, Act III.
6 Ibid., 237, Schmidt translation.
7 Ibid., 238, Schmidt translation.

References

Barton, Robert. *Acting: Onstage and Off.* 7th ed. Wadsworth Cengage Learning, 2016.
Chekhov, Anton. *Uncle Vanya.* In *The Plays of Anton Chekhov.* Translated by Paul Schmidt. New York: Harper Perenial, 1997, pp. 236–238.

TWELVE

Optimizing the Obstacle

Using Indicators of Csíkszentmihályi's Flow to Help Select, Test, and Experience Stanislavski's Obstacles

Fabio Polanco and Diane Bonfiglio

In his 1990 book *Flow: The Psychology of Optimal Experience*, Psychologist Mihalyi Csíkszentmihályi outlined the indicators present when an individual is in a state of flow or optimal experience. Flow is a psycho-physical state in which an individual in action is completely absorbed in the task at hand. In this flow state, the level of concentration, attention, feeling of fulfillment, and skill of the individual are amplified; the individual is working optimally. For Konstantin Stanislavski, inspired acting was a state of, "subconscious creativity."[1] The striking similarities between flow indicators and elements of Stanislavski's psychotechnique suggest that Stanislavski was searching for flow nearly 60 years before Csíkszentmihályi's coining of the term and that flow and inspired acting are nearly synonymous. Therefore, it follows that by applying knowledge of flow we can more deeply understand and effectively implement elements of Stanislavski's approach.

This chapter will focus on how knowledge of flow and flow indicators can be used to help actors select, test, and bolster the effectiveness of obstacles. It will culminate in our recipe for "Obstacle Cards." Obstacle Cards is a concept supported by consideration of "flow indicators," especially skill/challenge balance and how this balance, or imbalance, can impact concentration, attention, perception, actions, stakes, sensations, and feelings. It teaches actors and students of acting how properly calibrating the balance between the objective/task and the obstacle can lead to more dynamic and engaging acting.

What Is Flow?

Performers perform for many reasons. Undoubtedly, one of the reasons is the often-elusive sensation experienced when the performer, cast, material, space, and audience come together into what feels like perfect efficiency. Everything is working as it should. All is aligned, mentally, physically, spiritually. There is "order in consciousness."[2] The performer and the performance feel alive. It feels easy and the individual is utterly fulfilled. He or she is happy.

Outside of the performing arts, this optimal state is commonly experienced in sports. After a particularly outstanding stretch of play, athletes often speak of having been "unconscious," "in the zone," or in a "flow." However, this feeling is also experienced by individuals engaged in all kinds of endeavors: chefs, postal carriers, teachers, surgeons, pilots, amateur gardeners. Anyone who is engaged in an activity that is potentially absorptive can experience this optimal state. Although elusive, this feeling is so pleasurable that individuals of all kinds seek to re-experience it as often as possible. It is why below-average golfers may continue to golf. For, despite not being very good, once in every 18 holes they may hit a ball so "true" (optimally), and it feels so good to hit it so well, that they will return again and again in hopes of re-experiencing that sensation and level of happiness and satisfaction.

History of Flow

Twenty-three hundred years ago Aristotle concluded that, more than anything else, men and women seek happiness. Much has changed since Aristotle's time and yet on this most important issue very little has changed in the intervening centuries. We do not understand what happiness is any better than Aristotle did, and as for learning how to attain that blessed condition, one could argue that we have made no progress at all.[3]

In *Flow* (1990), Csíkszentmihályi set out to apply the tools of modern psychology to the investigation of when people feel most happy. In doing so, he not only discovered the factors or indicators present when people are feeling most happy, but also that, in that state, they may also be operating most optimally: not only do they feel at their best, they actually *are* at their best.

The Flow Indicators

Flow, like inspiration, cannot be reached through direct pursuit. However, flow and inspiration may both be reached indirectly. Stanislavski referred to it as tapping the subconscious through "indirect, conscious means"[4]. These indirect conscious means were the elements of the system. From a flow perspective, an individual might be able to induce a state of optimal experience by pursuing its indicators or creating the conditions in which the indicators may thrive. As Csíkszentmihályi writes, "Happiness (flow), in fact, is a condition that must be prepared for, cultivated."[5]

Csíkszentmihályi identified nine flow indicators. The first and second flow indicators are *goal orientation* and a high level of *concentration* on the task at hand (achieving the goal). When in a state of flow, an individual is in pursuit of a very specific well-defined and compelling goal or objective. As a result, it is easier for the individual to remain focused on its achievement.

Third is a *balance of challenge and skill*. The level of challenge they face is equivalent to their ability (skill) to achieve their goal. This is exemplified by Marlynn Wei's 2017 *Huffington Post* review of a solo dance performance by choreographer, dancer, and puppeteer Pepper Fajans:

> Despite the difficulty of this solo sequence, he accomplishes it with both intensity and great equipoise. He pushes himself to the edge, but never takes on more than he can handle. In doing so, Fajans takes the audience on this rewarding ride of "flow," a state described by positive psychologist Mihaly Csíkszentmihályi as a delicate point where one is challenged enough to be engaged, but not burdened to the point of being overwhelmed.[6]

When this relationship is out of balance, flow is not possible. When the challenge outpaces skill, the individual will experience anxiety. When skill outpaces challenge, the individual will experience boredom. This indicator is a pivotal consideration in effectively employing obstacles in an effort to achieve inspired acting.

The fourth indicator is *immediate feedback*. The individual is able to gauge, in real time, how effectively they are pursuing their goal and whether or not they have achieved it. A feeling of *control* is fifth. There is a sense of efficiency and command. Sixth is *ease* or *effortlessness*; a sensation that actions are being executed with minimal effort. An *altered perception of time* is the seventh. It feels as if time has passed very quickly. Eighth is the *merging together of action and consciousness*. The individual feels as one: mentally, physically, and spiritually. Finally, the ninth indicator is *autotelism*, meaning that the task is being pursued for its own sake, not for some external reason. In acting, these external reasons might include things like pleasing or impressing peers, teachers, or audiences.

The Relationship between Flow, Stanislavski and Inspired Acting

Stanislavski observed that when actors are at their best they are in a state of inspiration. He believed they were working from the subconscious, that the subconscious responds as in nature, and therefore those responses will usually lead the actor down "the right path"[7]. They knew what to do without thinking about what to do. Therefore, this subconscious state of inspiration should be sought by every actor engaged in rehearsal or performance. If this state were to come of its own accord, so much the better, and one leaves it alone. The issue is that we are often not in this state and no amount of wishing will lead us to it.

Aware of this conundrum and hoping to assist his pupils in resolving it, in Book One of *An Actor's Work*, Stanislavski, as Tortsov, tells his students that they must develop a conscious approach to the subconscious. They must find a conscious path to inspiration. That path is what he calls the psychotechnique. The psychotechnique is composed of numerous elements that can be used to prick the subconscious, including: objectives/tasks, actions/tactics, and obstacles.

Stanislavski's psychotechnique is effective. It has been employed over decades, elaborated on, and absorbed into the Western zeitgeist. His terminology continues to be what is most commonly used when actors, directors, and teachers communicate with each other in the rehearsal room and in the studio. But why does it work? Is it working in the way that Stanislavski described? And, if we can understand some of the science that underlies it, can we bolster its application?

For the purposes of addressing obstacles, and for this exercise, we will consider the following parallels between the elements of Stanislavski's system and the indicators of flow. These parallels begin with Stanislavski's most fundamental and impactful assertion, "Everything that happens on stage must occur for some reason or other."[8] The notion is that the character, and therefore the actor, is constantly in pursuit of something; there is a want, a need, a must-have. This is parallel to real life. We have needs and wants, they are pursued, met or not met, and then we move on to the next need or want. We want a sandwich, we get a sandwich, and so then we want the check, to pay, to leave, and so on. Stanislavski asserts that if we are in pursuit of an objective or task, and it is of significant interest, we have an opportunity to reach a state of inspiration. When we are in pursuit of the objective all else can fall away and we do things, actions, exactly as we do them in nature.

This concept mirrors Csíkszentmihályi's flow indicator, *goal orientation*. Csíkszentmihályi observed, just as Stanislavski did, that individuals in a state of flow or inspiration are oriented toward a goal of significant interest, be it swimming 100 meters, climbing a mountain, or any other task. This is instructive to both the actor as character and the actor as actor, because not only must actors identify and pursue objectives of significant interest to the character, but, perhaps more importantly, of significant interest to themselves. Again, Stanislavski made the same assertion: "It is important that every Task (objective) should appeal to you, and excite you."[9] In addition, it is especially ideal if the actor has significant interest in the role, the play, acting as a whole, and so on. Along with other elements like given circumstances and stakes, obstacles are a way to add significant interest to the pursuit of the objective/task/ goal.

The next parallel is between what Stanislavski refers to as "Muscular Release" (which encourages tension-free performance) and what Csíkszentmihályi calls *ease* or *effortlessness*. Stanislavski argued that it is only from a state of tension-free relaxation that an actor can be truly responsive. In flow, ease is the feeling that everything that is being executed is executed easily. It is done efficiently and with minimal effort. There is an absence of tension and the individual is operating at his or her best.

Concentration and attention are concepts offered very early in Book One of *An Actor's Work*. One reason for its importance to the system and prominence in the book can be linked to the flow indicators *autotelism* and *concentration*. Tortsov chastises his students for their concentration and attention on what he calls the black hole, the house. These students have their attention not on the world of the play, or their partner, an object within the world, and/or their objective, but rather on the audience and how they are being perceived. They are not acting for the sake of acting; they are acting to be admired, thought beautiful, or thought talented.

Tortsov suggests that they will never achieve inspired acting if they cannot turn their attention away from the black hole, and Csíkszentmihályi tells us that an indicator of flow is that the activity in which the actor is involved is *autotelic*. It is being executed for its own sake. When acting is autotelic the actor does not act for the approval of the audience, the critics, teachers, or directors, but for the sake of the work itself. We hope, and feel fairly secure, that all actors have had the experience of how much better they are when they focus on the work at hand for the sake of the work itself as opposed to the results. In addition, Csíkszentmihályi observed that when in a state of flow, individuals are fully *concentrated* on the task at hand.

Finally, we would also like to emphasize that the combination of the flow indicators of *balance of challenge and skill* and *goal orientation* plays a particularly crucial role in assisting the individual in establishing and maintaining concentration and attention and in the potential for achieving flow. If the goal is of significant interest and there is a balance of challenge and skill, it is relatively easy to establish and maintain concentration and attention. This perfectly parallels Stanislavski's assertion that objectives and all of our choices must be of significant interest in order to command and maintain our concentration.

Why Obstacles for This Exercise?

Simply put, obstacles provide the perfect intersection between the work of Stanislavski and the work of Csíkszentmihályi. First, because of the strong parallel between obstacles and the *balance of challenge and skill* flow indicator. Second, because *balance of challenge and skill* is an indicator that can be consciously controlled by either developing stronger skills or, more easily, through an adjustment in challenge level. For example, in order for a child to learn, it is important that the work they are being asked to do is at the appropriate level. It pushes them, it engages them fully, but it is neither too easy (leading to boredom) nor too difficult (leading to anxiety and frustration). It is also valuable to try to isolate obstacles and explore how different obstacles (including both physical and psychological obstacles) can be applied to the same objective and change the entire experience of its pursuit.

What are Obstacles?

Along with objectives/tasks and actions/tactics, obstacles are one of the most foundational elements of Stanislavski's technique. They are also inextricable from one another, since an objective is what you want, an action is what you do to get what you want, and an obstacle is what stands between you and what you want. They constantly impact each other. The choice of action is determined by the objective, for characters will attempt to get what they want by means that they believe have a reasonable likelihood of success. The action must be something that the character believes has a reasonable chance of overcoming or circumnavigating the obstacle and reaching the objective. Also, obstacles are partially determined by the nature of the objective. The obstacle must be something that the actor can reasonably believe might stand between the character and the objective. Finally, given circumstances impact everything: the objective, the actions, the obstacle, everything. In fact, not only do given circumstances impact obstacles, obstacles are given circumstances in themselves.

Why They Matter

Although we have already touched upon how obstacles work, we would like to elaborate on why they are important and useful. First, they are important because they exist, moment to moment, in our everyday lives. We are always in want of something; we are always doing things in order to get what we want; and there is almost always something standing in-between, some distance we must close, something we must overcome in order to get what we want, some obstacle. The challenge(s) presented by the obstacle(s) could be anything from "my refrigerator is not immediately next to me, therefore, I must cross my living room in order to get something to eat," to, "I must find my family, but they have been kidnapped and I have little clue as to their whereabouts."

Second, obstacles add difficulty to the achievement of objectives. This increase in difficulty promotes concentration and attention from the character and the actor and can initiate flow. The increased level of concentration and attention pulls actors away from the black hole and toward autotelic engagement with the task at hand (the achievement of the objective and acting itself) which may also initiate flow. Third, the increased challenge can initiate the experiencing of genuine sensations and feelings.

Finally, obstacles are important because they add conflict and interest. Our obstacles in life may often be small, but in drama they must provide enough resistance that there is doubt as to whether or not the characters' objectives will be achieved. They help to make each attempt at achieving the objective a tiny little play. They provide resistance and interest for the character and the actor. They can also be stacked one upon the other in order to add further interest and drama to the pursuit of any single objective.

Incorporation

It should also be mentioned that, like the relationship between the elements of Stanislavski's technique, the relationship between flow indicators is not linear but circular and that it is possible that when you engage fully with one indicator the others may follow. The key is finding the most welcoming point of entry into that circular continuum. That point of entry may be different for different people and may change from one day to another. Some days an individual might be able to enter into a state of flow through task orientation (objective), whereas on others it may be through ease. Exploring, defining, and understanding points of entry increases the actor's chances of entering a state of inspired acting or flow.

The Indicators Focused on for This Exercise

This exercise highlights and promotes the following indicators: goal orientation, a high level of concentration and attention on the task at hand, immediate feedback, ease or effortlessness, the merging together of action and consciousness, autotelism and, most importantly for obstacles, the balance of skill and challenge. Through focus on one or more of these indicators an individual may "light up" the remaining indicators and initiate a state of flow or inspired acting.

Exercise Goals

The goal of this exercise is to help actors (and students of acting) physically and psychologically understand, implement, and experience obstacles and their flow-stimulating potential. They will also experience how obstacles work in tandem with objectives/tasks and tactics/actions.

What You Will Need

You will need to create three sets of cards: Objective Cards, Physical Obstacle Cards, and Psychological Obstacle Cards. Ideas for Objective and Obstacle Cards are provided at the end of the chapter. In addition, you will need containers (index card boxes, jars, large envelopes, etc.) for each set of cards so that the students cannot see what is written on them when they make their selections.

Physical Setup

You may work in any empty space. However, it is beneficial for the space to include a door, chairs, other furniture, and props/objects that the actors may be able to use as obstacles, as part of objectives and/or as tactical aides in achieving their goals. An actor may work alone with this exercise, but it is optimal to work with other individuals who may serve as obstacles and provide outside feedback.

Directions

Exercise 1

Begin by focusing on the flow indicator of *autotellism*. Select two players. Communicate to Player 1 why they are engaging in the exercise. They are engaging in the exercise for the exercise itself, because they want to explore, because they want to expand their abilities, and because they love acting and creating. It is not to impress, to do it "correctly," as a performance, or to please you. Define and invite them to "turn away" from the black hole and toward doing the work for its own sake. Player 2 will be at the ready as some of the Objective Cards and obstacles require a second player.

Without looking, Player 1 will start by selecting an Objective Card. Example – You want to organize/tidy the space or you want to travel across the room and sit in a chair. The Objective Cards are the catalyst for the goal orientation flow indicator. Instruct the actor to make the achievement of this objective as high-stakes as possible (life or death). This will ensure that their objective is of significant interest and begins to activate the next flow indicator: a high level of concentration and attention on the task at hand.

Player 1 will execute the objective without an obstacle. Ask Player 1 to orally reflect on his or her experience. It is likely that Player 1 will share that the execution of the objective was quite easy. If not, ask them how difficult they found the objective or task and if it could be made to be more difficult.

Next, without looking, Player 1 will select a Physical Obstacle Card. Example – You can't open your eyes or Player 2 will not let you. Player 1 will then attempt to achieve their objective with the added obstacle. The *concentration* flow indicator will be strengthened by the increased level of attention and skill necessary to achieve the objective. The player should pursue their objective until it is achieved, it becomes clear that it will not be achieved or a period of no more than three minutes elapses. The immediate feedback flow indicator will communicate to them whether they are achieving or have achieved their objective. You will know that it is about time to end the exercise when Player 1 begins to recycle actions in his or her effort to achieve the objective. If it appears that Player 1 is fortunate enough to have entered or nearly entered a state of flow, is engaged and/or the pursuit remains alive, use your best judgment in allowing the exercise to continue longer: perhaps until the state of apparent flow and/or engagement is lost. You can also investigate what happens if it is allowed to go on for quite a long time, as we often underestimate what is sustainable.

When the exercise is complete, Player 1 will orally reflect on his or her experience and the ways that it may have differed from his or her initial obstacle-free pursuit of the objective. Was the obstacle strong enough to achieve balance between the challenge of achieving the objective and the skill level of the player, thereby creating the potential for flow? or is the player bored or anxious? Was it too easy to overcome? Was it too diffi-cult? What happened as a result? If Player 1 felt a sense of flow did it include the flow indicator – the merging together of action and conscious-ness? In other words, did they feel a sensation of unity in mind and body?

Player 1 will now add a second or even third Physical Obstacle Card to make the achievement of the objective even more challenging? Example: Player 1 can't open his or her eyes AND Player 2 will not allow Player 1 to leave the room. Player 1 will orally reflect on the ways that the experience was different. Did he or she begin to experience flow? Was there the potential to experience flow? Was it merely anxiety pro-voking? Did it release emotion? Could this be used to the actor's advan-tage? Did the objective change with the addition of another obstacle? Did overcoming the obstacle become the new immediate objective?

Exercise 2

Repeat Exercise 1 with a Psychological Obstacle Card in place of the Physical Obstacle Card. Is there a difference in experience between the Physical Obstacle Card and the Psychological Obstacle Card?

Exercise 3

Mix the physical cards with the psychological cards in one container and repeat Exercise 1. Example – You want to leave the room, but you are afraid of doors OR you want to leave the room, but you are afraid of doors AND you can't open your eyes OR you want to make Player 2 laugh, but you are petrified of rejection AND the entire class is standing between you and Player 2.

This stacking of obstacles will show how the balance or imbalance of goal and skill leads either to boredom, flow, or anxiety, and how flow and anxiety, in particular, lead to further sensations and feelings.

Exercise 4

Try the exercise with a duo, trio, or larger group selecting the cards and pursuing the objective together. Like a basketball team playing at its best, is there the potential to achieve a sort of group flow? What initiates this feeling of flow? What hinders it?

Inspiration (or Exercise Origins)

Obstacle Cards was derived from and inspired by the exercise "Character, Setting, Problem."[10] In many ways obstacles and problems are similar, for obstacles *are* problems, however problems also include the objective. The need for the objective is really part of the problem, for if that need was absent there would be no problem. In addition, we have expanded on the general concept of the exercise by infusing it with the knowledge we have gained from flow.

We came across Character, Setting, Problem in a document titled "Theatre Activities/Literacy Connections" developed by Karla Huntsman. Huntsman, a professional storyteller and former Theatre for Young Audiences (TYA) instructor, developed this exercise to teach the elements of narrative. It is similar to and falls under the umbrella of exercises and games often called "Character, Setting, Problem, Solution" that are used by elementary school teachers to address requirements of the common core. Huntsman's goal was to show teachers how they could meet common core standards through theatre games and techniques, and increase their students' exposure to the arts within the time constraints teachers face.[11]

Post-Exercise Reflections (for New Leaders to Consider as Discussion Points)

Although oral reflection is called for after each step of the exercise, the exercise as a whole should be followed by an overall reflection. In what ways did each step of the exercise physically and psychologically impact the player? When was there balance or imbalance between the difficulty of achieving the objective and the player's skill level? How was the player impacted by the balance or imbalance? What sensations and feelings did the player experience? What is the relationship between obstacles and the initiation of sensations and feelings? Are obstacles a key to experiencing genuine sensations and feelings on stage? Did the player experience flow or inspiration? What might the player do to increase the likelihood of experiencing flow or inspiration?

Ideas for Further Research

Flow is a powerful concept and state. It is synonymous with inspiration whether in everyday life, on a field of play, or on a stage. We are just at the beginning of understanding what is going on inside actors when they act and when they act well. By learning more about flow and its implications for, and applications to, acting methodologies, we can enhance the effectiveness of the methodologies, the acting exercises that advance them, and actors in performance.

Obstacle Card Ideas

Objective Cards

- You want to leave the room.
- You want to place a chair on the opposite side of the room.
- You want to travel across the room and sit in a chair.
- You want to find your keys.
- You want to write the word "objective" on a board.
- You want to crawl across the floor on your belly.
- You want to get Player 2 to leave the room.
- You want to get Player 2 to carry a chair across the room.
- You want to travel across the room and lie down on the floor.
- You want to unpack or pack your bag.
- You want to travel across the room and turn off the lights.
- You want to travel across the room and go into the closet.
- You want to organize/tidy the space.
- You want to find something to eat (but don't eat it if it is not yours).
- You want to hide from Player 2.
- You want to get someone to comfort you.
- You want to find water in the room.
- You want to find something extra to wear.
- You want to find a place where you feel safe.
- You want to get someone to give you money.
- You want to get someone to allow you to join them.
- You want to get someone to compliment you.

- You want to get someone to applaud you.
- You want to get someone to copy what you are doing.
- You want to create a sculpture with items in the room.
- You want to get someone to leave with you.
- You want to stack three blocks or chairs.

Physical Obstacle Cards

- You can't open your eyes.
- You can't use your hands.
- You can only use one hand.
- You can't walk.
- You can't use your arms.
- You can only move very slowly.
- You can't stop laughing.
- You can only move backwards.
- You can't look people in the eyes.
- Your joints are creaky and hard to move.
- You are not permitted to ask for help.
- Player 2 will not let you achieve your objective.
- You can only use your feet.
- You are physically exhausted.
- You can only take the longest possible distance between two points.
- Player 2 wants (and is trying to get) the opposite of what you want.
- You are four times heavier than you actually are.
- You are made of glass/fragile. You are easily shattered.
- You can't lift things.
- (Without touching you) The individuals in the class continue to stand between you and what you want.
- Player 2 is hugging your ankle.
- The room is filled with a noxious gas.
- You can't hear.
- You must always be in physical contact with Player 2.
- You may only travel along the walls.
- You may not touch the floor.
- You can only hop on one foot.
- The room is full of mosquitos.
- The floor is very sticky.
- It is very cold.
- It is very warm.
- Something in the room smells horrible.
- You desperately need to go to the bathroom.

Psychological Obstacle Cards

- You are afraid of people.
- You are afraid of moving.

- You fear rejection.
- You smell terrible and you don't want anyone to know.
- You have a desperate need to impress.
- You don't believe you can achieve your objective.
- You can't differentiate words or objects.
- You may not speak.
- Everything is confusing.
- You have never done this before.
- You fear success.
- Nothing is ever good enough.
- You are mentally exhausted.
- You can't stop laughing/Everything is funny making it impossible to communicate.
- You can't stop crying/Everything is sad making it impossible to communicate.
- Everything is frustrating/irritating.
- You can't do anything alone.
- You are incapable of articulating what you want.
- You think people are after you.
- You are afraid of light.
- You are a germaphobe.
- You are afraid of closets.
- You can't stay away from closets.

Acknowledgments

We would like to acknowledge and thank Kent State University students Madeline Barry, Rafaela Clerle Sadocco Pereira, Kaelin Curran, Luke Ehlert, Hannah Hensler, John Kost, Mikaela Ray, and Ronald Zak who volunteered to participate in a 2018 developmental workshop on Obstacle Cards.

Notes

1 Stanislavski, Constantin. *An Actor's Work*. Abingdon: Routledge, 2010. xxxii.
2 Csíkszentmihályi, Mihaly. *Flow: The Psychology of Optimal Experience*. New York: HarperCollins Publishers, 1990. 6.
3 Csíkszentmihályi, Mihaly. *Flow*, 1.
4 Stanislavski, Constantin. *An Actor's Work*, 17.
5 Csíkszentmihályi, Mihaly. *Flow*, 2.
6 Wei, Marlynn. "The Uplifting and Playful World Pepper Fajans and Brooklyn Touring Outfit." *The Huffington Post*, 28 August 2017. www.huffing tonpost.com/entry/the-uplifting-playful-world-of-pepper-fajans brooklyn_u s_59a1f0cde4b0d0ef9f1c14a2. Accessed 14 July 2018.
7 Stanislavski, Constantin. *An Actor's Work*, 17.

8 Ibid., 39.
9 Ibid., 151.
10 Huntsman, Karla. "Theatre Activities/Literacy Connections." byu.edu, https://education.byu.edu/sites/default/files/.../THEATRE–LiteracyConnec tions.doc.
11 Huntsman, Karla. Interviewed by Fabio Polanco. Personal Interview by Email. 21 December 2018.

PART III

IDENTIFYING TACTICS

THIRTEEN

The Tag-tic that Works

Lynn Deboeck

As a teacher or director, you may be asking yourself, "How can I break through those initial layers of inhibition in my actors quickly and subsequently make class and rehearsal time more productive?"

"Tag. You're it!"

Who among us hasn't played a simple game of tag? Most of our childhoods are liberally sprinkled with versions of this joyful pastime. Yet, this deceptively simple game carries hidden troves of skill-building and analytical training, which acting classrooms and rehearsal spaces need. Moreover, tag's form reminds us of the important place *play* should hold in our training. Using evolutionary psychology, cognitive science, and the tenets of Bogart and Landau's *Viewpoints*, I demonstrate how tag is the quintessential warm-up for fully engaging young actors because it not only physically engages the body, but it also loosens inhibitions, creates ensemble, involves the students' tactical faculties and awakens emotional centers.

Psychologist Dr. Peter Gray explains that we have evolutionary theory to thank for the reasons why we enjoy the game so much, which he likens to predator–prey behavior.[1] We are hardwired to delight in practicing the skills of evading predators. Tag is also the perfect primer for actors because it exercises each of Stanislavski's tenets. Tag provides immediate opposing objectives, offers improvisation and frequent changes in obstacles to overcome, and requires that the actor be nimble and flexible in how they adapt their tactics, whether it be to avoid who is "it" or to pursue someone to tag.

In addition, most students already know how to play a basic game of tag, having learned in childhood. Having this script at the ready, the students unknowingly improvise during the game. While the realization of what they are doing may not dawn on them in the moment, I argue this is exactly the way that the students should be exercising their acting muscles – as direct and unplanned *reaction*. The actors impulsively choose tactics in the game, which can be unpacked afterward to examine how improvisation can be used in scene work. I also experiment with various types of tag in an effort to prep my student actors appropriately for the work to come. For example, if a particular class is covering spatial relationships with scene partners, I may use a tag that requires more physical contact, such as "amoeba tag."[2] Or if the scene we are rehearsing necessitates a slower or more staccato tempo, I may utilize a variation of freeze tag. In essence, tag is the perfect Viewpoints exercise because it forces students (without the need for force) to engage as a group, as well as in response to a particular scene partner (whomever is "it"), and it requires particular movement that can change at any time, necessitating improvisation.

What follows is a recipe for activating young actors, specifically with the goal of revealing the skills they already possess. While no extra tools or equipment is needed for this exercise, you do need energy and a positive attitude to help your student actors take advantage of the exercise. While there are several different variations of tag, the standard setup includes choosing one person to be "it." There are many approaches to making this choice. Often, I give a brief, unexpected, instruction at the beginning of the period such as, "Whomever is the last to run up to me and give me a high-five is 'it'." Typically, it takes a moment for the instruction to sink in, but it is wonderfully illustrative to the group that one needs to pay attention! Once a selection is made, you initiate the game with a simple, "Ready, set, go!" and the person who is "it" tries to tag another person in the group. If they are successful, the person who was tagged becomes the new "it" and tries to tag another. As previously stated, there are also many variations on the game that might necessitate slight changes in this initial setup.

Acting instructors often use modified children's games for breaking the ice with students and increasing the comfort level of the class as a whole. But once the ice is broken, classwork usually moves to more standard acting instruction, the game being discarded as no longer applicable. A game of tag, however, can continue to be useful as long as you make the actors aware of the skills they are using that correlate to scene work. And while it may seem like a social risk too great for a young adult to make, according to neuroscientist Sandra Aamodt, students in this age range actually "become much more sensitive to peer pressure than they were earlier or will be as adults" and therefore "a 20 year old is 50 percent more likely to do something risky if [...] friends are watching than if he's alone."[3] In other words, even if a few students are reticent to join in a game of tag, they will still do so if their peers begin to play.

In this way, age is shown be a major factor in how actors engage with a game of tag. Demographic data about my students helps to understand where they are developmentally. My acting students typically range from 18 to 20 years old. Being young adults, their brains are still developing. According to recent research, scans show that brain development does not cease until 25 years of age.[4] These students are in a "middle ground" of sorts: not fully mature, but able to handle significant challenges better than children. According to Aamodt, the reality is that "the changes that happen between 18 and 25 are a continuation of the process that starts around puberty, and 18 year olds are about halfway through that process." She goes on to say that "their prefrontal cortex is not yet fully developed. That's the part of the brain that helps you to inhibit impulses and to plan and organize your behavior to reach a goal."[5] Far from being a hindrance, acknowledgment of this fact can help instructors reach their students. What better time is there to nourish growth in new actors than at this developmental moment? It is essential to take advantage of the fact that these students will, because of their lack of inhibitions, push the limits of improvisation farther.

Bogart and Landau describe their Viewpoints exercise as being used for: "(1) training performers; (2) building ensemble; and (3) creating movement for the stage."[6] The three corresponding lessons that tag teaches include: being fully present in one's own body; genuinely reacting to stimuli; and building upon what fellow actors offer in a scene. Tag prompts these skills in many different ways. One variation called no-touch tag involves eye contact rather than touching. Another, called "snake tag" engages the entire class in an ensemble effort with a modified crack-the-whip type of game where the person at the front of a line tries to tag the person at the end of the line. Another is Sharks and Minnows, wherein one person starts to tag the "minnows" as they cross the room and once tagged, they become "sharks" and help tag others. Tag's many strengths assist student actors in learning Viewpoints which exist at the heart of all acting lessons because they "involve *play*, the kind of play young children engage in – that of reacting to something that happens in a spontaneous fashion, without self-consciousness, judgment or hesitation."[7]

To initiate tag with a group of younger, or less experienced, actors, it is necessary to confront bodily presence. It can be quite challenging to get acting students *into* their bodies in our current culture that has trained them to repress physicalizing their emotions in exchange for texting emojis. Traditionally, new actors are indoctrinated through a series of exercises that will hopefully guide them toward a neutral state. While there are arguments to be made that the concept of "neutrality" and the body are contradictory, it is generally understood that if a neutral state can be attained, all gestures that follow will extend from the body fully and genuinely. By using tag in the manner I suggest, I am taking a chance with my actors. I throw them into the deep end of the pool with the faith that there is a neutral – or type of neutral state, for I believe there are many – within each student, and distance from that neutral state provides another perspective from which to see and access it. Just as the regular practice of yoga allows us to better feel when our bodies are out of alignment, so does tag – by deliberately and repeatedly pushing us away from a neutral state – allow us to realize when we achieve one. In other words, tag stretches us in order for our muscles to release the built-up, non-neutral physical norms we've forced our bodies to perform over time.

The physicality we adopt as humans reflects the norms of the society we live in. This physicality is what must be shed in order to find a neutral state. Tag enables this to happen because from the initiating point all members in the game are invested and, as instructor, I watch as bodies contort, writhe, and move with quickness and precision – all to tag or evade being tagged. These bodies are being stretched away from their norms in these first few games, but with time the new norm will be one of flexibility. Thankfully, this flexibility does not come at the cost of focus because with tag, much as with acting, "the task, the need, the now is all that you can know."[8] It becomes quite evident that people playing tag focus only on the game, leading to a plethora of teachable moments wherein individuals and the ensemble as a whole can retroactively unpack what it was they knew in that instant.

In addition to addressing bodily awareness and presence with the game, another step is to consider how to generate genuine reactions. Our tacit awareness of action – of physically reacting to external and internal forces – is most easily accessed when inhibitions are relinquished. Tag has the ability to effortlessly compel this release because it is a "script" that has already been memorized prior to the student actors' first meeting. In her book, *The Articulate Body* (1994), Anne Dennis emphasizes that, "each movement has a value and is done on purpose, as a result of the dramatic need."[9] The student running away from the person who is "it" *must* be fast. The audible reaction of a scream is *understandable* and even *expected*, because you could get caught at any second. There is no one that will question why someone moves the way they do in tag, because it is communally understood that those movements are necessary, and therefore allowed. The freedom granted to the actors during tag allows them to not only move out of their heads and into their bodies, but to react genuinely to the situation. It should be noted that the impetus is on the instructor or director to modify tag variations in order to best serve particular populations, such as those actors with disabilities. While I do not include a comprehensive list of options here; some examples of this include giving students laser pointers or flashlights to use to "tag" others, using variations that have pairs of people working together to tag, and verbal tag games that rely on being nimble on a more cerebral level.

Reacting genuinely to a scene partner is a fundamental skill that is coached in beginning acting classes. A genuine reaction is a response that should come from an action within a moment. Frequently, inexperienced actors try to "plan ahead" what they will do in a scene, which precludes authentic responses. Part of the issue is that the student actors do not know one another and, given their desire to fit in, may feel the need to plan in order to avoid embarrassment in front of strangers. As a childhood memory shared by most people, tag has the ability to cross boundaries and help people make instant friends by lowering inhibitions and prompting play. Engaging students in this game means they can play within the safety of a communal activity. Even those actors who hold a negative association with the game (usually the result of being singled out in some way) can be assisted by the instructor by starting with group-based tag versions. These are versions wherein a larger portion of the group works together toward a single goal of tagging another object that others of the group are guarding. By starting with this prequel, if you will, one can create a supportive environment that results in community – without which we cannot hope to be productive in theatre spaces. Regardless of the students' personal connections to the game, in my experience their basic knowledge of the rules seems to be the main element needed to create the kind of environment wherein growth and learning flourish. Without the pressure of learning something new, students can, and do, play. This play incorporates improvisational and genuine reactions – necessary skills in acting. The students, of course, have these skills already but may not realize it. Using tag in class consistently, I slowly awaken them to the realization of those skills they already have at the ready.

Once I have seen to the actors' body in time and space and addressed the necessary impulses toward reaction, I move on to building a scene together as an ensemble. Often, improvisation games such as "Yes, and" are used to challenge students to readily accept what the scene and other actors offer and to add to it.[10] The temptation for a new actor is to say "No" and to change the scene to be about what they are creating. Saying "No" gives the student the illusion of control and makes them feel more secure in their performance. It is the instructor's job to emphasize the importance of agreement. Without the assent of what the scene already is, there is no way to build upon it and make it something more. The game of tag eliminates the need for saying "Yes" or "No" because there are no other options – you are in the game and must play according to the rules. It also gives more control to the instructor as to how many options to provide the students for their own input.[11]

As an example, a traditional game of tag gives the participants two options – they can either run away or toward other people. Other rules can be instituted in order to give more options. One version of the game involves people being frozen in one position once they are tagged. This introduces the option of unfreezing fellow players. It is not required for those who are not "it" to unfreeze anyone, but it is an additional choice that creates more suspense and conflict as the person who is "it" may take advantage of the Good Samaritans by tagging them in the act of helping their fellow players. And though possibly illogical, if you consider the goal of the game is to avoid being tagged, in my experience empathy wins out because the more that students are frozen, the more students choose to take the risk and unfreeze their friends. The resultant "scenes" are then even more exciting.

As Bogart and Landau assert, "naming the Viewpoints allows us to dissect reality into something identifiable and perhaps repeatable on stage."[12] Tag enables actors to practice, name, and internalize the acting skills they will need in quite literal ways that will be kinesthetically remembered. Students can then draw from the game of tag and bring those skills into their scene work or rehearsal. The philosophic goals of Viewpoints: "Listen; Pay attention; Be open; Change; Respond; Surprise yourself; Use accidents; Work with fearlessness and abandon and an open heart,"[13] are all skills exercised in this simple, user-friendly warm-up game. But the true magic of tag is not that you build new skills into your actors, but that you help them find the tools they already possess and remind them how to use those tools productively as actors. In essence, you do not tell them what they can be. You remind them that they're "it" already.

Notes

1 Peter Gray, "Chasing Games and Sports: Why Do We Like to be Chased?" *Psychology Today*, November 5, 2008, accessed December 10, 2015. www.psychologytoday.com/blog/freedom-learn/200811/chasing-games-and-sports-why-do-we-be-chased.

2 "Amoeba tag" is played by pairing off the class and having all but one pair link arms. The unlinked pair are then the "it" person and the person being chased. The person being chased can link arms with one of the other pairs standing around and if they do, they are safe, and the person who is on the other end of the linked group of three is now the new person being chased. This tag game is referred to by other names as well.

3 Sandra Aamodt, "Brain Maturity Extends Well Beyond Teen Years," Brain Candy. *NPR*, October 10, 2011. [Radio] Accessed January 2, 2016. www.npr.org/templates/story/story.php?storyId=141164708.

4 Ibid.

5 Ibid.

6 Anne Bogart & Tina Landau. *The Viewpoints Book*. New York: Theatre Communications Group, 2005. 7.

7 Ibid., 209.

8 Ibid., 208.

9 Anne Dennis. *The Articulate Body*. New York: Drama Book Publishers, 1994. 51.

10 Touted as "the most important rule in improvisation" by Charna Halpern & Del Close, "Yes, and ..." refers to the rule that "whenever two actors are on stage, they agree with each other to the Nth degree. If one asks the other a question, the other must respond positively, and then provide additional information." Charna Halpern and Del Close. *Truth in Comedy: The Manual of Improvisation*. Colorado Springs, CO: Meriwether Publishing Ltd., 1993. 46.

11 For example, you might allow students to create a "base" that's safe from the tagger, or require them to say or do something before being "unfrozen" (for a game of "freeze tag"), or you might give them a "get out of jail free" card, if you will, by allowing them to call one or two "blocks" in the game – preventing the tagger from tagging them.

12 Bogart & Landau. *The Viewpoints Book*, 199.

13 Ibid., 204.

FOURTEEN

Improvising Tactical Choices Based on Status or "Who's Driving the Dramatic Action Bus?"

Jean Dobie Giebel

Some of Our Strongest Teaching Tools are Metaphors

I teach in an undergraduate liberal arts institution. My intro-level students come in with various levels of experience and training so it's challenging for them to come together collaboratively, particularly when rehearsing outside of class. To build a common language, I start with a common high school image. I suggest they take the classic triangular diagram of climactic structure and imaginatively lay it on the floor like a road map. If each beat has its own mini-climax that propels the action to the next beat, and the series of climactic beats build the overall structure of the play, their road map might look something like Figures 14.1 and 14.2.

Following that map means the characters must zig and zag toward the ultimate turn of the corner at the play's climax. The clarity of the zigs-zags keeps the audience on their toes, wondering who will win the core argument of the play.[1]

Students can embody the core argument by employing master improvisor Keith Johnstone's concept of *status*. Johnstone defined what I call the zig-zag of dramatic action through his "see-saw principle: I go up and you go down."[2] In other words, a character with high status is predominate to the low-status character(s), who lend focus by allowing the high-status character to drive the dramatic action of the play forward. Using the road-map metaphor, the high-status character drives the "dramatic action bus" along the road map by making strong tactical choices in the pursuit of their objective. That is, until the low-status character makes a move to take the wheel. Using status play to transition students from improvisation to text analysis, the following exercises teach students to identify beat shifts through changing dramatic status relationships. Defining beats with status allows students to improvise tactical choices moment-to-moment, building flexibility, collaboration, and improvisational play into their out-of-class rehearsal process.

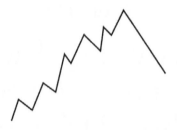

Figure 14.1 Climactic structure

Figure 14.2 Road map

Stanislavski believed that each scene in a play could be divided into *units of action*.[3] In each unit of action, each character has a sub-objective with supporting tactics that help to achieve the objective of the scene. A beat is defined here as one of Stanislavski's units; the building blocks of dramatic action that are delineated by a status transaction. Therefore, beat shifts are expressed by one or more characters changing dramatic status. In a two-character climactic beat, the character most actively pursuing their objective is called the high-status character and the character that is receiving information and is propelled to a reaction is the low-status character. When the low-status character makes a strong active choice that forces the high-status character to listen to the other side of the core argument, the status relationship changes. Low becomes high and high becomes low: the beat shifts.

Using dramatic status as a guiding principle, a character might use multiple tactics to work against an obstacle in one beat. The beat does not shift until there is a change in the obstacle; in other words, a change in the dramatic status relationship between the characters. To illustrate this principle, students are given two-character climactic scenes to analyze, in which they are tasked with discerning the dramatic status of their characters in each beat and how that changes throughout the scene. In a two-character scene beats are defined as having four possible status relationships: high/low, low/high, high/high and low/low. This transactional analysis is meant to correspond with the core argument of the play.

Looking at status another way, the first game my class plays to learn these principles is a rolling improvisational exercise, the goal of which is to collaboratively build an imagined kitchen. "The Kitchen"[4] then becomes a teaching metaphor for any imaginative play-space students build together. After warm-up exercises that teach improv best practices (most importantly always accepting and building on their partner's offers), students line up along one wall and as a group, build an imaginative kitchen through physical activities. Student X enters the space and begins pantomiming something a person might do in a kitchen. "Whatever happens in the kitchen, stays in the kitchen," so once an item is pantomimed, it exists and must be honored. For example, if Student X enters the kitchen to get a drink of water, they might establish a cabinet, a glass, a faucet (implying a sink) and countertop. As soon as the next student in line, Student Y, can identify what Student X is doing and is therefore able to accept the offer, Y enters the space and somehow greets their scene partner: "Hi!" "How're you doing?" "Yo, dude," etc. That greeting is X's cue to leave the space and Y begins a new activity, adding to the construction of the kitchen. This structure efficiently gives everyone in class an opportunity to play. To keep the whole class engaged throughout the exercise, I also usually have the first three students in line come back into the space, once everyone has had a turn, to describe the finished kitchen. Those three students then go to the end of the line, and a different pair of students begin the next pass.

Each time we play The Kitchen, the exercise expands. The first addition is a problematic given circumstance. Once X has established the beginnings of the kitchen, Y enters with a problem that can be solved in the kitchen. Their objective is to receive aid. It is important to note that, because all offers are accepted, any aid will do (which can result in some hilarious scenarios) because at this level of the game there are no obstacles and everyone in the kitchen is grateful. As soon as the circumstance is revealed by Y, X offers assistance. Going back to our example: if X enters the kitchen to get a drink of water, establishing a cabinet, a glass, a faucet, and so on, Y might enter the space and after greeting their partner with "Yo, dude," and they might add, "I am so hungry." From the imaginary counter near the sink, X might lift an object replying, "Have some pizza." Because everyone is grateful in the kitchen, Y responds with an expression of thanks, which now becomes the cue for X to leave and the next student in line enters with a new problem.

Once students understand the construct, conflict is introduced through the addition of obstacles and tactics. The student's activity in the kitchen becomes their objective and therefore the entering student's obstacle. The student in the kitchen can be instructed to resist giving aid until they have identified two, three, or any number of tactical choices on the part of the student making an entrance. Returning to the example above, when Y enters with the problem of "I am so hungry," this exchange might follow:

```
              Y
         Yo, dude.

              X
         Hey!

              Y
         I am so hungry

              X
         I'm getting a glass of water.

              Y
         Please, like I am really really hungry. (Tactic: to
         plead.)

              X
         And I am really really thirsty.

              Y
         I'll do your homework if you give me something to
         eat. (Tactic: to bribe.)

              X
         Dude, this water is so refreshing!

              Y
         Get me some food, NOW! (Tactic: to demand.)

              X
         Okay! Have some pizza.

              Y
         Thank you.
```

The offer of pizza is the shift in status. Each pass in the exercise is defined as a beat. X begins the beat in high status by establishing their activity and controlling the story. Y enters and initiates a conflict in which both students are working to control the dramatic action, in other words, to achieve high status. After the requisite number of tactics, Y wins control, X moves to low status; their status relationship has changed, so the beat shifts. Y expresses gratitude, which allows X to exit the kitchen. Y's objective becomes finishing the pizza as the next student in line enters with a new problem, beginning a new beat.

Building a kitchen together keeps an entire class participating, collaborating, and creating as they learn this basic anatomy of dramatic structure. When students have The Kitchen under their belt, they are ready to tackle text and create the zig-zagging roadmap for their dramatic action. As stated earlier, The Kitchen becomes the metaphor for any collaboratively built play-space based on given circumstances, so their first task is to identify the givens of their scene and build their kitchen. Once they have completed that task, it's time to identify the core argument and cook up their scene. Scene partners must come up with pairings of objectives that are in opposition. Objectives are defined as being immediately attainable positive goals so the conflict in the scene results from the pairing of opposing positive forces. X's objective becomes Y's obstacle, and Y's objective becomes X's obstacle. With that basic analysis, the students can then begin to populate lists of tactics.

Tactics are fundamentally what the actor brings to a scene to transform a written text into vital communication. The choice of tactics shapes the character, by expressing the length, depth, height, and breadth to which the character will go in the pursuit of their objective. Tactics are usually described as verbs or "action words," but I am also careful with undergraduates to differentiate them from emotional responses and states of being, such as being angry or glad. Tactics are therefore specifically defined as moment-to-moment choices made in reaction to the character's obstacle.

All humans have a range or vocabulary of tactics that they use to express their needs or desires; however, the most engaging tactical choices often result when a character is pushed outside that "comfort zone" into unfamiliar tactical territory. Therefore, the list of tactics the student builds for this approach to scene work should be long and broad in scope. When creating their list of tactics, students are directed to set the lines aside and work entirely with the given circumstances and their objective. Rather than preplanning tactics for each beat, the result is a list of choices to draw on in rehearsal. Then, working with synonyms and antonyms, students are directed to consider choices beyond the obvious. This work opens the student's mind to greater possibilities and allows them to choose the most enlightening array of tactics for the character to employ, thus revealing as much of the character as possible to the audience.

Once the objectives, obstacles, and tactics are gathered, preliminary beat shifts are identified in the text, based on shifting status relationships. Below is a brief excerpt from *Love and Country* by Alex Rubin,[5] with possible beat shifts marked based on status. In this play, Sydney and Kathy are sisters, but they have led very different lives. When Sydney tells Kathy that she is going to come out as a gay woman in country music, Kathy fears they'll both lose everything.

Beat one – Sydney high status, Kathy low status

SYDNEY is laughing to the point of breathlessness.

KATHY (CONT'D.)
What? What? Stop laughing! What is so funny???

SYDNEY
You are the – the worst impressionist!

Beat two – Kathy high status, Sydney low status

KATHY
Oh, because you're such a great actress yourself?
Like that CoverGirl commercial when you couldn't
remember, "Easy, breezy, beautiful."

SYDNEY
It wasn't that bad.

KATHY
You kept calling for line. It's three words!

SYDNEY
It got edited alright.

KATHY
And the guest spot on All My Children that they made
into a mute character.

Beat three – Kathy high status, Sydney high status

SYDNEY
They did not! They just decided that the character
could only express herself through song.

KATHY
And the ketchup commercial!

SYDNEY
If you know so much about it, why don't you try some
time and stop judging me? It's not as easy as it
looks.

KATHY
Neither is taking care of two kids on your own, and
I'm guessing you wouldn't want to trade.

SYDNEY
You're not on your own. You have Ray.

Beat three – Kathy high status, Sydney high status

KATHY
Well, he works a lot.

To keep students playing with their beats, I have them engage physic-ally, using the Johnstone "see-saw" metaphor as a simple way for them to feel the beats shifting. Placing two chairs facing each other, they read through the scene, standing when the character is in or is attempting to assume high status; sitting when the character is in low status. This simple exercise immediately allows them to physically check in with their choices and experiment with where to place their status shifts. For the introductory student, this simple movement exer-cise illustrates the organic connection between movement and struc-ture. By asking students to physically relinquish power by sitting, they begin to explore vulnerability when in low status. Most importantly, they begin to understand that the quality of the beat shift is specifically determined by the choice of tactic. Using tactics that are confident, sur-prising, or emotionally charged are some of the ways to seize high status. Characters assuming low status are often actively questioning, making concessions, or strategizing; falling back to regroup for their next attack. Playing with status, the final moments of the scene above might actually end up looking something like the following, if the beat change occurs two lines earlier.

SYDNEY
If you know so much about it, why don't you try some time and stop judging me? It's not as easy as it looks.

Beat four – Kathy high status, Sydney low status

KATHY
Neither is taking care of two kids on your own, and I'm guessing you wouldn't want to trade.

SYDNEY
You're not on your own. You have Ray.

KATHY
Well, he works a lot.

As scene work progresses, The Kitchen exercise serves as a reminder of the opportunity to employ multiple tactics within each beat. Students are coached to make more imaginative and subtle tactical choices, drawing on the lists of tactics they compiled. As Johnston recounts in his book *Impro* (1987), when teaching status, he directed his actors to:

Try to get your status just a little above or below your partner's ... and I insisted that the gap be minimal. The actors seemed
to know exactly what I meant and the work was transformed. The
scenes became 'authentic', and the actors seemed marvelously
observant. Suddenly we understood that every inflection and movement implies a status, and that no action is due to chance, or
really 'motiveless.'[6]

Students learn that the concept of low status is not meant to imply
a lack of motive or energy, but a tactical shift to active listening, while
lending focus to the character that the audience needs to follow to
understand the core argument of the play. Outside of class, they use
the technique to continue to playfully develop their scenes by actively
improvising their tactical choices moment-to-moment, connecting
improvisation to listening and working off of their scene partners,
while maintaining collaboration through the agreed-upon beat structure
of the scene. Students return to class with presentations in which they
are able to change tactics with every line, creating varied and specific
performances through a truly collaborative process.

One last metaphor: I tell my students that learning a new acting
technique is like breaking in a new pair of shoes. Our old technique is
worn in and comfortable, it conforms to who we are and where we've
been. As young actors grow, they need new techniques to move them
where they want to go, and when an entire class grows, they need
a technique to move them along together. They need a bus. The shifting status approach to beats is a technique that unifies a class in
a common language while allowing each individual actor the space to
play creatively. Status provides a clear and secure bridge from improvisation to scene work by giving young actors a structural context in
which to improvise tactical choices. In addition, the rudimentary connection to movement from the see-saw exercise can be reinforced and
expanded into gestures as animated as advancing, retreating, avoiding,
and diverting, or as subtle as shifting focal point or weight from one
foot to the next. The lesson is that movement connects to tactical
choices. Ultimately, in their out-of-class rehearsals, students are able to
play with each other within collaborative relationships while discovering the embodied tactics of their characters. In performance, they learn
the joy of taking their audience on a ride on the dramatic action bus:
a ride full of rich tactical scenery, that zigs and zags from one beat to
the next until it turns the inevitable corner, and rolls into the resolution.

Happy driving!

Notes

1 "Core argument" refers to the main conflict, or through-line of action. When I teach Aristotle to first-year students, rather than teaching "thought" or "theme," I focus on the *agon*, the struggle or argument that drives the play because students readily understand an argument has two sides that are engaged in a conflict, whereas a "thought" or "through-line" appears singular.

2 Johnstone, Keith. *Impro: Improvisation and the Theater.* Routledge. 1987. 36

3 Carnicke, Sharon Marie. *Stanislavsky in Focus: An Acting Master for the Twenty-first Century.* 2nd ed. Routledge Theatre Classics, Routledge. 2008. 214.

4 I first learned a version of this game as "The Laundromat" studying with interactive theatre artist Gary Izzo. It is a descendent of Viola Spolin's "Orientation" and "Where" games, descriptions of which can be found in her book *Improvisation for the Theater: A Handbook of Teaching and Directing Techniques*, Third edition. Northwestern University Press. Chapter 3, 51–104; Chapter 4, 118–134.

5 Rubin, Alex. *Love and Country.* Jane Chambers Award Finalist, AACT NewPlayFest Finalist. Copyright Alex Rubin Writes. All rights reserved.

6 Johnstone, Keith, *Impro*, 33.

FIFTEEN

Transformational Tactics

Engaging Students in the Heroic Pursuit of Their Objective

Kim Shively

I walk into an empty classroom. The space is filled with potential. Today is the day we work on tactics. I have asked my students to come prepared. They are working on the construct of character during this course, which serves as their last studio technique class at my institution. We acknowledge that character is tricky. The actor will not become somebody else. How can they? On a cellular level, they remain themselves. And yet, the experience of creating the role can change them. It can open up their eyes to some revelation or connect them to their humanity in a new way. This work can only happen when they know how to approach a character without judging the character and when they can heroically pursue their objective with fully embodied tactics. But getting to the heroic pursuit of an objective through these tactics is a journey for which there are few short cuts.

Like many of the Meisner teachers before me, I live in the realm of serving the text and telling the story while *living truthfully under the imaginary circumstances.*[1] That is what I teach my students. However, to crack open the code of this work as actors, I teach them Point of View (POV) work, an approach to playing a character. I have come to define POV as "A highly specific, emotionally evocative phrase which encapsulates the lens through which a character views the world, their situation or the other character in a scene."[2] POV colors the way the character sees the other character, pursues their objective, and the tactics they use to get that need met.

I think of the Meisner technique as a three-legged stool. The legs are action, need, and POV. Each of the legs is equally as important and all three legs must be equally balanced to make the stool secure. In their first acting course at my institution, students learn about playing an action (which eventually they come to understand as a tactic). In the next course, they learn about need (or objective). Finally, they learn

POV. And it is through the exploration of POV, that the need (object-ive) and action (tactic) fully come together in a solid technical approach. POV is only tested through the heroic pursuit of the object-ive. For our purposes, heroic means that the character behaves as if they are the hero of their own story, from their unique perspective. And for this purpose, the students must have tactics to get what they need. If their purpose is heroic from *their character's point of view* and they have crafted a clear objective (or itch that must be scratched) for the character, then the tactics become the *how* – how the actor attempts to get their need met.

I love the term "tactic" because it has a precise weight to it. It inspires images of carefully planned strategies or maneuvers. It is with precision and specificity that good acting is forged. And yet, nothing can be more detrimental to a performance than careful planning. Over-planning hinders impulses and makes the theatre dead and wooden. And *living truthfully* is what we all aspire to, which requires us to make something living – an honest and human experience. These tac-tics must therefore engage the actor to fully commit to their tactics in order to achieve their objective (or get their need met), which will then free the actor up to respond truthfully, impulsively.

This tightrope walk requires effective preparation and brave explor-ation, which can inform a performance and enliven the actor. On the day where we begin to play with tactics, there is a buzz in the air. The teaching and learning apprentices (TLAs) are excited, remembering their own discovery in class a few years earlier. The students have spent hours crafting their objectives and POVs. The students have also brought in lists of possible tactics, which would help them meet that objective in the scene.

The first pair have prepared the space for their scene and they have memorized their lines by rote, with no presupposition or inflections. They speak their POVs aloud as they look at one another. This is a ritual many choose to adopt in class. The actors begin the scene as they have rehearsed. The TLAs have the actors' sheets of tactics and begin to give the verbal cues for a tactic shift or side coach. They are not intrusive, but function like a voice in the back of the actor's mind. One actor may be given the tactic "wake up" and the actor takes a breath and changes their tactic to "wake up" on their line. The other TLA, in response to this shift, side-coaches the other actor to "teach" with their response. The discovery is fresh and fun and the actors are affecting one another in their pursuits and listening more deeply. These tactics remain for a few more lines, but then are shifted again. When the scene is over, the actors immediately begin to give feedback. They have made discoveries. They didn't think a particular tactic would work early in the scene, but it stirred their scene partner and brought something different to the moment and ultimately changed the way the scene played out. Perhaps a tactic didn't work out in a particular moment the way that the actor had thought it might, but instead, it gave insight into a moment not previously understood. The actors play again, but this time the TLAs exchange lists, but stay with the same actors.

After a few weeks of rigorous analysis and preparation, the room is electric with anticipation – they feel like something is really happening and they are *really doing* something – because they *are*. They are playing bravely and not a single person speaks of being stuck "in their head" for those few studio hours where they discover how to go after their need in a new way. The students also begin to articulate action differently, because they now have a new understanding of action working to get them what they need.

As an acting teacher, director, and coach, I have few missions more important than helping actors learn to use tactics to heroically change the other character/get what they need/solve their problem. Again, the actor is not being manipulative in their approach, but rather has justified their intention from a heroic perspective. To achieve this mission, I have learned that a solid POV, coupled with a specific objective, can open up a variety of possibilities for the tactics one could play for any given scene. I discovered the importance of these key pieces at the beginning of my teaching/coaching/mentoring career when I was coaching actors for auditions. I spent a majority of my time helping the actor formulate a great POV on the other character or their situation. We would then identify the objective so that we could play with possible tactics for a scene. This was particularly useful for actors who might have little to no training or for veterans who feel pressure to bring something new to their work after being type-cast. Once the initial work is done and possible tactics are compiled, the actor is ready and has the confidence to play. I also found that this work would keep the actor from making presuppositions or concrete decisions about the scene and getting into the rut of line readings.

The tactics activity described here offers exciting possibilities for engaging with tactics. It can be done in a classroom, rehearsal hall, or coaching session. One doesn't need teaching and learning assistants, as I have easily side-coached two actors at once. For that, I just need a table so I can bounce my eyes back and forth from the lists without shuffling papers. This activity helps solidify the work and gives students a way to approach rehearsal on their own after the work in class or a session has ended.

First, help the students identify the objective of the character and a POV that makes them the hero (this prevents "problem playing" or playing the negative action or emotion, and helps actors play to win – keeping the emphasis on *play*). To identify the objective, I encourage the students to read the piece multiple times (and the play, if applicable) so that they are absolutely clear on what they need from the scene partner. Keeping with the premise of the Meisner technique, they must know what they need from the other person. This will keep their attention on the other person and free the actor to get their need met, without watching themselves. The POV of the other person and the situation will inform how they can go about getting what they need. Once they have these two things sketched out, invite them to free-write for three minutes, compiling a list of simple tactics that will help them pursue their objective. Next, encourage them to identify five to seven of the most exciting tactics and find the opposite of each tactic, writing these down as well. When they share them, help them find the most positive way to express the tactics. An example of this is the tactic "to teach." The opposite tactic might be "to shut down." This has a negative weight, but "to suppress" or "to quiet" could be a more active spin on this action.

Now that the actor has a hearty collection of tactics at their disposal, they can play. The actor/s working will have a side coach. A two-person scene can have one or two coaches who work with the generated list of tactics. Prior to the start of the scene, there is a sequence of preparation for each individual actor. These steps can be executed for the partners simultaneously or one after the other, depending on the preference of the coach. The actor/s begin by stating their POV and objective. They then breathe in and "think in" the POV and objective. "Thinking in" can be done as the actors think about their POV and objectives – as if they travel through their body on the breath. I also might add the prompt, "Place your fingers on your forehead and softly close your eyes. Now, I invite you to breathe in your POV and object-ive and imagine it traveling through your brain, down your spine and into your belly." Finally, the actors repeat the POV and objective aloud one more time.

Next, the actor/s begin their work-through of the material. With each line of the scene, the actor will say the line with a chosen tactic and then the coach will offer a different tactic. With each tactic given, the actor will replay the line using the new tactic. The coach may allow the scene to evolve without side-coaching as the scene begins to take a new shape, but can jump back in with additional or contradict-ory tactics when they perceive it is appropriate or when prompted. These different tactics can be random or intentionally contradictory. If the student appears to be stuck in line readings, I have found using oppositional tactics back to back can be helpful to shake the action up. Once the initial work-through of the scene is complete, it is important for the actors to respond to any discoveries they made and to hear impressions from the coaches or teacher. The most helpful feedback is most often the areas where the piece came to life and where the actors were most enlivened by the pursuit of their objective.

Once the student understands the activity viscerally, they can apply this work to their personal rehearsal, which is often a challenge for the student and professional actor alike. I often encourage students to work through various tactics while working on a few lines of text to see what discoveries might be made. When solo rehearsal often becomes more about memorizing lines or a specific way to perform a scene, giving tangible activities that further exploration is helpful to any actor, regardless of their level of training. After really pursuing their objective and playing to win in the exercise, they know what it feels like and they can begin to play on their own. Talking students through this process is important, as some will make the connection to out-of-class rehearsals, while others may not.

Explaining that this work can be done alone is important. I have found it helpful to give examples of how an actor might work through a particular set of lines with multiple tactics, which can be played to a chair or a spot on the wall. This is most helpful for auditions and on-camera acting, as there are often demands on the dramatic imagination which challenge the parameters of the situation. Also, when working in the medium of film and television, the ability to give opposing deliveries of lines or a scene is often required and the actor will find themselves flexible in their pursuit of the objective if they have prepared in a dynamic way: particularly when on set and playing to a mark rather than the other actor, as is often the case.

I love this exercise because it demystifies the "magic" or the pressure to "call down the fire from the gods" before a performance or audition. Often, actors without a solid, personal technique feel as though they are dependent on supernatural inspiration. Instead, this exercise prepares the student to deliver consistently fresh and living work by giving them something solid *to do*. This work empowers actors to understand that the pursuit of the objective is the action. It also helps solidify the concept that ultimately the theatre is a place where something special happens; therefore, their objective is important and makes for tactics that become transformational as those tactics are used to help the actor pursue their objective.

In a world where people can anonymously engage online, being cruel has never been easier. Some students have expressed that they struggle with maintaining a healthy perspective and self-image while engaged on social media. I have observed that students now are balancing more criticism, stress, and self-awareness than in previous years. Finding the heroic perspective in a culture of disconnect is paramount to keeping humanity connected. When it really matters, human beings listen. And when we listen, we can be changed. And when we understand these basic principles, we can find and utilize tactics that transform.

Notes

1 Meisner, S., and D. Longwell. *Sanford Meisner on Acting*. New York: Vintage Original, 1987, 87.
2 Shively, Kim. "Point of View: An Exploration of One Meisner Teacher's Journey to Character Development." *The Player's Journal*, 2018. Available at www.theplayersjournal.org/articles/point-of-view.html.

SIXTEEN

Hunter/Hunted

Experiential Learning and the Actor's Craft

Valerie Clayman Pye

One of the biggest challenges that students can face is translating their intellectual understanding of Stanislavski's concepts into the actual work they do in practice when they are up on their feet. They may have already learned and integrated Stanislavski's vocabulary into their own vernacular, but they still find it difficult to identify which components of Stanislavski's teaching they employ at a particular moment. When working through a scene, they may sense an inherent change, but question, "it is a beat change or a tactic change?" Or they may have written a perfectly actionable verb for their objective, but play – or show – the *idea* of that verb rather than engaging fully in the action. And if the notion of an objective is new to them, if they are really early in their training (or if they are facing a lapse for whatever reason: a challenging scene, lack of preparation, blocks in their work, or issues with their scene partner) they may be stuck in the cycle of playing emotion, rather than an actual objective.

Teaching the concepts of objectives, obstacles, and tactics through practice, through experiential learning without any mention of those concepts or the ideology behind them, enables students to forge a deep understanding of each concept by *doing* the thing itself. Just as one can only fully understand the experience of riding a bicycle by acquiring the tacit knowledge one develops by doing the riding[1], introducing an embodied experience of those concepts helps to create a lexicon that underpins the studio work and anchors the actors' understanding of Stanislavski's tenets through their lived experience. Once students have experienced the components practically, the tacit knowledge of the craft serves as a lexical shorthand for future explorations and rehearsals.

The following exercise works across a range of expertise, from the novice who has never taken an acting class to an actor who is well versed in Stanislavski's objectives, obstacles, and tactics; it is as well suited to the non-major as it is to BFA and MFA acting students. In parallel to the exercise itself, I would like to introduce you to this variation of "Hunter/ Hunted," then identify what the exercise does and how it enhances both your teaching and the students' understanding of the actor's process.

Hunter/Hunted

Exercise Goals

- To demonstrate clearly what an objective is, what a tactic is, and what an obstacle is.
- To identify a "beat change".
- To provide a model for the phrasing of objectives.
- To expose how "emotion" results from/is revealed by pursuing the objective through a variety of tactics.

What You Will Need

- A bandana/blindfold for each student.
- Chairs (equal in number to students participating, plus one for the leader).
- A highlighter pen.

Physical Setup

Position the chairs in a wide, open circle. The circle should be as large as you can manage, but not so large that students are unable to reach out and close the circle, if necessary.

Directions

Explain all of the directions before you begin, then ask the students to put on their blindfolds.

- Each student sits in a chair within the circle, blindfolded.
- While the students are blindfolded you will do two things:
  - Hide the highlighter somewhere within the circle.
    - Please note: you can remove your shoes in order to minimize potential noise; you will want to keep the location of the highlighter concealed for as long as possible.
  - Select two players, by tapping them.
    - Please note: you will want to select two players that are not seated directly next to one another in order to maintain the integrity of the circle (players must remain in the playing space).
  - When both tasks are complete you will return to your own empty seat and announce that "Two players have been selected."

- o Once you have made the announcement that players have been selected – and *ONLY* once that announcement has been made – will both players enter the circle.
- o The students who have not been selected will remove their blindfolds and serve as spotters for the selected players.
- o Both blindfolded players (Seekers) have the same objective: to find the highlighter and become the Hunter.
- o When the highlighter has been found, you will announce that "We have a Hunter."
- o Once the highlighter has been found and the announcement has been made, the objectives change:
  - – The Hunter's objective is to catch the Prey by tapping the Prey anywhere with the highlighter.
  - – The Prey's objective is to return to one of the empty seats and find safety.
- o The seated students also have an objective: to keep the players safely within the circle:
  - – Student spotters are to keep the players within the playing area by creating a physical barrier that lets the players know they are at the edge of the circle.
  - – Spotters can communicate that a player is about to attempt something dangerous or impossible by gently tapping the player twice.
- o Please Note: it is vital to remind the students to remain absolutely silent during the exploration so that they don't reveal key information to the players, whose senses are already heightened.
- • Feel free to create a safety word that causes all action to stop immediately. For a previous trust walk, I used the word "bananas" so that is already a part of our ensemble's vocabulary.

Inspiration

This exercise is a variation of Hunter and Hunted taught to me by Rose Bonczek.[2]

The key differences in this adaptation are:

- • The roles of Hunter and Prey are not assigned, but are determined by the outcome of the first objective.
- • This variation features the introduction of a "beat change".
- • The weapon is considerably smaller than a rolled-up newspaper.
- • The Prey's safety is dependent on the players selected rather than a fixed location outside of the circle (the room's exit or a wall).

This exercise is also influenced by Clive Barker's exercise, The Fight in the Dark.[3] Barker's exercise centers on the theft of a "precious object" (in this case, the weapon), and also features seated observers (in a square configuration). However, Barker's "precious object" is always in a fixed location, in the center of the space. This variation of Hunter/Hunted heightens the actor's pursuit of the objective because the location of the object is always unknown. Therefore, the actor must *actually* find the object in order for the first objective to be completed successfully.

At the start of this exercise, it appears to be little more than a game of skill for students who grew up on a diet of post-apocalyptic YA novels. Right from the beginning, as they sit blindfolded in the circle, there is a heightened sense of readiness (or for those hoping to avoid selection, of protection) in the body. When blindfolded and in that state of readiness, your players' senses will become more acute; they will be actively awaiting your next instructions. Some of them may want to begin as soon as you have selected them, so you will want to remind the group that they are not to enter the arena until you say "Two players have been selected." When your spotters remove their blindfolds, it's not uncommon for them to take a moment to orient themselves to see where the highlighter has been hidden and who has been selected as the players. I make sure that when I hide the highlighter, I avoid patterns of where it has been hidden; the only proviso is that it must remain in the circle, which includes the chairs that make up the circle. I will hide the highlighter as often between the spotters' feet as I do in the center of the playing space or under the chairs.

The first time the game is played, potential strategies have not yet had the opportunity to develop; both players often employ similar tactics in the first round. Sometimes they begin from a standing position, until they realize that there was no stipulation that they remain on their feet. When kneeling, they may begin with small sweeping hand motions as they feel around the floor for the highlighter. They will continue with their initial action for what seems like an unusual amount of time, until they realize that their strategy is not yielding the desired result. Then, instinctually, they try a different tactic, often with increasing creativity and complexity: they engage their lower body, they roll across the floor like a log, they make imaginary snow angels. Note when these changes take place: they are touchpoints that you will want to return to in your discussions after everyone has completed the exercise.

The seekers will remain fully committed to their strategy until they reach the tipping point of exasperation and try an alternate method. These moments are golden teaching opportunities, for they also tend to accompany the release of some emotion: the seeker may become frustrated, frantic, or confused; even angry or giddy by their lack of success. Seekers may simply stop for a moment to recalibrate; they sit in stillness, waiting for a new strategy to emerge before they resume their task of finding the highlighter. Their objective (to find the high-lighter) is so clear that it remains front-of-mind, despite both an internal and an external obstacle (they are blindfolded, and they have a competitor). The seekers cannot "play the end of the scene" because they have no idea what that will be. They cannot "end-gain" because until they achieve their objective of finding the highlighter, they have no way of knowing whether they will need to search for their Prey or seek safety. This acute sense of presence is another point to which you will want to return.

When the highlighter *has* been found, you will announce, "We have a Hunter," and this beat change is so distinct that this moment of practice will become another anchoring point for your training. The players' body language changes immediately, as they commit to their new objectives. The playing space becomes charged with urgency, as they each set about to achieve their new objectives: finding the Prey, finding safety. The commitment to the new goal may also reveal play-ers' emotion; they may exhibit the pride and confidence that accom-panies their success, or the fear and vulnerability that accompanies their pursuit.

As you move your ensemble through this exercise, you will notice that the tactics become more sophisticated with each pair that is selected; they have had the opportunity to observe which tactics they feel are more successful. This won't diminish the efficacy of the explor-ation for they still won't know where you have placed the highlighter. Those tactics that they have pre-screened as effective may or may not be so for that particular round, as each round is very different. Players often underestimate the obstacle that their blindfold presents. They may *think* that they have strategized successfully, but when they are in the arena they are met with the unexpected.

Committed audience engagement is an unforeseen, yet welcome, con-sequence of this exercise. Spotters will squirm in their seats, stifle their gasps, and communicate their non-verbal responses to the exercise across the circle. The suspense created, as the players narrowly miss finding the highlighter, is palpable. The spotters are riveted witnesses to the event. In discussion, you can address with them what captured their rapt attention.

Reflections

As you reflect on the exercise, please keep the following points in mind:

- Each student pursues an objective, faces an obstacle, and engages a variety of tactics.
- Players weren't concerned with *showing* their objective, they simply pursued the objective fully.

- Full pursuit of the objective reveals emotion; emotion is a result of playing the objective fully.
  - Players did not concern themselves with showing that they were becoming frustrated by the exercise, they became frustrated by failing to find the highlighter (but their objective remained "to find the highlighter").
- Why or *how* did the audience "read" a particular emotion from the actor's actions?
- There is an "event" (the highlighter is found) that changes the remainder of the "scene".
  - Although each player may have engaged a variety of strategies (tactics) to find the highlighter (the objective), the objective: "to find the highlighter and become the hunter" was one "beat".
- What physical changes did you observe during tactic changes? During the beat change?
- What caused the audience (spotters) to engage with the event?
- How does the use of blindfolds affect the actors?

I like to phrase objectives in the following way: "I need to/want to [action verb] (subject) in order to/so that [desired result]." For example: "I need to find the highlighter in order to become the Hunter." This gives the actor the playable action as well as the desired result; what they hope to gain by executing the task. I also insist that the objectives be phrased positively, so that they can be as active as possible. For example, "I need to avoid answering the question so that I can keep the truth a secret" is more active than "I don't want to tell him where I was." *Avoiding* something is active and actively playable. The positive phrasing gives the actor something to play. Sometimes students may struggle to articulate the objective. They may view the objective in relation to the event's results without a clear sense of what they can do in order to achieve that outcome ("I want to keep my partner from winning"). Hunter/Hunted helps to clarify the differences between the two by illustrating what it takes to achieve that desired outcome. When students lead with the results, you can refer back to their experience with Hunter/Hunted. "Let's go back to Hunter/Hunted," I tell my students. "In Hunter/Hunted, you wanted to keep your partner from winning; that's the result. What was the action that leads to that? What did you have to *do* in order to keep them from winning? *Find the highlighter*." The examples they've experienced in Hunter/Hunted are so clear, and that "scenario" isn't complicated by text, which makes it much easier for them to decipher what the objective is.

Hunter/Hunted can also be revelatory in terms of illustrating what a beat change is. Players have one goal, to which they are fully committed. There are many ways in which they try to achieve their goal; although there are changes in their attempts, the need remains constant. Something happens that changes that need *entirely*. Players cannot pursue what follows the beat change and still play their action. If they are looking for safety – or for their partner – before the highlighter has been found then they have lost sight of their objective.

The experience actors have in practice through this active exploration provides the tacit knowledge that helps to shape their craft. They understand in their bodies what these concepts mean, and they observe how actors that pursue their objectives fully engage the audience and organically release the emotion required by the text, without having to work on their own emotional state of being. When my students are challenged by their scene analysis, or when things lack clarity, I often remind them: "Just find the highlighter."

Notes

1 Pears (26–27), featured in *Practice as Research in the Arts: Principles, Protocols, Pedagogies, Resistances* by Robin Nelson (9).
2 Featured in Bonczek and Storck (200–202).
3 Barker (57–61).

References

Barker, Clive. *Theatre Games*. Drama Book Specialists, 1977.
Bonczek, Rose Burnett, and David Storck. *Ensemble Theatre Making: A Practical Guide*. Routledge, 2013.
Nelson, Robin. *Practice as Research in the Arts: Principles, Protocols, Pedagogies, Resistances*. Palgrave Macmillan, 2013.
Pears, David. *What Is Knowledge?* Allen & Unwin, 1971.

SEVENTEEN

Tactics and Action Drives

Stanislavski Meets Laban

Conrad Alexandrowicz

Two of the greatest pioneers in related areas of performance of the 20th century, Rudolf Laban and Konstantin Stanislavski, never met. It is fascinating to speculate what might have ensued between them if they had, given that such affinity abides between their respective sets of concepts and practices. But perhaps it would not have mattered if they had encountered one another: they were both "prime movers" who were devoted to their own journeys of discovery and invention. It has fallen to countless instructors in both text and movement training for actors to bring them into conversation with one another in the classroom and rehearsal studio.

However, there are institutional impediments to such a conversation taking place because of the customary division of actor training into the three sub-disciplines called "acting," "voice" and "movement." What does this use of language communicate? That "acting" is, well *acting*, while the other two pursuits are somehow ancillary? Surely what "voice" instructors do is to teach "acting" with an emphasis on vocal production and the technical aspects of text, while "movement" specialists teach "acting" with an emphasis on the body and the physical dimensions of performance. I find this division both arbitrary and counter-productive, in that it engenders compartmentalization in the way students engage with their training. I feel we ought either to eliminate it or find new language for the different emphases it attempts to denote.

I propose that the matter goes further: this hierarchy in itself says much about the kind of theatre that continues to enjoy dominance in Western culture(s), and also in the acting pedagogy that supports and feeds it; theatre that is text-based, founded in realist representation, and exemplified by the historical examples of the drawing-room comedy and the "well-made" play, as well as much contemporary drama. This approach to training also lends itself to the photographic

realism of film and television. In recent decades theatre as an art form
has moved on, and assumed a wide range of expressions that are based
outside of realism, and that often call upon the expressive potentials of
the actor's body. Hans-Thies Lehmann, in his landmark work *Postdramatic Theatre* (2006), attempted to collect and analyse all these varieties of performance under the heading "postdramatic," [*sic*] and
argued that "[i]t is essential to accept the coexistence of divergent theatre forms and concepts in which no paradigm is dominant."[1] But, for
the most part, our approach to the formation of actors has not kept up
with these developments: I believe the traditional construct of "acting"
as the meat and "voice" and "movement" as the potato and vegetable
in the meal that we serve as actor training remains largely in place.

It is intriguing to consider that Stanislavski considered Vsevolod
Meyerhold – a pioneering exponent of physical theatre – "my sole heir
not only in our own theatre but in general."[2] That is, while the
"Method" is so often treated and taught, certainly in North America,
as primarily a cognitive pursuit, it was developed by an artist and
pedagogue who was deeply invested in the corporeal life of the actor.
Ann Bogart and Tina Landau, authors of *The Viewpoints Book:
A Practical Guide to Viewpoints and Composition* (2005), make some
trenchant comments on the way "acting" tends to be taught in
a culture so thoroughly influenced by cinematic realism: "Our misun-
derstanding, misappropriation and miniaturization of the Stanislavski
system remains the bible for most practitioners. Like the air we
breathe, we are rarely aware of its dominance and omnipresence."[3]
This may be traced to the Moscow Art Theatre's début in New York
in 1923, when, as the authors note, "Americans grasped onto what
turned out to be a severely limited aspect of Stanislavsky's 'system,'
and turned it into a religion."[4]

Scholar Sharon Marie Carnicke has done vitally important work on
this subject, revealing the complex history of Stanislavski's work and
the historical reasons for its chronic misrepresentation. She complains
that American acting teachers – I amend that to *North* American –
assume a ready knowledge of the Russian master and his work; that
he was:

> [e]xclusively committed to realism as an aesthetic style and per-
> sonal emotion as the primary wellspring of great acting. In fact, he
> viewed the actor as an autonomous artist, saw realism as only one
> in a myriad of equally profound theatrical styles, and developed
> a compendium of acting techniques, with 'emotional memory' as
> the most capricious and least effective.[5]

She notes the severely truncated nature of the translations of his work by
Elizabeth Hapgood, which have nonetheless been treated almost as holy
writ.[6] And she reminds us that his "psychophysical experimentation with

Yoga and his interest in modern dance deserve a closer look by those seeking new approaches to the actor's physical training."[7] Indeed, Stanislavski seems to have become more devoted to embodiment as his work changed and developed over the years. One of Carnicke's research interests is the history of "Active Analysis," the approach Stanislavski developed in the very last years of his life when he lived in a kind of internal exile in Moscow. Having been chosen by Stalin as the Soviet regime's embodiment of socialist realism he was at once lionized and subjected to intense scrutiny and control.[8] "By invoking the Aristotelian notion that drama is an imitation of an action, Stanislavski redefines a play as a score of actions ... just as musical notes record melody."[9] This return to a radical concept of the nature of "playing" makes Stanislavski's work applicable to all genres of theatre, as well as to dance and opera, in which he was intensely interested in his later years.[10] Carnicke observes that "the Soviet political machine constructed the Stanislavski myth by suppressing Active Analysis and replacing it with a politically correct version known as The Method of Physical Action," the phrase by which it is widely known.[11] She proposes that we are finally making progress on this subject when we admit that "the 'Method' in the US and the 'Method of Physical Actions' in the USSR established our common, but far from complete, knowledge about him."[12] This topic, while fascinating, is outside the scope and purpose of this chapter. Suffice to say that Stanislavski's "system" – he apparently preferred the small "s" and quotation marks[13] – was far more concerned with the "movement" angle of the actor training triad than we commonly credit.

This is where Laban comes neatly into play. His work may be described as both a "method of physical action" and a form of "active analysis," albeit rooted in the realm of dance. The exercise which I analyze and describe here may be summed up as follows: *Students create a physical score based on dramatic text using the Action Drives from Laban Movement Analysis.* It is therefore very much in the spirit of Active Analysis alluded to above. In order to engage in this activity one must, of course, learn how to use the Action Drives, and in order to do *that* one must learn the basic principles of Effort, one of the four cornerstones of Laban's system. For the sake of this study one ought to begin with a thumbnail sketch of the work of this pioneer of 20th-century performance.

Without going into biographical detail, which I invite you to do independently,[14] it is enough to say that Laban was a dance artist and theorist who invented and developed, along with Irmgard Bartenieff and Warren Lamb, individuals who worked with and after him,[15] the most thorough and comprehensive system that we know for describing, visualizing, interpreting, and documenting all the varieties of human movement. The edifice of his ideas is denoted by the acronym BESS: Body, Effort, Shape and Space: four interlocking categories, of which our present concern is with Effort, which may be defined as "movement," but is best understood as "behavior," the reason why it is so useful for acting teachers. Effort breaks down into: (1) Flow, which underlies all movement, is linked to Emotion, and operates between the poles of Free and Bound; (2) Space, which is about Attention, and runs the gamut between Direct and Indirect; (3) Time, which connects to Decision, and which moves between Sustained and Urgent; and (4) Weight – or Force – which implies Intention, from Light to Heavy. It is important to stress that these factors operate on continua: one's movement is *more or less* bound or free, Direct, or Indirect, etc.

If Flow is about Emotion, then one might say that the process of socialization is about learning how to *bind* one's flow. Children tend to be in free flow, whereas, I suggest, people in most business environments tend to be in bound flow, at least *usually*: at the office Christmas party one might see a good deal of free flow. Therefore, adults who are in the most free flow will be those in transports of Emotion, those who are intoxicated, or in delusional states, such that they break with social norms. This applies also to mostly physical conditions: One is in free flow when dancing, or engaging in high-energy sporting activities; one is in bound flow when trying to move in a dark room, or walking on ice that one suspects might be unreliable.

With Direct Attention in Space, one perceives one's goal to be unobstructed, and moves to it in a linear fashion, while with its opposite one has to bend and turn. This can apply both to purely physical practices, such as weaving through a crowd, or in the realm of dramatic action, where one is either confident of achieving one's objective, and encounters no obstacles, or has to resort to various tactics in order to achieve one's objective. (This improvisation is itself a model of how Laban intersects with the basic operations of acting.)

The Time Factor is about one's *relationship* to time, not simply about *tempo*: does one have lots of time or very little of it? Is one walking on a beach on holiday, or running late getting to the airport to *go* on holiday?

The Weight factor is about degrees of resistance: is one's passage through Space free and easy, or does one have to fight all the way, as though struggling against a strong wind? Laban specialists, called Certified Movement Analysts (CMAs), use language that is very useful for actors to describe the opposite ends of the Effort continua: they write about "fighting and condensing" Attention in Space, Decision in Time, and Intention in Weight, that is, Direct, Urgent, and Heavy; or "indulging and expansive," namely, Effort values that are Indirect, Sustained, and Light.[16] These two sets of terms are equivalent to high stakes on the one hand and low-to-no stakes on the other. To say that the Time Factor is moving from Sustained to Urgent, or the Weight factor from Light to Heavy is as much as to say the stakes in the scene are going up: one is strolling in the park until one notices one's house is on fire. This is also true of one's Attention in Space, but is most evident in terms of Decision and Intention.

Table 17.1 Action Drives

Action Drive	Space	Time	Weight
Float	Indirect	Sustained	Light
Glide	Direct	Sustained	Light
Press	Direct	Sustained	Heavy
Wring	Indirect	Sustained	Heavy
Flick	Indirect	Urgent	Light
Dab	Direct	Urgent	Light
Slash	Indirect	Urgent	Heavy
Punch	Direct	Urgent	Heavy

The eight Action Drives are composed of combinations of elements from Space, Time, and Weight. *It is crucially important for instructors to understand that Flow is NOT a part of the Action Drives!* They are "flowless," meaning they are transitory and discontinuous, and are therefore ideally suited to stand as movement metaphors for the shifting play of tactics within performance. However, in order to learn them effectively students must sustain their engagement with them over time, in effect entering into a whole different set of Drives which are not the subject of this chapter, and which I consider to be "too much information" for student actors' purposes.

Table 17.1 lists the eight Action Drives, which are are Float, Glide, Press, Wring, Flick, Dab, Punch and Slash: I teach them in this order, moving from Sustained to Urgent Time, and Light to Heavy Weight; that is, from relative ease of expression to that which is more demanding, both emotionally and physically.

Using Action Drives to Play Tactics

Exercise Goals

The overall goal of this work is to physicalize actions fully so that the student will have experienced full embodiment in the playing of a piece of text. Too much seated analysis of a dramatic passage, largely a cognitive, disembodied process, will only get the student so far. This is particularly important for beginning actors, many of whom seem to think – on the basis of how they present themselves in audition monologues – that acting is about learning your lines and saying them in the proper order while standing politely in place. And this is why I use this exercise as the key in-class component of my introductory term of "movement."

The students must engage in a process whereby they remove the text from the score of playable actions completely, explore the movement content as an object in itself, and then eventually restore the text. This generally means reverting to whatever blocking has been set for the scene, given that these texts are generally excerpted from plays in the realist canon.

It is hoped that at least three learning outcomes will be realized from this activity:

- The residues of such work will remain with student actors even when they revert to what may be relatively constrained staging in their "acting" classes, playing with more specificity and dimension.
- This activity supports an understanding of the total plan of the performance text, of which dialogue is only one component. (As my first directing teacher, very much of the of the old school, once remarked, "Always remember: the theatre is primarily a non-verbal medium!")
- This work also gives them a glimpse of the possibilities of theatrical performance in which text is either absent or minimally deployed.

What You Will Need

Instructors will need to learn the basics of Laban Movement Analysis (LMA), which sounds like a tall order, but which can be accomplished by working with a number of very good books on the subject.[17] While learning LMA from a book might have been easier for me given my dance background, I believe that anyone can acquire and practice the basics of LMA; it is about human movement – that is, human *behavior* – and is inescapably democratic and *democratizing*.

However, in the recognition that learning is a lifelong process, and that the acquisition of new knowledge is a pleasurable thing for most instructors, I also recommend finding a Certified Movement Analyst with whom to work. In my case this was a matter of confirming my understanding and embodiment of the principles of the system, refining what I knew, and learning new information, which I may or may not have included in my teaching. While the Action Drives form only a small part of the whole body of knowledge that was developed by Laban and his successors, these are the tools most commonly used by acting teachers and directors; in effect they are the most useful elements of the system for acting instruction.

Physical Setup

This approach is all about movement, which the instructor needs to be able to model effectively for students: "Do as I do *and* as I say."

- While it is possible to engage in a great deal of movement expression in a limited space it is preferable to have lots of room to move. If there is a choice in terms of your access to more than one space, do opt for the bigger one.
- It is of course preferable to have a sprung wooden floor: concrete floors and human movement *do not* go together! However, if concrete floors are unavoidable, instructors must take care to modify students' level of exertion – foregoing jumping, for example – in order to avoid injuries.
- Both students and instructor need to wear clothing that allows full freedom of movement.
- I recommend dispensing with street clothes because they bring the social world with all its distractions into the space of the acting classroom. I suggest the wearing of "practice clothes" unless and until costumes are brought into the class.
- Music can be a great support to learning how to work with the factors of Space, Time, and Weight, but once the move is made to working with text it ought to be set aside as it will intrude on the "emotional music" of the monologue or scene.

Directions

In order to teach students how to use the Action Drives to play tactics, one must first convey the materials out of which they are made; that is, students must have a thorough experience of Flow, Space, Time, and Weight so that they can learn and embody concepts accurately and comprehensively. My classes are 80 minutes in duration, and I generally spend half the working time available for each Effort factor. Therefore, it will take students about a week to assimilate all the material before they begin to learn the Action Drives.

Students must learn to work with Flow, even though it does not form part of the Action Drives; recognizing what *not* to do is part of any learning process. In any case, using Flow will prove to be an unavoidable part of the process, as most learning involves sustained engagement with a task, and this is no less true with learning the Effort factors and then configuring them as Action Drives. Begin by asking the students to improvise free-flowing movement all over the room; get them to play like five-year-olds. Shift to bound flow: the given circumstances might involve carrying very full cups of tea in a room with cream-colored carpets; ask them to imagine that they are at a party where they know only the host, and are very shy.

Space

Choose a place in the room, go directly to it with singular focus, and complete some simple task, such as moving a chair from one place to another: this is "fighting and condensing Attention in Space."[18] Now take a very Indirect path with lots of different overlapping points of focus, as though searching for something, or trying to follow the movement of fireflies. This opposite embodies "expansive and indulgent Attention in Space."

Time

I provide students with the following sequence of prompts: "Imagine you are in a wonderful art gallery, and linger – portraying 'expansive and indulging Decision in Time' – as you take in all the paintings and sculptures. Now imagine that you have an important interview – perhaps an audition – and you cannot find your keys to lock your apartment before you leave: this is an example of 'fighting and condensing Decision in Time.'"

Weight

I usually get the students to try and move one of the walls. We do this for scant seconds as it's heart-breaking in its futility, but it's a good example of the use of Heavy Weight, that is "fighting and condensing Intention in Weight." I then ask them to float around the room as though they were dandelion seeds someone has blown from its puffball, that is, "indulgent and expansive Intention in Weight." In order to convey the notion that Weight is about Intention, and any dramatic scene is about *opposition* between competing intentions, I ask students to find partners of roughly their mass and to brace against each other palm to palm, each trying to dislodge the other from their stance. Later we do this exercise with bits of text.

I proceed to the Action Drives with gestures – which is where they actually occur in human behavior – and then in the same class move to full-body engagement in order to deepen students' experience of them.

To create a **Float** Action Drive, combine Indirect Space, Sustained Time and Light Weight: "With one hand, produce an easy, drifting gesture. Then incorporate these qualities with the whole body and float all over the room. What internal sense does this activity engender? What might be the given circumstances?"

Change the Space factor to Direct to perform a **Glide**, a Direct, Light, sustained line in Space. Now Glide across the room, noting how much stately power it can have: a wedding, an inauguration, a coronation all entail Gliding action.

To stage a **Press** Action one changes the Weight to Heavy: I ask the students to imagine they are not very bright thieves and have stolen a grand piano which they are attempting to push across a parking lot.

We then arrive at the **Wring** Action Drive, which is particularly salient for actors as it embodies all kinds of intense but contained Emotion: anger, anxiety, and grief, but also physical pain. I ask them to wring out a soaking facecloth, and then to *be* the facecloth being wrung out, to end up in a knot on the floor, and to note the painful psychic state this produces.

We then move to the Drives in Urgent Time: I ask them to **Flick** various things away: fluff on one's clothing, dandruff or bugs, and to note that to Flick something away is also to dismiss it. (I find that this moment is the first explicit connection between an Action Drive and an acting verb.)

To Dab one changes the Space factor to Direct. The students play tag: one uses a **Dab** to make someone 'it.'

I save the most strenuous Drives, Slash, and Punch, for the end. I ask them to imagine they are cutting thick jungle vines using a machete in each hand, a classic **Slash** Action Drive. We then switch to **Punch**, being careful to convey its Direct Attention in Space. With a partner, and lots of space between each player, students practice Slashing and Punching, noting that both are about combat. I suggest to them that the difference in the Space factor is not significant in this situation: a boxer uses both jabs and hooks in in the ring; that it's all about fighting

The above explorations are repeated, including the voice, using "unconstructed" sound rather than intelligible speech. I get the whole class to improvise, calling out the various Drives at random. (Warning: This can get very loud, and one might want to use a whistle to get the class's attention.)

Students then form two lines and face each other across the width of the room, identifying their partner. (Or *partners*: in the case of an uneven number a trio will have to take turns playing one against two.) We continue to explore the Drives, adding a minimal bit of language. Students need to be able to physicalize the Drives with full embodiment, but voice and text must be brought into the process early on so that students can get a feel for how they will be used in text-based scene study; that they are not just about physical improvisation. We proceed one team at a time: one student calls "Hey!" five times to her partner, adding their name at the end; they then reverse roles. They may use as much or as little of the space between them as they feel in the moment. (One could call "Hey!" any number of times but five has a good feel to it.) As they play the Action Drives I ask the students to decide what they might be playing to their partner. Are they taunting them when they Dab? Dismissing them when they Flick? Begging them when they Press? Condemning them when they Slash?

The addition of a piece of neutral text is part of this layering process, in which one aims to execute the Drives accurately while increasing the components of the task. Some days before we move to this activity I ask them to find a recipe and reduce it to two or three sentences, retaining as many verbs as possible – mix, beat, stir, whip, fold, etc. – so that they may play any action without being influenced by the actual *semantic* meaning of a piece of dramatic writing.

I distribute a list of acting verbs, such as the kind found in *Actions: The Actor's Thesaurus*. Students try to play select verbs – there are lots of synonyms, of course – as accurately as possible, and in doing so find a suitable Action Drive; in other words this is the reverse of the improv using "Hey!" with which they began, where one played the Drive and then tried to guess its dramatic value. This activity is done in a free-for -all using the whole room, as well as in partners. Students may use any part of the text in any order, or its entirety.

When I feel that the whole class is able to play acting verbs as Action Drives accurately with full embodiment we turn to the actual textual material with which they are concerned, both monologues and scenes. (I consult with my colleagues on this matter and inform them that we will be engaging in this crossover activity, and to watch for any changes that may arise as they continue to work with these texts over the course of the term.) Students must articulate the overall objective that the character is pursuing, and then identify as rigorously as possible all the units of action, or beats, in the text;[19] that is, all the tactics to which the character resorts in pursuit of that objective.

They construct a score based on these choices, and play the speech or scene, emphasizing – exaggerating – each Action Drive as they perform the piece. They then create a movement composition based on the sequence of Drives without any text at all. In the case of a scene this means they will make a duet or trio. They are instructed to make this movement piece as expansive and abstract as possible – a piece of choreography, in fact. These pieces are shown to the rest of the class. When they revert to the text they must reduce it to proportions appropriate to the style in which it will be played, usually, as noted above, those that are suited to realism, but attempt to retain the vividness and specificity afforded by movement expression of the whole body.

Inspiration (or exercise origins) Like many instructors who have incorporated Laban Movement Analysis into their work, I have assembled this approach over many years of experimentation in the studio, gradually adding pieces to it, and am unable to credit any one instructor for it. However, I have also incorporated ideas of how to teach the Effort factors from *Acting Essentials* (2015) by Brigid Panet, a text I recommend. My use of neutral text derives from an acting class I took from Toronto-based actor and director Alan Jordan; Donna Redlick is the CMA I worked with in Vancouver.

Post-exercise Reflections (for new leaders to consider as discussion points) After the exploration check in with your students with questions such as the following:

• Do the Action Drives make sense as a kind of formula for acting verbs in general?

• Did you find that reducing a text-based scene to a movement score helped you connect with the text? Or did it seem like a distraction from it?
• How do you experience the relationship between the text-as-thought and thought-as-movement?

I am struck once again by how much overlap there is between Stanislavski's "system" – considered in all its range – and Laban Movement Analysis. Both these pioneers were concerned with understanding the bases of human behavior as action. While Stanislavski's interest was in the work of professional performers Laban was concerned with all human movement, not just that of dancers, and his work can be seen as a tool with which to analyze Stanislavski's "system." Every performer, even those in the most abstract expressions, is doing – *playing* – something while on stage, and therefore these approaches are valid for the training of actors, dancers, singers, and even orchestral musicians. In this way Laban Movement Analysis helps us to acknowledge and embrace the kinship that exists between all the practices of the performing arts.

Notes

1 Hans-Thies Lehman, *Postdramatic Theatre*. Abingdon and New York: Routledge, 2006, 20.
2 Jean Benedetti, *Stanislavski: A Biography*. London: Methuen, 1988, 345.
3 Ann Bogart and Tina Landau, *The Viewpoints Book: A Practical Guide to Viewpoints and Composition*. New York: Theatre Communications Group, 2005, 16.
4 Ibid.
5 Sharon Marie Carnicke, "Stanislavsky and Politics: Active Analysis and the American Legacy of Soviet Oppression," *The Politics of American Actor Training*, eds. Ellen Margolis and Lissa Tyler Renaud. New York and Abingdon: Routledge, 2010, 15.
6 Ibid., 17.
7 Ibid., 26.
8 Sharon Marie Carnicke, *Stanislavsky in Focus: An Acting Master for the Twenty-first Century*. 2nd ed. New York: Routledge, 2009, 40.
9 Carnicke, "Stanislavsky and Politics," 22.
10 Carnicke, *Stanislavsky in Focus*, 190.
11 Ibid., 18.
12 Ibid., 3.
13 Jean Benedetti, *Stanislavski and the Actor*. New York: Routledge, 1998, x.
14 I suggest *Mastering Movement: the Life and Work of Rudolf Laban* by John Hodgson (London: Methuen, 2001).
15 Barbara Adrian, *Actor Training the Laban Way: An Integrated Approach to Voice, Speech and Movement*. New York: Allworth Press, 2008, 6.
16 Adrian, *Actor Training the Laban Way*, 117–18.
17 I can recommend the following: Newlove's *Laban for Actors and Dancers* (New York: Routledge, 1993, 1995), and *Actor Training the Laban Way: An Integrated Approach to Voice, Speech and Movement*, by Barbara Adrian (New York: Allworth Press, 2008). There is also Brigid Panet's *Essential Acting: A Practical Handbook for Actors, Teachers and Directors*

(London and New York: Routledge, 2015), which includes LMA within a very wise and useful book about acting instruction in general. These were the texts with which I worked.

18 All quotes from Adrian, *Actor Training the Laban Way*.

19 It is intriguing to note that the term Stanislavski used was the Russian word *kusok*, which translates as "bit," but which became "beat," part of the mistranslation to which his was work subjected. See Jean Benedetti. *Stanislavski and the Actor*. New York: Routledge, 1998, 151, and Carnicke, *Stanislavsky in Focus*, 63.

References

Adrian, Barbara. *Actor Training the Laban Way: An Integrated Approach to Voice, Speech and Movement*. New York: Allworth Press, 2008.

Benedetti, Jean. *Stanislavski: A Biography*. London: Methuen, 1988.

Benedetti, Jean. *Stanislavski and the Actor*. New York: Routledge, 1998.

Bogart, Ann, and Tina Landau. *The Viewpoints Book: A Practical Guide to Viewpoints and Composition*. New York: Theatre Communications Group, 2005.

Calderone, Marina, and Maggie Lloyd-Williams. *Actions: The Actor's Thesaurus*. London: Nick Hern Books, 2004.

Carnicke, Sharon Marie. *Stanislavsky in Focus: An Acting Master for the Twenty-first Century*. 2nd ed. New York: Routledge, 2009.

Carnicke, Sharon Marie. "Stanislavsky and Politics: Active Analysis and the American Legacy of Soviet Oppression." *The Politics of American Actor Training*. eds. Ellen Margolis and Lissa Tyler Renaud. New York and Abingdon: Routledge, 2010.

Lehmann, Hans-Thies. *Postdramatic Theatre*. Trans. *Karen Jürs-Munby*. Abingdon and New York: Routledge, 2006.

EIGHTEEN

Stanislavski in the Voice Studio

Deric McNish

Stanislavski was deeply committed to holistic actor training: body, mind, and voice. Early aspirations to be an opera performer were replaced by acting and directing, but he remained preoccupied with the actor's voice. He encouraged a twofold approach to voice training: rigorous and long-term exercise to expand the voice's capabilities, along with inner justification for every sound the actor makes. Weaving Stanislavski's system into voice training helps students to more quickly achieve a vibrant connection to the inner life of the character, resulting in compelling vocal expression.

In today's actor training programs, voice classes typically begin at the same time or immediately following a fundamental acting class that introduces Stanislavski's system. Armed with a budding grasp of terms such as objectives, obstacles, and tactics, students often put those aside as they begin their voice training, focusing instead on the physiological aspects of voice work. This is a missed opportunity to reinforce important concepts and to tie voice work to the trajectory of their overall growth as actors. Incorporating objectives, obstacles, and tactics into foundational voice exercises helps to contextualize the work and to put the actor on a path towards greater integration of varied approaches in their training.

In *My Life in Art*, Stanislavski articulates a primary concern of voice teachers today: "The habit of saying words without any meaning for the sake of the exercise of sound, and not in order to express inner feelings and thoughts, breaks the direct connection between soul and word, voice and emotion."[1] In seeking to strengthen the connection between "soul and word," voice teachers explore diverse topics, from the practical, such as the physiology of vocal production, to the abstract, such as the relationship between imagery and sound. In my experience, students tend to naturally gravitate toward one or the other. Exercises that prove profound for one student may leave another disconnected and bored. Rockford Samson presents this as "art versus science" and he convincingly argues for a mix of approaches in voice class.[2] The indispensable experiential part of this process can achieve greater student buy-in when framed not as an abstract supplemental exploration, but as an essential acting technique that ties indelibly to the Stanislavski system. This view of voice pedagogy offers active ways of achieving healthy, honest, compelling, spontaneous, and emotionally transparent expression but never, as Stanislavski says, "for the sake of the exercise of sound."

Vocalizing without having an objective will never sound authentic to the listener. Incorporating objectives without also imagining obstacles may feel disengaged. Lack of specific tactics leads to generic vocal choices and, as Stanislavski warned, "'In general' is the enemy of all art."[3] By including objectives, obstacles, and tactics as fundamental elements of voice and speech curriculum, a student actor will begin to understand how every sound we make is only convincing when connected to a playable tactic. The honest impulse to speak must come from an immediate need to affect change. By fleshing out the inner life of the character and assigning obstacles, objectives, and tactics to these voice exercises, our voices are imbued with purpose. They become colored by our imaginations and we promote greater spontaneity while avoiding general qualities.

Exercises

There is no exercise we do in a voice class that can't be enhanced by asking the actor to flesh out the inner feelings and thoughts that motivate vocalization. Even the simplest of warm-ups becomes more effective when the actor frames each sound as a tactic used to achieve an objective.

Raising the Stakes with the Exaggeration Circle

Exercise Goals

In its simplest form, the "Exaggeration Circle" is used to promote expressivity, to encourage actors to make bold choices, and to enhance ensemble. This adaptation goes one step further and connects to text, helping the actor to identify their character's primary objective and to explore it vocally and physically. Through group work, it enhances what is usually a personal, introspective process. It encourages a playful approach to breaking down a character's motivations. Exaggeration Circle, sometimes known as "Sound and Gesture," appears in many different collections of improvisation games for theatre and education and has been taught at the iO Theater in Chicago. Many theatre games began with the "mother of theatre improvisation games," Viola Spolin. Her exercise, called "Extended Sound," may have inspired Exaggeration Circle.

What You Will Need

At the time of the exercise, each actor should be working on a piece of text. This can be a scene or a monologue. At this point in the process, it does not need to be fully memorized, but it helps if the student has read the entire play and has an understanding of the character's objectives and obstacles. Otherwise, the only thing that is required is space for movement.

Physical Setup

The actors stand in a circle with room for movement.

Directions

This activity works best in four parts.

Part 1: Play the traditional version. To play Exaggeration Circle, ask all actors to stand in a circle, leaving themselves plenty of room for movement. The instructor begins by making a sound and a gesture. Choose something simple, subtle, and clear. For example, the instructor might flick her hand at an imagined gnat and say, "ugh." The person to the instructor's right must do the same thing, but with a slight exaggeration. This doesn't necessarily mean louder; it should be a slightly more committed and (in this case) disgusted response. The gesture and the sound should reflect that. Each person exaggerates what the person before them did, until it reaches the end of the circle. By the time we get to the end of the circle, it should be an incredibly over-the-top exaggeration. End each round by asking what the objective of the sound and gesture was, whether or not it changed as it moved around the circle, and what motivated the change.

Play a few rounds of this simple version, shuffling the circle frequently to give people the opportunity to experience the beginning and end of the circle. Coach students to respond *immediately* to the person that came before, rather than taking a moment to think about what they will do. Likewise, do not hesitate to "rewind" when someone has lessened, rather than exaggerated, the sound, movement, or energy. Finally, remind students to exaggerate exactly what came before, in order to promote listening and spontaneity by keeping them from planning ahead.

Part 2: Give students some time to work independently with their monologues or scenes. Ask them to speak the text as they begin to identify a simple sound and a gesture that encompasses their character's objective. This should not be solely an intellectual activity, but one that happens simultaneously in the body, voice, and mind. Instructors familiar with Michael Chekhov will recognize this as an element of "Psychological Gesture."[4] Remind students that they are exploring what *drives* their character, what their character wants or needs, and not the character's emotional state.

Part 3: Bring everyone back to the circle. This time, as we run each actor's rehearsed sound and gesture through the Exaggeration Circle, the actor that begins will actually go twice; they will be the first person to go *and* the last person to go. Doing this allows them to experience both spectrums of the sound and gesture they created. The actor provides the spark that begins the circle, watches it transform and grow in the bodies and voices of the other actors, then provides the most exaggerated version that ends the circle.

Part 4: Finally, have students work solo once again. They should begin by revisiting the sound and gesture they created that connects to their character's objective. They should repeat that until it feels connected, then immediately launch into the first few lines of their text. Then encourage them to repeat that process but experiment with different levels of the sound and gesture, remembering the full range that was explored by other actors in the circle. Ask them to look for the level where the sound and gesture feels energized, alive, engaged, interesting, connected to objective, and still truthful. Have them bring that work back to the perimeter of the circle and share their modified sound and gesture immediately followed by the first few lines of their text.

Post-Exercise Reflections

I have had great success with this exercise. It begins as a joyful game and becomes a memorable lesson. Students return to the circle with big, embodied, supported, and vocally interesting choices. I ask students to journal about the experience and they have found it to be very useful at focusing on objectives and "getting out of their heads." By exploring their character's objectives, they confidently make bolder physical and vocal choices. Students are usually surprised by the quality of work that emerges. Consider setting aside a few minutes immediately after the exercise for journaling, then using some of these questions to spark discussion.

- What skills did we practice during the first part of Exaggeration Circle?
- What surprised you in your work? What surprised you in the work of others?
- How did it feel to see your sound and gesture adapted by others as it went around the circle?

- Do you feel a stronger connection to this character? Why?
- How might you use this in your future work?
- How did this physicalized objective affect your voice? Think about pitch, tone, tempo, volume, rhythm, placement in the mouth, areas of strong resonance, and breath.

If you choose to do this exercise multiple times, take Stanislavski's advice: "Never repeat an exercise without a fresh objective."[5]

A Motivated "Mm"

Exercise Goals

Beginning a vocal warm-up by gently humming awakens the vocal folds and begins a process that readies the actor for the demands of vocal production. As a next step, to warm up facial resonance, actors may simply hum on an "mm" sound with the goal of bringing the vibrations forward to the outer edges of their lips, where the forward placement may allow the sound to travel further. "Mm" for the sake of "mm" is a purely physiological activity, a dissociated sound that is technical in nature. Adding inner justification for the sound and connecting it to scene partners helps the actor to more quickly achieve a forward, resonant sound. This warm-up is adapted from one taught by Louis Colaianni in his 2013 "Joy of Phonetics" workshop at the Celebration Barn Theater in Maine. Colaianni's brilliant Phonetic Pillow technique for teaching the International Phonetic Alphabet (IPA) focuses on the sensual experience of sound. In his model, IPA becomes an active and exciting tool for expanding expression. This adaptation of his work focuses more specifically on Stanislavski's language – objectives, obstacles, and tactics – by experimenting with the inner motivation for sound.

What You Will Need

An effective demonstration can be made if you have some fruit or candy at hand. No other materials are required.

Physical Setup

Actors dispersed around the studio with room to move, standing comfortably.

Directions

Part 1: Begin by asking for a gentle and easy hum. This should be a tension-free sound. Ask the actors to sense where their hum is vibrating most strongly in their bodies and to place their hand on that spot.

Then ask the actors to place a hand over (but not touching) their lips, and to send that "mm" sound towards their fingers. Give them a moment to explore how to consciously send that sound towards the outside of their lips.

Part 2: Explore "mm" as the outward expression of a character's inner motivation. "Mm" speaks volumes when it is influenced by objectives, obstacles, and tactics. Ask for a volunteer to taste the snack you have brought – a blueberry, for example. As the actor begins to experience an enjoyable flavor: "mm" is a natural expression. Encourage that by asking the actor to send their "mm" to specific people in the class, with the intention of sharing their experience with the listener. Encourage specificity in their choices. For example, the actor might choose to make one person's mouth water, to make another person jealous, or to tease. When others in the class begin to empathize with the actor's authentic experience, instruct them to respond by joining in the "mm," with the intention of convincing the rest of the class. Obstacles will be inherent; some students in the class don't like blueberries. Others simply need more convincing. The converted will have to work until all students in the class have joined in.

Part 3: Once the entire class has begun to "mm," invite them to begin to move around the space. Encourage them to let the sound be their motivation for moving. Stay focused on Stanislavski's terms by changing the nature of the "mm." Begin by asking them to think of the "mm" in the tactic "to promise." See how that affects their quality of movement, tempo, rhythm, and energy. Try this with several other words, such as "mash," "mope," "mangle," "mollify," "mangle," and "mortify." Remind them to be specific, sending their "mm" tactic to specific individuals as they move about the room. Keep an eye out for students that are pushing, as this should remain a gentle warm-up that doesn't cause strain or tension.

Part 4: Finally, ask actors to pair up and have an "mm" conversation. The only sound they can make is "mm" and their tactic should be "to mock." Afterwards, change the tactic to "menace" and experience the difference. Encourage specificity in the exchange. Ask students to think of other "mm" tactics for these scenes.

With these directions, "mm" is used as a tool connected to a specific tactic. The vibrations leap forward into the lips much more readily than without any context. The specificity naturally leads to more resonance.

Post-Exercise Reflections

Here are some topics for post-exercise discussion.

- At the beginning of the exercise, you placed your hands on the place of greatest resonance. Did that place change when the sound

was connected with intention? For those that, at first, felt chest resonance, did the sound move forward?

- How did the placement of vibrations and the vocal quality of the
  "mm" change when you had the specific goal of reaching a scene
  partner?
- The room was filled with vibrations. In what ways did you experience that sound? How did it move you? Did you feel connected to
  the others in the class? Could you feel a shift when their tactics
  changed?
- In *An Actor's Work*, Stanislavski wrote "pushing not only ruins
  their voice production and diction but their inner experiences as
  well."[6] What does pushing mean in this context? How does this
  quote relate to your experience in this exercise? Discuss how clarity
  and good projection emerge from a desire to communicate.
- What is it about "mm" that feels right when it appears in words
  like "murder," "mean," and "menace." What is it about "mm"
  that also feels right for words like "mother," or "more?" This can
  lead to an interesting discussion about the origins of language or
  the inherent emotional quality in certain consonants.

Conclusion

This approach is less prescriptive and provides alternate ways to measure success. Actors become practiced in connecting voice to the objectives, obstacles, and tactics that work best for their characters.
Prioritizing inner justification rather than aesthetics facilitates a different
way of assessing voice work. This training model departs from arbitrary
standards of what is aesthetically pleasing (which are often intrinsically
biased to favor certain groups) and offers a measure of student success
that is much more nuanced. Things like "standard speech" become less
important when the actor's success is measured by how well they
achieve their objective.

Stanislavki's system is a valuable tool that expands the potential of
the actor's voice. Asking the actor to try a different objective or tactic
yields more surprising and organic results than simply focusing on the
quality of the speech. Every vowel and consonant is an opportunity to
affect your scene partner in some way. When speaking with intention, in
order to move someone or to cause something to happen, the actor's
voice does remarkable things without conscious manipulation. Each
vowel and consonant becomes another pigment to paint with and
another nuanced way of playing a unique tactic to achieve an objective.

In *Voice into Acting: Integrating Voice and the Stanislavski
Approach*, Christina Gutekunst and John Gillett offer a thorough road-
map for voice curriculum based on Stanislavski's system.[7] Central to

their approach is a commitment to Stanislavski's concept of *as-if*, the idea that the actor's honest commitment to given circumstances will trigger an unmediated and spontaneous vocal response. No sound will feel disconnected or cerebral if it emerges from a richly imagined inner life. When an actor commits to character, voice "becomes dropped in, rooted, on the breath, and resonates the experiences of the character within the whole pitch range."[8] If you are interested in this approach, I recommend reading their book.

All voice work on stage and screen must be character-driven. When we focus not on the sounds we make, but on what we want to achieve, we find ways that physical action can translate into genuine emotional response. Incorporating Stanislavski's vocabulary into voice and speech training for the actor is an opportunity to weave various pedagogies into one holistic approach.

Notes

1 Stanislavski, Constantin. *My Life in Art*. Translated by J. J. Robbins. New York: Routledge, 2013. 84.
2 Samson, Rockford. "The Unspoken Voice and Speech Debate [or] the Sacred Cow in the Conservatory." *Voice and Speech Review* 10. 2–3 (2017): 157–168.
3 French, Stephanie Daventry and Bennett, Phillip G. *Experiencing Stanislavsky Today*. London and New York: Routledge, 2016. 21.
4 Chekhov, Michael. *To the Actor: On the Technique of Acting*. New York: Harper and Row, 1953. 63.
5 Rumyantsev, Pavel, and Stanislavski, Constantin. *Stanislavski on Opera*. Translated by Elizabeth Reynolds Hapgood. New York and London: Routledge, 2013. 10.
6 Stanislavski, Konstantin. *An Actor's Work*. Translated by Jean Benedetti. London and New York: Routledge Classics, 2016. 398. In this translation, Jean Benedetti combines Stanislavski's *An Actor Prepares* and *Building a Character*.
7 Gutekunst, Christina and Gillett, John. *Voice Into Acting: Integrating Voice and the Stanislavski Approach*. London: Bloomsbury, 2014.
8 Ibid., 199.

NINETEEN

Stimulating Embodied Tactical Actions

Lesley-Ann Timlick

I have been teaching acting, voice, and movement to culturally diverse college students for most of my career. Many of these students have suffered the pains of displacement; they struggle with loss, English is their second language, and they must adjust to a new, bicultural way of life. My desire to meet these students' needs has led me to conduct extensive research on different approaches in performance pedagogy. As student demographics continue to change, I have expanded my research to include actors who are neuro- and gender-diverse.

Through much experimentation, I discovered that almost all of my students made greater advances by using explorations which integrate movement, breath, sound, and text. The actions of respiration, phonation, and physical movement take place in the body where we are fundamentally similar and help lead to a unified assimilation required for strong acting. I developed a series of exercises merging ideas from the work of Feldenkrais, Laban, Michael Chekhov, Lecoq and multiple vocal practices (i.e. Berry, Linklater, Lessac, and Rodenburg). These lessons helped a wide spectrum of students to increase awareness, release tension, improve psycho-physical connection, free their imaginations, understand qualities/sensations and develop clearer physical/vocal specificity. As a result, these investigations enhanced my students' ability to find more connected differentiations in their voices and bodies and generate possibilities for vocally and physically articulate outward actions to unite with inner actions. The audience receives the essential information when the action is both visually and audibly coherent.

The foundation of my pedagogy stems from the New York masters of the post-Stanislavski systems (e.g., Adler, Meisner, Hagen). I define acting as an activity where inner action is divulged and clarified through outer actions. The inner and outer action are inextricably linked and flow together. The inner action is an objective the character seeks to

185

fulfill. The external actions are tactics or various strategies done to another character to achieve the objective. Tactics are expressed in action verbs that you can do to your partner (i.e., to lambast, to seduce, etc.).

I offer the following two lessons to activate embodied tactical actions which connect to an objective. These exercises increase physical awareness, clarify vocal and physical connection to the pulse (time), space (directions) and the imagination.

Lesson One: Expanding Awareness and Pulse of Time

Lesson one is an adaptation of a classic Feldenkrais Awareness Through Movement® lesson[1] which deepens the awareness of time and tension in the body. I introduce this exercise in the first semester of my movement and voice classes.

Goals

- To sense how acquired tensions can hinder movement.
- To arouse the body–mind connection.
- To increase the awareness of the movement quality of time and the sensations it stimulates in the body:
  - Movement Quality: how something moves, its essential aspects, feature (i.e. time can be slow or quick).
  - Sensation: a physical feeling, reaction or state, from something that connects to the body, it can be from both an internal or external stimulus.
- To expand movement capacity and vocal variation with the exploration of pulse:
  - Pulse: rate of speed/tempo (fast/slow) during a movement activity.
- To notice physical changes from and responses to different pulses of time.
- To experience how the inner and outer sensations of pulse can unite to shape the voice and body to establish articulate tactical actions that can be easily seen and heard by an audience.
- To explore a three-to-five-beat monologue using a pulse of time to affect the pursuit of an objective and to express tactics through unified visual and audible connections in the body and voice:
  - Tactics are various strategies that win the objective. Tactics are expressed in action verbs that can be done to the other character (i.e., to lambast, to seduce, etc.).
  - Beats are thought changes. Each beat uses a different tactic to overcome the obstacle.

What You Will Need

- One 90-minute class period (I have put a suggested time for each step of the exercise in parentheses).
- Movement clothing, no shoes.
- Tumbling mats, large flat floor space, memorized three-to-five-beat monologue, which has been analyzed (i.e. objective, tactics, beats, and obstacles).
- Instrumental music that creates an environment (Will Ackerman[2], Penguin Café Orchestra[3], Liquid Mind[4]).

For clarity, I have italicized comments on the exercise. Once the students are situated on their mats, I describe the exercise to the entire class in the following way:

I am going to guide you through a sequence of movements. Each movement is performed slowly about four times and is executed in a contained way. Feldenkrais discovered that the body and mind can only learn when movements are small, slow, and repeated. After a sequence of movements, there is a resting period. In these pauses, you will be guided to notice changes in the body. The lesson begins with a body scan to tune into the body and assist with your ability to sense differences.

Steps 1–8, Time: 30 Minutes

1. Please lie on your back on the mat and let your arms and legs lengthen. Notice how your body feels on the floor. Does one side of the body feel longer than the other? What parts of the body seem more in contact on the floor than others? Does the right side of the back of your head feel more in contact with the floor than the left? Which shoulder blade feels more in contact with the floor? Which leg feels more in contact with the floor? Sense all the lengths, curves, and pressure points of your body. Become aware of your breath and feel the movement of your inhalation and exhalation.

2. Bring your knees to standing with your feet flat on the floor. Begin opening and closing your right hand effortlessly. Where else in your body can you feel that movement? Spread your legs further apart so you have to increase effort to hold them up. Open and close your right hand and see what effect the leg position has on the hand. Keep moving the hand and slightly move the right foot away from you and move the left foot a bit little closer to you. How does this change in balance effect the quality of opening and closing your hand and your breathing? Balance your legs again and see if that changes the quality of the unfolding and folding of the hand.

3. Continue the movement of the hand and squeeze the floor with the bottoms of your feet. What does that do to the hand

movement and breathing? Decrease the effort in the feet and let them be soft. What else softens in your body when the feet soften? Keep your hand moving easily. Let your legs lengthen, and rest. Is there any change in how you are lying on the floor?

4. Fold and unfold your hand, establish a nice rhythm and slowly roll on to your right side. The tempo of your rolling should be in harmony with the opening and closing of your hand. Roll back and forth between your side and back several times. Let the hand determine the softness and speed of the rest of your body. Where do your eyes go? Let your legs lengthen, and rest on your back while keeping the hand going. What has changed?

5. Continue moving your hand as you roll to the other side. Maintain the rhythm and quality of the moving hand. Let the quality of the rolling be determined by the quality of the hand folding and unfolding. Roll back and forth several times. Pause and rest your back with your legs long. What has happened to your relationship to the floor?

6. Once again begin folding and unfolding the right hand. You may be getting a bit tired of this, but the body learns from repetition. Roll from side to side letting the hand dictate the quality of your movement. Let the arm go easily overhead as you roll. Pause and rest on your back. What has happened to your relationship with the floor? How does the left hand feel compared to the right?

7. Fold and unfold your hand; make it effortless. Roll in either direction onto your stomach while the hand continues to open and close. Your hand dictates everything you do. Roll back and forth between your stomach and back. Rest on your back (legs long) notice how the floor supports you.

8. Open and close your hand slowly, without disturbing the hand or stiffening your body roll and come up to sitting. Come easily to standing, letting the hand dictate the movement. Stop the movement of the hand and feel the difference in the two arms. Walk around and feel the arm swing of the hand that was opening and closing. I will continue to prompt you with questions to think about during this lesson and in rests. After the full sequence is finished, we will discuss your experience.

Now Let's Investigate Pulse and Movement (10 Minutes)

9. Begin opening and closing your hand and let the rhythm of your walk and breath be determined by the pulse of the hand. Then explore different movements (i.e. sit, stand, walk, gesture) with this pulse. How are each of these movements transformed by the pulse? Do any feelings arise internally from the pulse (i.e. do you feel anxious because it is slower?).

Next Let's Explore Pulse with Breath, Voice and Text (10 minutes)

10. Stand with your feet a hip-width apart, slightly bend your knees and let your tailbone drop under your spine. Put your hand on the space between your belly between your navel and your pubic

bone. Feel your breath moving in and out in its natural rhythm (a few seconds).

11. Pick a line of text from your monologue. Inhale enough breath to support this line of text and begin to speak it at a comfortable pulse for you. Repeat this about three times at this pulse. (5 minutes)

Then begin to find the same hand pulse you explored in steps 1–8. Match your breathing rhythm to this pulse. Begin to speak this same line of text. Go back and forth between your preferred pulse and this hand pulse. How does the hand pulse and its variations change your delivery of the line (i.e. rate, articulation, intonation, resonance)? Do any of the changes from the pulse bring up any feelings? (5 minutes)

Let's Explore How Pulse Can Link with Breath, Voice, Movement with Longer Sections of Text (10 minutes)

Next take a section of your monologue that stands out as a separate thought unit (beat). Pick a tactical action (i.e. to soothe, to elevate) that suits the energy of the hand's pulse and the monologue's objective. Let your breathing rate match the rhythm of the hand. Try walking and solo-speaking this section of the text with the hand pulse. Pause and don't open and close the hand but retain the inner impression (sensation) of the pulse. Speak this part of the monologue playing the tactical action to an imaginary partner and allowing it to be affected by this inner pulse. Repeat this twice. Let the entire body and voice give in to the inner sensation of the pulse. Allow your outer body and voice to radiate out the internal characteristics. How does this pulse change the unit of the monologue? Do you notice vocal or physical changes to the beat?

Musical Exploration of Pulse Variation (20 minutes)

To prepare for the next section of the exercise, have the music you have chosen ready to go.

12. Listen to some fast-paced music (i.e. Penguin Café Orchestra). Feel the tempo of the music and begin to find its pulse in your hand by opening and closing it. (5 minutes) Next, listen to this lyrical, legato, slower-paced music (i.e. Liquid Mind). Feel its speed and start to discover its pulse in your hand. (5 minutes)

Now have the students repeat steps 10 and 11 with these newly inspired pulses. (10 minutes)

How do these tempos change external delivery of the lines and beat?

Extended Monologue Exploration (10 minutes)

13. Finally, let's explore three beats of your monologue utilizing these new pulses with tactical actions. Try using a different tactic (i.e.

to lift, to overwhelm, to wear down) for each beat as you pursue your objective. The pulse might be well matched if the voice, body, and emotions create effortless changes and you sense an amplified connection to the text, tactic, and objective. Allow the tactic to affect you and select a pulse which suits your tactical action. For instance, the tactic to overwhelm may become even more active and alive with the pulse you discovered from music by the Penguin Café Orchestra.

As the actor speaks to an imaginary partner and uses this pulse they may feel their articulation becomes crisper, vowels shorten, and gestures are lighter and faster. Michael Chekhov would refer to this as being more staccato, and Laban might refer to this as being more sudden in time. These changes from pulse may inspire the actor's connection to the character, changes in breath, voice, and body clarify tactical actions.

Lesson Two: Space (The Six Cardinal Directions)

Lesson Two is inspired by fundamentals of the systems developed by Rudolf Laban and Michael Chekov. Chekhov's and Laban's use of space creates strong psycho-physical connections within the actor.

Goals

- To improve the body—mind connection.
- To increase the actor's understanding of the six cardinal directions in space (right, left, up, down, forward, backward).
- To expand movement capacity and vocal variation.
- To notice if psycho-physical connections arise from different directions in space.
- To discover how direction incites qualities of movement and arouses sensations in the body.

What You Will Need

- One class period (about 90-minutes long).
- Movement clothing, dance shoes.
- Large flat floor space.
- Memorized three-to-five-beat monologue, analyzed for objectives, obstacles, tactics, and beats.

I describe the exercise to the entire class in the following way:

1. Stand in "zero position," a state of readiness, with your feet hip-distance apart, your knees slightly bent, your weight evenly

distributed on both feet. Feel your breath moving in and out in its natural rhythm. (5 seconds)

2. Now you are going to physically explore these cardinal directions by stepping into them. We will lunge slightly into these directions. Turn your body to face right and step into this direction with your right foot, without moving the left foot (weight distribution 70 percent on the right foot and 30 percent on the left). Reach your arms out in front of you at shoulder level, pointing right with your palms facing downward. Send all your attention and energy in this direction. Imagine little sparks of light streaming into this direction from your fingertips. First inhale and then release your breath on an unvoiced "fff" sound- (fff as in far) into this direction. Inhale again and then release the breath on a voiced "hahh"-(h as in hat and ahh as in father) keeping this same position. Finally, inhale and then release the word "Hello" in this direction.

3. Return to the "zero position." Notice any changes of sensations or feelings in your body. Do you feel a stronger connection to this direction? Repeat the same movement, breath release, sound, word, and gesture to the left, up, down, forward, and backward directions. Keep your shoulders down and chest wide for all these movements. Make all the movements with a sense of ease, elongate the muscles rather than shortening and tightening them.
   Note on exploring the upward and downward directions: When you move upward, stay in the "zero position," reach your arms above your head, fingertips toward the ceiling. Then tip your head down and back so you can look up. When you move downward, roll through your spine, leading down with your head. Reach your arms down, fingertips toward the floor and step backward with one foot to get closer to the floor.

4. After you have completed exploring all the directions, pause and stand in "zero position." Do you now feel a clearer awareness of the six directional forces within the body? *My students often tell me they sense a greater connection to space and feel more present.*

5. Inhale and then release the word "Hello" and send it into all these directions. Again, imagine those sparks of light but now they stream out into all the directions from your voice and body.

6. Pick a line of text from your monologue. Repeat steps 3 and 4 with this line of text and add a tactic (i.e. to tease, to threaten) Do the directions bring up any feelings or add vocal/physical changes to the line?

7. Next, take one beat of your monologue and read each line aloud with your tactical action (i.e. to entertain, to butter up, to get sympathy). Allow the tactic to affect you. Sense where line and tactic want to move together in pursuit of your need. Are you being more direct and want to move forward or are you trying to avoid and move indirectly to the right or left? Your urgency will increase

when the words, tactic, and direction connect. You may also want to change your tactic because the direction inspires a change. Perhaps the next line doesn't move but pulls you upward because your strategy is to lift someone up. Maybe the next line moves you downward because you are trying to evoke sympathy.

8. Move through all beats of the monologue, line by line, applying changes in direction with your tactic. The directions may be compatible if the voice and body make natural shifts and you feel a heightened connection to the text, tactic, and objective. In performance of the monologue, the actor will not always physically move into all these in all the explored directions. They might feel them internally and subtly make a shift while standing or sitting in one spot.

Concluding Thoughts

Currently, it has become increasingly challenging for student actors to connect themselves fully and to integrate multiple components in their work. Clear communication requires effort skill, reflection and physical/vocal specificity. These lessons aim to help students discover an inspired, integrated connection between all aspects of their instrument: physical, vocal, and psychological. It is my goal to help advance acting training by enhancing unified articulation in the body. I have found that hybrid approaches which unite breath, sound, movement, and text help actors become more dynamic performers who can create more expressive shifts in tactical actions.

Notes

1 The Feldenkrais Method is a form of somatic or movement education that was developed by noted educator and scientist Dr. Moshe Feldenkrais (1904–1984). The method is a fusion of biomechanics, motor development, psychology, and martial arts. Feldenkrais developed two aspects of his movement education method: Awareness Through Movement® and Functional Integration®. Awareness Through Movement® in group sessions where the Feldenkrais practitioner verbally guides the students through movement sequences. Functional Integration® takes the form of oneon-one sessions, where a trained Feldenkrais practitioner communicates the learning process of the lesson through slow gentle hands-on movement. The movement that is communicated in both Functional Integration® and Awareness Through Movement® lessons can change habitual patterns and establish new learning opportunities for the neuromuscular system. The method enables students to improve alignment, flexibility, coordination, heighten the body mind connection, release movement tensions and patterns and improve self-image. Most importantly, the method assists the nervous system to self-organize and gain the ability to produce actions that are more intelligent and effective. The Feldenkrais portion of this lesson is based on an Awareness Through Movement® lesson, introduced by Feldenkrais trainer Frank Wildman during Professional Feldenkrais Training in November 1993, Miami, FL.

2 Will Ackerman: American guitarist who founded Windam Hill records, new-age music label.
3 Penguin Café Orchestra: avant-pop band founded by Simon Jeffes in the UK.
4 Liquid Mind: relaxation and mediation music developed by keyboardist, Chuck Wild.

References

Chamberline, Franc., and Michael Chekhov. *Performance Practitioners*. London: Routledge, 2004.

Chekhov, Michael. *On the Technique of Acting*. New York: Harper Perennial, 1991.

Chekhov, Michael. *To the Actor*. London: Routledge, 2004.

Feldenkrais, Moshe. *The Elusive Obvious*. Capitola, CA: Meta Publications, 1981.

TWENTY

NRGs and the Nature of Action

The Lessac Tactic Circle

Caroline Good

Ask beginning actors what they want in a scene, and their answers often include how "angry" or "frustrated" or "happy" their character is. In a nutshell, they tend to do one of three things: they immediately attempt to analyze and play (or force) the general "emotion" of the character; when they do play an objective, they often overcomplicate the process, which causes them to become stiff; they over-intellectualize their objectives and find it challenging to fully pursue those objectives actively. This paralyzes the body and disengages the actor from fully committing to affecting their partner.

Goals of the Lessac Tactic Circle

Through the "Lessac Tactic Circle" exercise, actors learn how to:

- Pursue a single objective.
- Employ a number of tactics.
- Play a range of physical and vocal behavior[1] *within* each of those tactics.

Inspiration/Origin of the Tactic Circle

I searched for a technique that would distill and simplify objectives, obstacles, and tactics – one that students could grasp in a short time, that would direct their focus toward their scene partner and not on playing an emotion, and that would propel them into specific physical and vocal behavior. I studied many of Stanisklavski's texts and, in the spirit of his efficient system of physical actions that leads the actor toward purpose rather than emotion, I strove to streamline an approach for my students – and to find a way to incorporate the invaluable body energies (NRGs)[2] of Arthur Lessac (1909–2011). Lessac developed the body NRGs as a complementary component to his vocal training to offer a broader, more holistic, and practical approach to actor training. We utilize these body NRGs in a variety of ways every moment of our lives; it is useful to be aware of them and to more intentionally apply these physical tools to add dynamics and specificity during the rehearsal process and in performance.

The body NRGs (*potency*, *buoyancy*, and *radiancy*) are not only useful in creating character and stimulating the imagination, but also in communicating a wider physical vocabulary from which to draw when pursuing objectives and employing tactics. Each body NRG has within it more specific qualities of movement, intensity, tempo, and nuance that broaden the physical and vocal choices within any given tactic and can add a whole new creative dimension to any scene.

Context for the Teacher

Lessac Body NRGs

Within each tactic lives a wide range of specific and individualized physical and vocal behavior. The NRGs are identifiable natural behaviors that manifest physically within a variety of familiar circumstances. Incorporating the texture of the body NRGs while employing tactics will allow the actor to utilize these manifestations more creatively and intentionally. Briefly introducing these (potency, buoyancy, and radiancy)[3] during the "Tactic Circle" gives students a chance to experiment with how they can affect the tactics.

The first body NRG is potency. When doing tai chi, asserting ourselves within a confrontation, or playing a superhero, we naturally move in a slow, condensed potency NRG that takes up space with a reaching, powerful quality. Two forms, or "dialects,"[4] of potency are *reaching potency* and *writhing potency*. Reaching potency derives from the stress-reducing impulse of the yawn; when we get out of the car after a long car ride, our impulse is to not only yawn but also to stretch, or "yawn" *all* of our muscles reaching outward and upward. We observe it when a cat stretches or stalks its prey. It is slow, controlled, and sustained. When we are in pain, we contract inwardly with "muscle yawn"-concentrated,[5] writhing potency. We close, or draw the body inward. Infusing the entire body with potency, more confrontational tactics such as *threatening*, *forcing*, or *probing*, and inducive tactics such as *pleading*, *imploring*, *luring*, or *seducing* will add a greater level of physical commitment and specificity to our movement.

The second body NRG is buoyancy. When we sigh with relief, relax into a chair, or smile with euphoria, we tend to float in buoyancy.

The three dialects of buoyancy are *rising buoyancy, floating buoyancy,* and *settling-down buoyancy.* Buoyancy can be attributed to our stress-reducing impulse after a long day on our feet, or relief from a stressful situation; we tend to want to float in the tub, relaxing the body and relieving the tension. Rising buoyancy is an upward anti-gravitational wafting that lengthens the spine, subtly lifting the limbs and the crown of the head toward the ceiling. Floating buoyancy is a more back-and-forth floating, an equilibrium suspended between upward and downward motion. And settling-down buoyancy is the downward tendency, not heavy or sluggish, but light as a feather or leaf settling down to the ground. Instinctive application of more conciliatory tactics like *caressing, comforting, calming, soothing,* or repelling tactics like *dismissing, evading,* or *ignoring* are conducive to buoyancy.

When we revert back to more electric, playful, or humorous behavior, we are experiencing a dialect of the third body NRG, radiancy, called *child-like radiancy.* Another dialect of radiancy, *vibratory radiancy,* manifests with shaking, shivering, perhaps as a result of nervousness or fear. And, a third form of radiancy, *anticipatory radiancy,* can occur when on alert, as a guard on watch or while walking through a dark alley at night. Anticipatory radiancy can also occur as a runner awaits the starter pistol, or as a cat readies itself for just the right moment to pounce on its prey.

Infusing a body NRG to play an "opposite" acting choice can elicit an entirely new dimension for a character. For example, an instinctive NRG choice while threatening would be potency, however, engaging buoyancy while threatening provides the actor with a more dynamic choice, thus conveying a more complex characterization. Perhaps, instinctively, we would choose buoyancy while taunting, but could also employ radiancy as an alternative choice. Table 20.1 contains some examples:

Table 20.1 Creating dynamic choices with opposing NRGs

Tactic	Instinctive Choice	More Dynamic Choice
threatening	potency	buoyancy
taunting	buoyancy	radiancy
pleading	potency or radiancy	buoyancy
apologizing	buoyancy	potency
demanding	potency	buoyancy
mocking	buoyancy	radiancy

The Lessac Tactic Circle Exercise: Setup/Directions

In the Lessac Tactic Circle, actors are encouraged to *discover* the tactics first, through physical behavior – to allow them to acknowledge their own instincts – and then apply those instincts intentionally. (Beneath the exercise, you will find a short list of immediate playable objectives (IPOs) and action-packed tactics.)

You will need:

- Small cards (index cards cut in half work nicely) with a tactic written on each.
- Small cards with one IPO, such as "I want you to smile" or "I want you to bow before me," along with three tactics on the same side of the card that would be conducive to that IPO. For instance:

    I want you to smile.
    cajoling, entertaining, pleading

- Write 10–20 tactics on the board for examples to use later in the game or, ideally, on a flip chart that can easily be revealed at the appropriate time.
- Write several IPOs on the board or flip chart for students to see as examples they could choose from when they create their own in the later rounds. Beneath the exercise is a list of my "go-to" tactics and IPO examples.

The basic exercise sequence is as follows:

Round #1: Participants form a circle with one volunteer in the center. To demonstrate, instruct several students (one at a time) to use a single nonverbal strategy to get the center person out of the circle (without making physical contact). (Beforehand, establish some parameters regarding physical contact and proximity.) Give each participant only 15 seconds and instruct the center person to refuse. Afterward, inform the participants that the "strategies" they were employing were "tactics," and that their pursuit of removing the center person from the circle was their "immediate playable objective" (IPO).

They may have used tactics such as bribing, enticing, tricking, or forcing the person out. This demonstration is rooted in natural human behavior. Offer them an example: "For instance, if a child wants a cookie from his mother, he will instinctively employ a series of tactics such as charming, pleading, negotiating, and finally demanding, changing from one tactic to the next with each refusal." It is important to emphasize that this behavioral strategy is observable in everyday human interaction.

Round #2 (Tactic Card): Now, hand each participant a tactic card and instruct each person around the circle (one at a time) to pursue their IPO of removing the center person from the circle ("I need you to leave") while employing the tactic on the card. Instruct them to only play the tactic on the card nonverbally, and not to revert to other tactics. Pursuing the IPO and employing the tactics nonverbally will stimulate physical behavior and commitment as they are relying on that alone to achieve their goal. Instruct the center person to creatively refuse each attempt, responding to each player truthfully.

Round #3 (Add Non-Specific Text): During the next round, non-specific text is given to the students, such as, "Twinkle, twinkle, little star" as they repeat their tactic (or create their own new tactic); the center person responds with "How I wonder what you are." (You can use "Row, row, row your boat" with the response, "Gently down the stream," or even alternate the letters in the alphabet as non-specific text.) The IPO remains the same ("I need you to leave").

The person in the center is instructed to refuse each attempt, as before. However, during this round, the center person may choose to continue to refuse, or to give in to the tactic-player. A player who achieves their IPO replaces the center person and the game continues.

Using a non-specific text urges the actor to continue to pursue the objective, to attempt to overcome the obstacle, and to employ the tactics with physical behavior and to focus less on just letting the words do all the work. The refusals from the center person represent the obstacle, and thus, the students will experience the impulse to change tactics.

At the end of this round, take just a few minutes to ask the students if they could identify an adjustment in their physicality or their voices depending on which tactic they played. For instance, when playing a more aggressive tactic, like punishing, we often fuel our voices with more tone, or use more emphatic extended gestures. On the other hand, when playing a more inducing tactic, like coaxing, we tend to use less tone in our voices and softer, lighter, and more fluid movements.

Round #4 (IPO/Tactic Cards): Next, each person around the circle is given a card with an immediate playable objective (IPO) on it, such as "I want you to smile" along with three tactics. The tactics on the card may include cajoling, tricking, and gently teasing.

During this round, each one pursues their immediate playable objective, while employing the set of tactics using the same text from Round #3, or another non-specific text. If they use their own improvised text at this point to help them accomplish their goals, they may revert to letting the words do the work and utilize little, if any, physical engagement. Encourage them to be more physically involved, to make physical contact, and to use specific physical proximity.

As in the previous round, a player who achieves their IPO replaces the center person, and the game continues. Point out that THIS is where the emotional reaction manifests naturally with exhilaration, frustration, anger, disappointment, etc. These feelings surface as a result of winning, or not winning, the goal. It is also important for the young actor to understand that when we react to certain circumstances, we are motivated to DO something. So, if they say that their characters are angry, ask them then, "What does your character DO to others when they are angry?" Most likely, they will answer with a list of psychological tactics! Consider asking them WHY they are angry, and what is the source of that anger; this enlivens the pursuit with vivid imaginary circumstances.

> **Round #5 (Create IPO/Tactics):** This next round involves the same format as Round #4, only for this round, the students will be creating their own IPOs and tactics, based on the ones they played above and the examples on the board, along with their own improvised text, preferably a text that does not directly state the IPO so that they will be more physically engaged in the subtext. It is perfectly acceptable for different students to choose the same IPO/ tactic.
>
> **Introduce Body NRGs:** Once the students seem to grasp the concept of IPOs and how tactics are employed, briefly introduce the body NRGs (potency, buoyancy, and radiancy)[2]. It might be useful to write these on the board for reference and to move in each NRG with the students as you introduce them:
> - Starting with potency, ask the students to "muscle yawn" with their entire body, by reaching and extending as if they just woke up, or as if they just got out of their car after a ten-hour drive, feeling the fueled, condensed energy of the "yawn." Breaking out of the circle, encourage them to move around the space with this slow-moving tai chi-like energy that feels controlled, powerful, and strong, like a superhero or a wizard.
> - Ask them to shake that off, and begin to slowly float through the space, anti-gravitationally with this buoyant energy that feels light and free, like an astronaut walking on the moon, a feather gently settling down to the ground, a ballet dancer, a frond of seaweed anchored to the ocean floor swaying side to side with the current, or a balloon floating upward unattached. This is buoyancy.
> - Ask them to shake that off, and begin to shake gently at first with shivering, then more vigorously in vibratory radiancy, like a cowering animal, a child wild with anticipation, or an aged person with tremors.

- Once the students have explored the NRGs for 3–5 minutes each, allow them to revisit their IPO-tactic pairing and text from Round #5, only this time infusing one of the three body NRGs. Going around the circle, one at a time, instruct each student to pursue their IPO/tactic in a body NRG to the person next them in the circle using the same text. This will save time and accomplish the goal of allowing them each to intentionally explore the added element of the body NRG.
- In order to demonstrate how the body NRGs can introduce students to more dynamic choices, instruct them to engage the following tactics with these body NRG pairings. Going around the circle using the text, "What are you doing," instruct each student to simply employ: (1) interrogating in buoyancy, (2) calming in potency, or (3) warning in radiancy to the person next to them. Encourage them to take note of how these choices offer greater complexity and build upon the instinctive ones. Ask them to note how their physicality and their voices were affected by the body NRG. Did they feel more or less tone? Use a higher set of pitches? Did they move in a more fluid, or abrupt, manner for instance.

Round #6 (Putting It All Together): For the last round, a new center person takes their place and, going around the circle, each player creates another IPO and series of tactics as Round #5, but this time they will layer in a body NRG that more specifically guides the physical and vocal behavior.

Examples of IPOs and Action-Packed Tactics

10 Immediate Playable Objective Examples

I want you to give me your hand.*
I want you to bow before me.
I need you to give me a hug.
I want you to tie my shoe.
I need you to leave the room.
I want you help me find my ring.
I need you to spill the beans.*
I need you to agree to my plan.
I need you to smile.
I need you to go to sleep.

*Note: Depending on the character and their situation, "I need you to …" has a stronger urgency than "I want you to …" and therefore the IPO can be stated using either, but it is helpful to discern which is more appropriate.

20 Tactic Examples (these are Just a Few)

scolding, pleading, bribing, ordering, enticing, coaxing, scolding, warning, instructing, seducing, flirting, mothering, commanding, shocking, nagging, cajoling, befriending, threatening, tricking, interrogating.

Post-Exercise Discussion

• What vocal/physical manifestations of specific tactics did you observe in yourself and in others?
• What gestures seemed to organically emerge?
• How did you use physical proximity?
• How did you engage in any physical contact?
• What body NRGs could you identify in yourself and in others?
• What role did the NRGs play within the tactic?

Conclusion

After completing the Lessac Tactic Circle exercise, I have found that students are much freer, more fully engaged, and actively attempting to affect their scene partners. They have widened their physical vocabulary and discovered a full range of behavior through the body NRGs, all through a playful experience.

Notes

1 "Behavior," in Lessac terms, is often used in place of "body language." It encompasses movement, gesture, and includes both physical and vocal expression.
2 NRG = Neurological Regenerative Growth, the acronym Arthur Lessac uses in his *Use and Training of the Human Voice* to describe "energy" as "pure, harmonic, intrinsic, vitalistic motion as opposed to movement." In Lessac, Arthur. *The Use and Training of the Human Voice: A Bio-dynamic Approach to Vocal Life.* 3rd edition. McGraw-Hill, 1997. 273.
3 Lessac, Arthur. *Body Wisdom.* San Bernardino, CA: Lessac Institute Publishing Company, 1981.
4 "Dialects" is used to describe the more specific subcategories of each of the three main body NRGs.
5 The tightening of muscles caused through force or strain is replaced by the benign, strength-inducing "muscle yawn" of potency.

TWENTY ONE

Relaying Action – from Breath to Text

Aaron Alpern and Rebecca Covey

What is it to act? To do. A character is always in action, wanting something and using different tactics to get it. Ask students to define "action" words and they ultimately will answer "Verbs!"

However, it can be challenging for students to choose and then use compelling verbs that bring a text to life. To begin, it is important to clarify that not *all* verbs work as playable actions or tactics. Students need to be able to recognize strong active tactics and distinguish them from weak actions that are not helpful to the actor. The following guidelines set out simple criteria for identifying strong playable tactics and avoiding weaker verbs.

Pre-Exercise Discussion: What Is a Tactic?

- A playable tactic must be an "action verb," that is to say that it must express an action that a person (or animal, or thing or force of nature) can *do*. I write on my blackboard "To Do Something."
- A playable tactic must also be a "transitive verb." A transitive verb has two qualities. First, it is an action verb that expresses a doable activity. Secondly, it must have a direct object – someone who receives the action directly. To test a tactic, use the following fill-in-the-blank sentence. "Jill _____s her daughter." Students should ask themselves if their character can *do* this action to the other character in the scene? I then write on the blackboard "To Someone."
- A playable tactic must be evocative or make you feel **excited to play** it. Students should find powerful visceral words ("push," "tease," or "interrogate.") that they can do to the other character in the scene. Students should be advised against using lifeless verbs like "reiterate," "recite," or "question." If merely saying the tactic out loud can make your heart beat a little faster, you are on the right track.

To help solidify these guidelines write the following sentences on the blackboard and then review them one by one as a class.

Sally pushed Clair. Lexi laughed bitterly. Lincoln cleaned his blanket. Marco charmed Susan. Armand sneezed shyly. Mary Shelly teased Lord Byron. Inez joined the meeting. Sheila was sad the professor had died. James tricked Ernst. Fran fell down. Ali belittled William and he cried. Marialexia stated her case.

After you have written the sentences on the board, ask the following questions:

- Which of these sentences has strong playable actions?
- Which of these sentences have actions one person can do to another person?
- Which of these sentences has weak non-active verbs, adverbs, or emotions?

At this point the class should have a have a working understanding of a playable tactic.

Exercise: Tactic Verb Relay

Exercise Goal

To drive home the concept of a strong, playable tactic.

Physical Set Up

A space that can accommodate two lines of students and a chalk/dry erase board.

What You Will Need

- Large chalkboard at one end of your space.
- At least two pieces of chalk/dry erase markers.
- An eraser and a timer.

Directions

- Divide the class into teams A and B. Each team nominates a captain. The teams line up behind their captains at one end of the room facing the board. Draw a line vertically down the middle of the chalkboard to separate the teams' responses. Give the class the following instructions from step 2.
- Each team will have five minutes to write as many playable tactics on the board as they can. Starting with the captains, teammates will run to the board and write a tactic verb on their team's side of the board.

- Players will race back and pass the chalk to their next teammate in line. Each player will rotate through their line as many times as possible until time is up.During the relay there is no talking. Answer any questions and then begin the race.
- Once the relay is complete, the students return to their seats. Go through with Team A the list of tactics written by Team B. Team A and the instructor, vote on whether each word is a strong playable tactic. If there is a consensus that the verb is not a strong tactic it is erased. Once Team A has finished evaluating Teams B's list, Team B evaluates Team A's list.
- If there is a genuine dispute as to whether a tactic is playable – guide the students with the following questions. Ask the student who is defending the word to play that action on a simple neutral line (such as "Sam, I am going to the store now"). Then ask the other students if they observe the tactic influencing the student's voice and body. If the students all agree that the tactic can be played, the tactic stays on the board. This process underscores that the purpose of tactics is not academic but to use in performance. If a tactic energizes your performance, it works.
- After counting up both lists, the team with the most tactics wins. Erase any duplicates and what is left is a list of strong active tactics. Remind the class that there are more active tactics than are written down on this list and the ultimate test of whether a tactic is effective is if it activates the actor.

Exercise: Tactic Breath, Sound and Movement Exchange

Exercise Goals

To connect actors with their partners, to connect tactics with breath, and finally to connect tactics, breath, and sound with physical actions.

Physical Setup

Ideally, the verbs from the tactic relay are visible for easy reference and there is space to work in pairs, either sitting on the ground or in chairs.

What You Need

If the board with the tactic verb relay is not available, an easily accessible list of playable verbs will work well, too.

Inspiration

These exercises are inspired by Robert Benedetti's Trading Breath[1] exercise as well as by Kristin Linklater's[2] Sound and Movement work.

Directions

I start by connecting the impulse for action with the breath. Often students focus so hard on a verb that they forget to breathe! I remind them that the word *inspiration* can mean more than a sudden, brilliant idea. Inspiration also means the *drawing in of a breath*. Creative action begins with a breath.

Step One: Breath Exchange

- Partners sit comfortably aligned opposite each other.
- Each puts a hand on their belly and allows the breath to drop in so the abdominals are soft and move in and out in the rhythm of their natural breath.
- Next, as one partner releases breath through opened lips, the other allows the breath in through open lips.
- Partners continue until they find a shared rhythm – one breathing out and the other breathing in. This doesn't have to be perfect but they should do their best to allow the breath – like the tide – to flow between them.

> Note: Students may choose to maintain eye contact during the Breath Exchange. However, this may be overwhelming for some. In this case, they may look at their partner's ear or cheek.

Step Two: Tactic Breath Exchange

- Partner A silently chooses a tactic verb from the board or sheet.
- Partner A then allows the breath to drop in through open lips then plays the tactic through the release of *breath* in order in order to affect the partner. There is no sound or text at this point. The concept is that the breath picks up the quality of the tactic verb. For instance, the breath might tickle, attack, or caress the partner.
- Partner B allows herself to respond to the tactic – again, just with breath. Her breath may push away, calm, or tease her partner, for example.
- Then Partner B chooses a tactic, allows the thought of that verb to bring in the breath and plays the tactic through her breath. Partner A allows himself to respond with breath.
- Repeat this cycle until the instructor feels the students are committing to their impulses and letting the tactics affect them.
- Students sometimes add a smile, wink, or other gesture that can prevent them from truly connecting. Breathing may bring up uncomfortable feelings and students may rely on habits to protect themselves from feeling vulnerable. Coach them to release the

facial muscles and to convey the tactic (and whatever emotion comes up) primarily through breath.

Step Three: Pause for Feedback

Partners now check in as I guide them with questions:

- Were you able to find a breathing rhythm together?
- Were there moments where you really connected to the tactic and to your partner?
- Did any feelings or story come up for you?
- Was there anything new, unexpected, or intriguing?

Students may be excited to guess the exact actions played. However, the focus of the exercise is connecting the breath to action and playing it fully so the partner will have an authentic response.

Don't be surprised if emotions start to come up when students allow themselves to connect to their breath. They may touch into the diaphragm/solar plexus area – what Kristin Linklater calls "the emotional receiving center"[3] – and release energy held there. If this does happen, it is an excellent opportunity to reinforce the difference between action and emotion.

You can't play "to sadness someone" but you can play an action such as "to beg."

And that action may *create* an emotion – such as sadness. Emotion is therefore a byproduct of action. Or, as I might add, emotion is the love child of action and breath.

Step Four: Tactic Sound Exchange

- As above, each partner chooses a tactic verb, but now the partners play the tactic with vocal sound (NOT a word).
- They allow the thought of the tactic to drop in with the breath and release that verb through a *sound* to their partner. The choice of verb should be quick to avoid overthinking. I encourage them not to plan the sound in advance, but to let it be spontaneously inspired by the tactic.
- When Partner A plays his tactic on sound, Partner B can respond spontaneously with whatever sound comes to her. They continue until Partner A has changed or affected his partner in some way. In one instance, Partner A played "to command" until Partner B fell in line and made a "Huh!" sound like a GI in basic training.
- Next, Partner B plays her tactic through sound and Partner A responds.
- Since each tactic is a new idea, the sound should never be exactly the same. The voice becomes transparent to the thought.

- After the exchange, the actors can give each other feedback. Before they reveal their verbs, they can share their reactions and whether any story started to emerge between them.

Step Five: Tactic Sound and Touch Exchange

Preparation for This Step

For the final step, it is imperative to establish physical "no-fly zones." My research involves helping neurodiverse students succeed in theatre training so I strive to be clear in my communication. I spell out that no-fly zones are areas of a person's body that shouldn't be touched. These include the genitals, breasts, bottoms, and insides of mouth, ears, and nose. After the inevitable giggles subside, I point out that this is a good time to tell partners of any bruises, injuries, or any other spots they don't want touched today. This discussion may serve as an introduction to intimacy guidelines or reaffirm those established at the beginning of the course.

Just as they can express tactics through different pitches, resonators, and qualities in their voice, they can also touch with different parts of the body – not just the hands. What might be expressed with a touch of an elbow? Or a toe? Or a back?

- Partners now *stand* in alignment, four feet apart.
- They put their hands on their belly as a reminder to let breath drop in.
- Partner A chooses a tactic. To keep the sense of spontaneity, I ask them to close their eyes and point at random to a verb on the board or sheet. Then they open their eyes and allow the thought of that tactic to drop in.
- Partner A now plays the tactic with both sound and *touch*. Partner B responds with sound and a physical reaction. This can be a touch, withdrawal, or physical shift in the body.
- They switch.
- I coach students to release their throats if they are gripping and to use their backs, their legs, their hips – not just their hands.
- When each has played and responded to a few tactics, I signal for partners to simultaneously give feedback on their experience to each other.

Step Six: Post-Exercise Discussion

To conclude, I bring the group together to reflect on their experience and place it in the larger context of objectives, obstacles, and tactics. For example, one student played "to stroke." He stroked his partner's arm but she didn't have his desired reaction: her body language communicated discomfort and later she confirmed that "He creeped me out and made me feel really uncomfortable." This was *not* his objective. So, without changing his tactic, he changed the *way* he performed his tactic – to softly stroking her hand and softening his tone. She admitted that this change "made me feel safe."

Both were strong reactions to a simple sound and touch.

My students have responded enthusiastically to this series of exercises. They see the connections between acting and voice and begin to understand that action begins with impulse and breath. By quickly choosing verbs they get out of their comfort zone and play tactics they would not consider otherwise. They admit to being emotionally affected by their partners' tactics, in ways that they don't anticipate. This visceral experience shifts the concept of tactics and action from the intellectual to the experiential. It is no longer about finding the perfect verb, it is about using a tactic as a tool to affect the partner to get what the character needs.

Exercise: Text a Tactic

Exercise Goals

This is a simple yet engaging game to illustrate the power of playing tactics.

Physical Setup

A chalk board or dry erase board that is visible to students next to a stage or acting space.

What You Need

The list of tactic relay verbs on the board or on sheets of paper handed out to students.

Smartphones.

Inspiration

I have a love/hate relationship with smartphones. I love mine and I hate yours, or to be more specific, I hate my students' smartphones. They are a pervasive distraction that can undermine a classroom.

One day I entered a jam-packed elevator crammed with students staring at their phones. I observed that this technology is something my teachers never had to contend with. Then I thought, is there a way to *employ* smartphones in acting class instead of banning them?

What follows is an acting game that focuses on tactics and uses cell phones. It was inspired by an improvisational exercise called Jump taught to me by Lou Palter at The California Institute of the Arts.

Directions

In this exercise, student A picks another student B to be their scene partner. A establishes their relationship and something that A wants B to do. B can and should be tempted by A but should never give in. This ultimately requires A to try different tactics to try to influence B. The class can easily see via the scene the effectiveness of playing different tactics. The result is a game called "Text a Tactic". Students will be texting actions to students onstage so make sure that students willingly consent to sharing their contact information. Anyone who is at all hesitant should be encouraged to watch or participate with a friend's phone. I frequently find that my classes are already involved a group chat.

- I use the blackboard that students filled with strong active tactics from the previous Tactic Relay.
- I invite one student to jump up onto the stage and bring a partner.
- The actors on stage write their own cell numbers on the board.
- The students in the audience sit with their phones on – screen side down in their laps.
- The two actors, A and B, begin to improvise their scene. A begins the scene and establishes the relationship with B and his/her objective – what A wants from B.
- Students in the audience may use their phones. However, to control the flow of content, students may text the actors in the scene only when I point at them.
- When an audience member is pointed at they may stand and use their phone to text a tactic from the blackboard to the actor they are helping.
- After texting a tactic, the audience member sits again, returning their phone to its previous position. The actor who received the text does their best to remain in the scene while playing the new tactic.
- The instructor then ends the scene after several tactics have been tried.

Post-Exercise Discussion

Following the scene I ask for feedback from the actors:

- How was that for you?
- Were some tactic verbs easier to play than others?
- Which verbs were easier and why?
- Do you find some verbs that worked that you didn't expect to?

I also ask the audience for their observations:

- Could you tell when an actor switched actions?
- Could you tell what action they were playing?

- Were some sections of the scene more successful than others sections? Why?
- How do you think playing tactics affected the performances?
- What did you experience when you put down your phone after texting?
- Were you tempted to give focus to your phone instead of the actors on stage?
- If so, why do you feel that was?
- If not, what did you find more compelling about the action on stage.

The use of the phone in this game may not be much more than a gimmick. However, when my students play this game I always witness a clear and palpable enthusiasm. The game's fundamental lessons of spontaneity and action are highlighted while the technology inspires excitement and keeps the audience engaged. This exercise may also serve as a launch point for dialogue about the healthy use of phones to stay present in the moment and connected to community.

There are undoubtedly many creative ways of using smartphones in the acting classroom. Bring them on. I am now seeking to change my attitude from "How can I keep this technology out of my classroom?" to "How can I use it?"

The group of exercises laid out in this chapter introduces to students the notion of tactics and to the process of integrating the concept into their work. We proceed first intellectually – by helping the student identify playable actions. Then we help them process the technique by letting tactics play through their breath and body in order to affect a partner. Finally, we work creatively through improvisation to develop the student actor's facility and ease with tactics. Our goal is that through this layering process the student actor gains a visceral understanding of tactics to carry into the next phase of their training.

Note: You may need to check your institution's privacy policies to ensure that sharing phone numbers does not violate Family Educational Rights and Privacy Act (FERPA) guidelines.

Notes

1 Benedetti, R. *The Actor at Work*. Pearson, 2009.
2 Linklater, K. *Freeing Shakespeare's Voice*. Theatre Communications, 1992.
3 Linklater, K. *Freeing the Natural Voice*. Drama Publishers, 2007.

TWENTY TWO

Using Improvisation to Identify Tactics

Nathan Stith

Generally speaking, I find that students understand objectives conceptually. They can analyze the text and determine what the character wants fairly easily (with occasional prompting or guided questions). They also have little difficulty with finding beat shifts through close examination of the text. However, students sometimes struggle with determining what tactics a character is employing in pursuit of their chosen objective, and they are often hesitant to think beyond the text in determining possible tactic options. Because the concept of shifting tactics in pursuit of a single objective can be intimidating, students will often land on a single tactic early in their rehearsal process and play that tactic throughout the entire scene. Even if the tactic is active and engaging, the scene or monologue becomes monotone and lacks any sense of spontaneity. Using improvisation as described in the exercise below has proven to be an effective tool which allows students to explore the possibilities of using multiple tactics in pursuit of a single objective as well as how to shift from tactic to tactic while maintaining focus on a single objective for their character.

Inspiration and Exercise Origins

My Introduction to Acting course begins with three weeks of improvisation work where students explore the basic tenets of improvisation through games and exercises. Through improvisation, the students gain trust in their classmates, understand the value of working together as an ensemble, and, most importantly, can utilize these improvisation skills as we shift towards working with the Stanislavski system and the concepts of objectives, obstacles, and tactics. Beginning the semester with improvisation is especially helpful for the mix of students I have in my Introduction to Acting course which serves both as a requirement for our Theatre Major (BA) and is equally populated by students looking to fulfill their general education arts requirement for the university. The course is capped at 16 students; however, the exercise below can work with a class of any size. Once students are comfortable with improvisation (and each other) they are ready to move on to incorporating the techniques of the Stanislavski system into their work. The system is first introduced through assigned readings, group text analysis, and class discussions where students gain an intellectual understanding of these concepts.

The following exercise was originally inspired by an exercise developed by Robert Cohen in his text, *Acting One*. In his chapter, "Acting with the 'Other'," Cohen describes an exercise called One Two Three Four Five Six Seven, which is "intended to deepen your concentration and extend your repertoire of communication tactics"[1]. In this exercise, Cohen asks his students to attempt to "make" their partners do a series of tasks using only the words "one two three four five six seven"[2]. Instead of concentrating on tasks with limited dialogic options, I begin the exercise by focusing on tactics and tactic shifts using improvisation and then adapt Cohen's exercise to help the students understand how to use gesture, tone, inflection, and subtext in pursuit of an objective.

Exercise Goals

The central goal of this exercise is to help students think of the basic principles of the Stanislavski system not as theoretical concepts, but practical approaches to enhancing their character development and overall acting. In addition, this exercise will:

- Provide students with a deeper understanding of how to find active, engaging tactics in pursuit of a clear objective.
- Help students understand the value of identifying multiple tactics within a scene.
- Allow students to recognize when a tactic is not successfully achieving the objective.
- Give students the ability to shift more seamlessly from one tactic to the next in pursuit of a single objective.

What You Will Need

- Prior to class, type a series of "I want" objectives on slips of paper and put them into a hat. There should be at least enough objectives for each student in the class. The "I want" phrases should be open-ended and relatively simple, but always in relation to the scene partner: "I want to terrify you," "I want to amaze you," "I want to discourage you," etc.

Physical Setup

- An open space, such as a typical acting studio or black box theatre, with clear delineation between performance space and audience space.

The Exercise: Round One

- Introduce the exercise as a simple improvised scene, with clearly
established relationships and given circumstances; however, the
focus of the exercise will be on employing Stanislavki's concepts of
objectives and tactics.
- Bring two volunteers onto the stage (or performance area) and
have them each take an "objective slip" out of the hat and read it
without showing their partner or the rest of the class.
- Give the students the basic given circumstances of time, place, and
relationship. For example, "you are on a first date, in Central
Park, at 7 pm."
- Instruct the students to choose a specific, active tactic to play in
pursuit of their chosen objective. For example, if the chosen objective is "I want to terrify you," the tactic "to be scary" is a state of
being; it's not active or playable, instead the actor might play the
tactic "to surprise" by jumping out from behind a set piece, or
they might attempt to terrify their scene partner by playing the
tactic "to disturb" by locking eyes with their partner and not
blinking.
- Allow the scene to progress, but keep a close eye on when a tactic
isn't working. If the student is not coming closer to achieving their
objective, the tactic isn't working and they need to shift tactics (the
scene partner wasn't terrified when the actor surprised her by
jumping out from behind a piece of set, so now the actor must
shift tactics in order to achieve the objective). Often, in this first
round, students will choose a strong tactic initially (jumping out
from behind a set piece to terrify), but because they don't fully
understand the concept of tactic shifts, they will simply repeat the
same tactic over and over. When this happens, simply point out to
the student that the tactic isn't working and encourage them to
find another tactic.
- The goal should be for each student to play at least three tactics in
pursuit of their objective. However, keeping in mind that there are
three rounds to this exercise, with discussions between each round,
the scenes should be relatively short (probably no more than 90
seconds per scene). Determine how long each scene should last
based on the number of students and the amount of time allotted
for the class. Either allow the scene to end naturally or call
"Scene" to end the scene. Each actor can then reveal their chosen
objective to the class. It can also be interesting (and helpful) to ask

the class to guess what each objective might be. This allows you to gauge the degree to which your students are understanding the concept of objectives.

Round One Discussion

- After each scene, ask the class to identify each tactic they witnessed the actors attempting, by naming the tactic. For example, if the chosen objective was, "I want to encourage you," the actor may have tried to convince her partner that she was beautiful. When the scene partner put up obstacles to this tactic, such as pointing to her big ears, the actor may have then praised her partner's writing skills, and so on.
- Encourage the students to name the tactics with active verbs ("to convince," "to praise," etc.).
- Ask the entire class to identify other possible tactic options for the scene ("to reassure," "to inspire," "to raise her spirits," etc.).
- Guide the discussion by offering other possible options for tactics which might make a person feel "encouraged" ("to uplift," "to compliment," etc.).
- Encourage your students to think "outside the box" to find more creative tactics. For example, if the objective is "I want to encourage you" the *tactics* don't necessarily have to be what one would normally think of as "encouraging." Perhaps the actor must lie to their scene partner about a boy who is in love with her to make her feel encouraged, or perhaps the scene partner would feel encouraged if she was able to rescue her scene partner, thus the tactic could be "to lie," or "to create a dangerous situation for myself."
- Create a list of eight to ten additional tactics which the actor could have attempted to achieve their given objective. In preparation for Round Two, write the additional tactics on the board so that the entire class (including the actors) can see them.

Round Two

- Have the actors improvise the scene again with the same chosen objectives and same given circumstances. While the dialogue can (and likely will) be similar to the first scene, especially at the beginning of the scene, you should encourage the actors to explore new dialogue when they are shifting to tactics which were not a part of the original scene.
- Instruct the actors to refer to the list of possible tactics on the board during the improvised scene and to shift tactics whenever they sense that a chosen tactic isn't working (either because the tactic isn't active enough, or isn't successful in achieving the objective within the given circumstances).

- If an actor is struggling, side-coach by suggesting possible opportunities to shift tactics, using the list of possible tactics.
- To make this round more challenging (and fun!) for the actors, allow individual students watching the scene to shout out "shift" at any point to force an actor to immediately shift tactics.
  - A word of warning: while fun, this can sometimes get out of hand. Make sure the students know that the goal isn't to harass those performing, but rather to challenge them. Remind your students that their objective is to introduce tactic shifts, not to manipulate the exercise (or their classmates!). The actors must have clearly established a tactic they are playing in pursuit of the objective before anyone in the class can shout "shift."
- Keeping time in mind, try to allow each actor to shift tactics at least two to three times during the scene.
- The goal of this second version of the improvised scene is to give students a clear understanding of what it feels like to first play a specific tactic, then abandon the tactic when it isn't successful in achieving the objective, and finally, to shift to a new tactic, all in pursuit of the same objective.

Round Two Discussion

- Ask the students viewing the scene to describe the specific moment when they witnessed a tactic shift occurring. Guide the discussion by asking the following questions:
  - Why did the actor choose to shift tactics at that moment?
  - Was the initial tactic effective in pursuing the objective? Why or why not?
  - Which tactics were most active? Why?
  - Which tactics were most engaging? Why?
  - Which tactics not used (from the list) might have been more active and/or engaging? Why?
- Two new students then create a new improvised scene with two new objectives, and so on until all students have had a turn.

Round Three

After all students have had a chance to do both versions of the improvised scenes, the entire class is familiar with each of the given objectives in the hat and have a mental list of possible tactics. They also know what it feels like to pursue a single objective with multiple tactics. The objectives slips are placed back in the hat for the third round.

- Using Robert Cohen's One Two Three Four Five Six Seven exercise as a guide, this third round asks the actors to pursue an objective and shift tactics without the benefit of complex dialogue.[3]
- Ask the actors to choose a new "objective slip" and do a new improvised scene in which they attempt to achieve the selected objective. This time, however, the only spoken dialogue that is permitted are the words, "one, two, three, four, five, six, seven." For this reason, the given circumstances become less important. I have found success with using the same given circumstances from the first two rounds *and* with providing new given circumstances for the third round.
- Encourage the students to use the tactic options discussed during the first two rounds, but they should also have the freedom to choose a completely new tactic if they are inspired to do so.
- Because they have seen the objectives from the previous round and participated in the discussion of possible tactics for each objective, their focus isn't on choosing a tactic, but instead the students must find a way to convey the tactic and achieve the objective through tonal shifts, inflection, gesture, and subtext. For example, if the chosen objective is "I want to terrify you," the actor can begin with a kind, soothing tone, then shift to a deeply resonate voice "to intimidate" their partner, then the actor could use threatening gestures, such as a raised fist, "to bully" their partner; then the actor could speak the dialogue with an overly sweet, soft tone while playing the subtext "to frighten." If the chosen objective is "I want to amaze you," the student could choose inflection shifts "to impress" their scene partner by starting each number with a very low pitch and shifting to a very high pitch; then shift to the tactic "to astound" by using physical gestures such as standing on one leg while miming juggling, and so on. Not every objective can effectively use tonal shifts, inflection, gesture, *and* subtext, but encourage your students to explore as many vocal and physical options as they can. Because the text is limited, the need to use their bodies and voices to clarify tactic shifts usually evolves organically from the students due to their newfound expertise in finding tactics, but offer suggestions for possible tactic shifts if a student is struggling.
- Students learn that sometimes what a character says may not be relevant to the objective or may contradict the tactic being played, but it is still possible to pursue the objective once they've identified a multitude of possible tactics. By removing dialogue, students often gain a quicker sense of when a tactic isn't working. Often the tactic shifts come much more quickly and because the focus is on physical and vocal choices rather than dialogue, students become more focused and the objective itself becomes much clearer.

Round Three Discussion

- Following the same guidelines as above, lead the class in a discussion of each scene:
  - What objective was being pursued?
  - What tactics did the actor play in pursuit of that objective?
  - When did you see a clear shift in tactic? Why did the actor choose to shift tactics at that moment?
  - What specific vocal choices did the actor make while playing each tactic? Where those choices effective in pursuing the objective? How so?
  - What specific physical choices did the actor make while playing each tactic? Where those choices effective in pursuing the objective? How so?

This exercise has undergone several iterations over the years. Sometimes, students struggle with creating a scene in which two students are pursuing two different objectives at the same time, when they don't know what their partner's objective is. If students find it difficult to actively pursue their objective while also realistically reacting to their partner's pursuit of their own objective, it is sometimes necessary to pause the scene and have one actor pursue their objective first and then later create a new scene in which the second actor pursues their objective. Once both actors have successfully pursued their objectives using multiple tactic shifts, you can, if time allows, return to the original scene and have both actors pursue their objectives simultaneously. I have also occasionally found that when the class is composed of students with limited background in theatre it is more effective to only play the first two rounds of the improvised scene rather than adding the dimension of limiting dialogue. If you're not sure how your students will handle the third round, it is advisable to create enough "objective slips" so that each student has the opportunity to work on two improvised scenes. However, I have also had experiences in which students found it difficult to think of ways to shift tactics (even when options were posted on the board) during a typical improvised scene, but had much more success when they didn't have to think of dialogue and could simply focus on playing and shifting tactics in pursuit of their chosen objective. What I appreciate about this exercise is that not only does it give the students the opportunity to play with objectives and tactic shifts through improvised scene work but it is also easily adaptable to each individual student's understanding of the concepts of objectives and tactics *and* to their own abilities and comfort level as actors and improvisers.

Ultimately, after engaging in this exercise, which generally lasts the full two hours of class time (but could easily be split between two shorter class periods), students have a deep understanding of the value of identifying multiple tactics in pursuit of a single objective within a scene; they can recognize when a particular tactic is not working; and they have the ability to shift more seamlessly from one tactic to the next. In addition, once discussion shifts to applying this concept to scripted monologues and scenes, the students already understand the value of finding multiple tactics (including "outside the box" tactics); they know how to find moments in a text when a tactic shift might occur; and they appreciate how the use of tone, inflection, gesture, and subtext can be used in playing a tactic in pursuit of an objective.

Notes

1 Cohen, Robert. *Acting One*. 5th ed. New York: McGraw Hill, 2008. 35.
2 Ibid., p. 36.
3 Ibid., pp. 35–36.

TWENTY THREE

Activating the Actor with Game Theory

Using Gamification to Create Playable Tactics on Stage

Jeanne Leep

Often, beginning acting students confess they don't quite know what to do with their scene partner beyond repeatedly running the scene. Outside of class, rehearsals seem to be only about running lines, and maybe adding some blocking, but students don't always know what they are seeking in rehearsals, or if they do, they don't know how to get there beyond running the scene repeatedly. Many students use only their time to discuss the scene and don't use it to actually experiment with it on its feet. Experimenting with a scene can sound confusing to beginning actors, especially when correct memorization is expected and required for scene work, and they are desperate to "get it right." And this isn't confined only to beginning students. Running a scene over and over without any major changes or new risks doesn't help to evolve tactics or to enrich the objective. Adding a game, however, can. A game can be a new way to experiment with a scene and get new results that will inspire actors to explore further and make discoveries.

Employing games in text based scene work can help clarify the objective and create new tactics. Games lower the stakes for players, increasing the fun of the work and, ultimately, enhancing the scene. Through the use of games, empowered learning, and problem-solving, a new understanding of the scene is revealed. Let's consider the quest for playable tactics that are meaningful in light of game theory: active learning, play and risk taking, and designing your original interpretation of a scripted scene.

Game theory is not exactly new. For some people, game theory's mathematical applications which deal heavily in quantitative, data-driven inputs spring to mind. However, game theory has been more recently re-examined by educational theorists, which links to the work in the theatre studio, as game playing in theatre remains standard operating procedure for acting classes and warm-ups. Improvisation is frequently used to round out a character's background, or perhaps deepen a play by improvising the scenes that are not in the script while still in the rehearsal hall. There are many books and resources for warm-up games or improvisational performance scene work, but game playing in theatre as a tool for active learning on stage in the context of a written scene is less examined. As an acting coach or director, it can be challenging to think about using improvisation with a script, especially when training beginning actors. Employing various improvisational games in rehearsal, especially in light of game theory in the field of education, can create a hands-on approach to tactics work in the studio. And it can do so with a mood that sparks creativity instead of stifling it, while providing another option when investigating the never-ending quest for deeper, truer, and more interesting tactics in the tradition of Stanislavski and all his theatrical heirs.

As an educational theorist, James Paul Gee[1] discusses the power of a good game, particularly video games, to teach. In his 2005 article "Learning by Design, Good Video Games as Learning Machines," Gee maintains that the kind of education where students just cite facts is on its last legs, and the education that sparks creativity, innovation, and problem-solving skills is where education must go. Video games do this – a good video game teaches the player as it unfolds. Players learn what they need as they play, and they learn, as one does in all games, through failure. As a player puts in the hours, that player gets better; there isn't a test at the end of a game – a player has completed the game, so it is mastered. And that mastery, achieved through hours of practice and game playing, is the assessment – not a written test. Gee's research shows that games relieve pressure on learners and create a sense of fun and play in a learning environment.

Rather importantly for theatre, every worthwhile game has a clear objective. Even board games have clearly stated objectives – they have them on the sheet of rules or on the side of the box. Gee explains in his book, *Situated Language and Learning: a Critique of Traditional Schooling*:

> For humans, real learning is always associated with pleasure and is ultimately a form of play – a principle almost always dismissed by schools. There is one crucial learning principle that all good games incorporate that recognizes that people draw deep pleasure from learning and that such learning keeps people playing. Good games allow players to operate within, but at the outer edge of, their competence. At lots of moments, a good game feels highly challenging, but ultimately "doable." Perhaps the player fails a few times at a given task, but good games show how much progress the player has made on each try and the player sees that this progress is increasing each time he or she "fails." Eventually success comes. This feeling of the game being highly challenging, but ultimately doable, gives rise to a feeling of pleasurable frustration, one of the great joys of both deep learning and good gaming.[2]

Successful games in a rehearsal or classroom setting create an instant objective that is actually playable. They simultaneously create tactics that are discovered in the moment as they are played and can be discussed after the scene is done – they evolve naturally from the objective of the game, and if the rules of the game shift even slightly, the tactics can shift too. Helping students to find an objective and playable tactics that makes sense in the scene can start with goofy, low-stakes fun and evolve into something much richer, deeper, and interesting. It can also create a path for students to continue to play the games with their scene partners on their own, which in turn can create a toolbox for the actors that they continue to develop well into their professional careers.

The sciences have embraced the idea of experimentation – students learn science by actively doing science in labs. They conduct experiments and fail a lot. Theatre has borrowed from science in the past: creating theatre "labs," using Grotowski's' theatre laboratory vocabulary, and quoting Samuel Beckett's famous "fail better" mantra. Juxtaposing the experimental quality of a science lab with the low-stakes risk taking of game theory and the studio model of scene work can create a vibrant opportunity to explore tactics.

Exercise: Physicalizing the Quest for Tactics with Games in Rehearsal

Goal

To find new tactics using some of the basic tenets of game theory. More specifically, playing games with the text in rehearsal aims to:

- Layer a game-like objective into a scene, helping students to create playable, achievable tactics on their own, in rehearsal work.
- Make an objective that was unclear to a student clear through the action of changing tactics.
- Tweak the rules of the game continuously to further change and build tactics.
- Transform an objective that makes sense on paper, but seems unachievable and unplayable to an actor, to an achievable and playable one through the process of playing.
- Take a lackluster scene with no useful physical choices and create motivated movements for the actors in the scene that help clarify tactics to an audience.
- Evoke a mood of creativity and fun while helping to create new tactics for beginning actors, or for more experienced actors who are "stuck."

Perhaps the most useful element of this exercise is the mood it can create in the rehearsal hall. Actors, and students especially, can be tense when first showing their work. Criticism, however kindly given, can feel very personal when the only tool actors have is themselves. They want to do it "right." They don't want to look stupid. That can be motivating and useful, but when the personal stakes are too high, creativity can often be blocked and the mood of the whole session can be stressful. Playing a game and introducing it as "only a game" brings a visible sense of relief to actors. The stakes are lowered and the tenets of game theory, where we learn by repeated failure, are evoked. At the start, no one expects much of a game. Except, perhaps, a little fun.

What You Will Need

Actors and a scene – memorized or not. If standard acting class levels of physicality have not already been established, then permission for actors to physically touch each other in non-invasive ways would be useful, such has hands on shoulders, holding hands, hands on face, side-hug, etc.

Physical Setup

Whichever rehearsal furniture that is needed for the scene. Usually three distinct areas with a scenic/furniture anchor in each area works for most basic classroom scenes. Any truly vital rehearsal props are important, too.

Directions

Two (or more) actors are working on a scene, either in class or in the context of rehearsal. For this example, we'll use an acting class setting. Actors have been asked to work on *Proof* by David Auburn.[3] It's a great play for undergraduate scene work as three of the four characters are young and relatable to college-aged students. A pair of actors perform their scene. Before many notes are given, a game is introduced. The game might make the scene appear to come unhinged, but the discussion that follows can shape clearer, playable tactics that not only make sense within the context of the scene but also use the unique gifts of the individual actors. For this exercise, we'll look at two scenes.

Background of Play

Auburn's Pulitzer Prize-winning script looks at a crucial time for Catherine, a college-aged daughter who left school to care for her ailing math professor father, Robert. Robert has just died, and Catherine's sister Claire has come to help with the arrangements. Robert's former grad student at the university, Hal, has also arrived at the house to go through Robert's papers, searching for any possible theories or glimmers of past brilliance. Catherine has her father's talent for math, but is also worried that she has her father's tendencies for madness. Claire sees an exhausted and troubled Catherine making choices that seem unstable and wants to help her sister. Catherine wants to be thought of as strong and capable, to (perhaps) have a real relationship with Hal, to be recognized for the work she has done in both math and caregiving, and not to be seen as ill, but she has her own doubts about that last point.

Physical Setup for the Example

The entire play takes place on the deck of a house in Chicago in autumn. Students can set up the deck how they like, but giving them direction to include three distinct areas on the deck can be helpful. A standard setup involved with this play can make it easy to use in class, as every scene can have more or less the same furniture, even if the layout is changed slightly for different scenes. For this example, let's assume there is a patio table and two chairs, center. Add a bench or stool or two in each downstage corner – but not so far downstage they cannot be completely encircled. A serving table of some kind that can have a few props, could be up left.

The Work

Actors do their scene as usual. Two actors work on a scene early in the play, which contains a lot of emotional complexity. The sisters share familiarity but also tote a lot of baggage in their relationship. Claire and Catherine are having morning coffee on the deck. The previous night, Catherine has called the cops on Hal, thinking he has stolen some of her father's work. She does not know that Claire is aware of this. Catherine was wrong about Hal's theft of intellectual property, and is struggling with her flirty, romantic feelings for Hal and her frustrations with Hal's condescension of her and her own mathematical abilities. She both resents Claire swooping in when her dad is dead, yet is relieved that Claire is there to organize things for the funeral. She battles her mix of grief and relief at the passing of her father, and her own morning grogginess.

Claire is struggling with her own grief juxtaposed against the joy of her own recent engagement; she struggles to find the balance between those extremes of emotions, and to break this happy engagement news to her sister during a sad time. She wants to help Catherine, and is deeply concerned by the run-down state of the house and the fact that her sister is evasive and appears to be doing poorly. The police came the night before to respond to Catherine's call. They returned that morning and talked to Claire. Claire is attempting to get information from Catherine about what happened with the police, and what happened the night before that made her want to call the police.

Usually, the details of given circumstances and relationship contexts are lost on a first scene with beginning actors. Actors are worried about their lines. Often, they make almost no physical choices to enhance the scene.

So, two actors perform the scene off book. Typically, they sit at the table and do the scene, never moving. The rest of the stage is mostly ignored because they do not know how to use it. They have a lot of expression, a lot of vocal variety, but not a lot of bold physical choices. While they are aware of objectives and tactics, they are often putting all their energy into the speaking of the lines and forgetting how physical choices can communicate.

The Game

After a preview of the scene, with very little discussion, I say to the actors, in a bright, upbeat tone: *Hey, let's play a little game with this scene. You might not do this in the context of the scene when you actually perform it, but let's just try it. We are going to do a little bit, not the whole scene, and I'll cut you off, because it's only a game.*

Claire, you are going to play Viola Spolin's Contact exercise, and every new thought you have, every line at the least, you are going to have physical contact with Catherine.[4]

Catherine, you are going to play The Get Away Game: without leaving the stage, you are going to try to get away from Claire on each new line or thought while still having this conversation.

Feel free to go over the top – let's just see what you find – like I said, probably not all this stuff would work if we were doing the play for real, but let's just play.

What usually happens: chaos and laughter ensues. Catherine zooms away from Claire, while Claire follows her all around the stage, trying to pat her shoulder or touch her arm in some comforting and benign way. They do a few lines, and the scene turns into a weird game of tag. Everyone laughs. Often, we stop because if they are working off book, they cannot remember their lines. This is brushed off – concerns about lines are explained as a byproduct of playing a new and nutty game.

Redirect: next, I'll sharpen this a bit. *Okay, okay, that was crazy! Let's try that bit again but now Catherine, you cannot move more than five steps away at a time on your line* (or three if the space is small). *And if Claire gets to you, you just have to take it. Claire, if Catherine is sitting, you need to sit by her, if she is standing, you need to stand by her. Whatever she is doing, you need to try to match it.*

What happens next: Catherine is roped in and now uses other tactics to get away for Claire. She moves to the stool and sits. Claire follows and sits next to her, or drags a chair over to sit by her. Catherine moves again, this time back to her chair at the table and sits, but now Claire comes by her and sits on the arm of her chair. Catherine gets up and moves behind the bench, and Claire comes and stands behind her, giving her a little side-hug, Catherine rolls her eyes and breaks off from that, moving to the bench and laying on it such a way that Claire cannot possibly sit on it, so Claire, with no place else to go, just sits on her sister.

And, once again laughter ensues. And, again, these are not the kinds of choices that would ultimately work on stage, but now formality has broken, and the tension of trying to be "right" is gone. Here, we discuss: *So, what worked here?* "Well," says the actor playing Catherine:

> when she said the police came while I was in the shower to check up on me, I really truly wanted to move away from her, so I did. It was like I wanted more time to think of how I would respond and the moving gave me that time to think and then talk.

Ah, so you want to switch tactics here from being belligerent and sarcastic in order to get Claire to leave you alone and have your coffee in peace, to being guarded and defensive to get Claire to leave you alone and have your coffee in peace. That shift was very interesting and you made it when you learned something new. That worked. Keep it. And when you went to the bench that worked too, but maybe don't lay down. Keep experimenting with movement that matches what you want to accomplish.

Next, the actress playing Claire says, "I liked how I was able to give her a little side-hug, that seemed like a good place for that." *Okay, why?*

> Well, I'm telling her there is a lot to think about and I ask her how she feels, and it just seems to fit – I'd been trying to get the truth out of her without rattling her cage too much, so the side-hug worked there, but when I told her what I knew about the police, it seemed to really shake her up but I was getting somewhere, so I wanted to keep that momentum, so I just sat on her.

Oh, so you had been trying one tactic, to be kind and comforting with the side-hug, but in this moment your tactic shifts when you reveal the truth, and then you become more relentless?

"Yes."

Keep that idea. Keep the side-hug. But what else can you do besides sit on her? Maybe moving to her and standing over her will be enough. And hey, know what? when the tactics shift on paper that is almost always a good place to move on stage. So let's play a new game. Get your script and every time you think there is a tactic shift, move somewhere else on stage.

Next, we're workshopping the scene again, this time with actors looking at the page and discovering places they think the tactics can shift and putting them into action. Sometimes one actor will move a lot and the other not much at all. This calls for a redirect: *Claire,*

I noticed you haven't moved a lot here, so let's add a new layer. This moment seems to be all the same tactic for you, but every time you are rebuffed by Catherine, try moving. After a few minutes of this new game, we seem to have discovered some micro-tactics for Claire, some small playable shifts that she can physicalize. For example, when Catherine is sassy to a very reasonable question, Claire doesn't stop trying to get the truth with kindness, but she tries a different kind of kindness. Is there a place for tough love there? We try that. Ultimately, not all the moves are going to work in the context of the scene, but they can be boiled down to a spine-shift, a head-turn, or a crossed arm rather, than a huge stage-cross. The physical indication of a tactic shift is the discovery. They can then explore and incorporate that discovery when they next rehearse together outside of class.

The magic of using games to find and workshop tactics is the mood it creates – that both coach/director and actor are seeking these tactics together, and the atmosphere is merry. The director isn't just layering on tactics, the game creates a collaboration – we are on the same team, trying to win. The game also breaks down tensions and formalities that are barriers to most actors taking big risks and failing. The game itself as performance would be bad with terrible blocking, and weird out-of-proportion choices. But shaping the game by using the moments where actors find something as a launching pad to discuss new tactic shifts is deeply useful. They can then take that work into their own rehearsal time together, and continue to build on that game, to move when a new tactic- shift appears. Ultimately, not all the movements will work either, but the outward physical choice initiated through play creates an internal pathway for the actors to understand they need to show their tactics. Actors who do this are more confident and brave, but most importantly, more truthful and thoughtful in finding new tactics and playing them fully.

Another example: in the opening scene of the play, Catherine is interrupted late at night by Hal, who has been working in her father's study going through his notebooks. Catherine starts to think that Hal is trying to sneak her father's research out of the house so he can use it as his own research. She demands to see his backpack. He refuses, saying she just said there was nothing in the study worth researching so she does not need to go through his backpack. And she retorts that he does not, then, need to return. It's a nice little beat in the scene that involves a lot of flirty, wordplay wit. Wordplay is the downfall here for the introductory acting class, because there is a tendency for actors to simply work with vocal shifts. But there is an actual backpack in the scene. So, in this example, we'll use the same stage setup. They know their lines, and they can see there is a tactic change here, but they do not know how to play with it, or how to use their own physical selves to enhance that.

After they perform the scene once, I say: *Okay, good. Now, let's play with it. Let's play a good old fashioned game of keep-away. Hal, you want to keep the backpack away from Catherine; Catherine you want to get it. Don't worry about the lines. Just see what happens.* Physical games need another set of rules: *The only rules are don't hurt each other and stay in the boundaries of the stage.* Some duos need to be side-coached to actually try to get the backpack, or move away. If an actor playing Hal is taller than Catherine I will side-coach for that actor to use that height, and the class will delight as the actress playing Catherine jumps for the backpack. This goes on for a very short time for those watching: 30 seconds to a minute. The actors, however, report that it seemed to go on much longer. So now we add the lines. I will ask the actor playing Hal, *When do you hold up the backpack? Why? Is simply holding the backpack up a tactic shift?* Let's say that Catherine decides to tickle Hal or step on his foot or find some way to get him to lower his arm to get the backpack. We play with that for a moment, but the text leads us to discover that she wins this beat not by winning the game of keep-away, (Hal won that) but by outsmarting Hal with her wit. They play the game "Who Will Ultimately Get What They Want?" and Hal wants more research. Catherine wants to see inside the backpack, to make Hal leave, but mostly to prove to Hal that she is as smart as he is. Catherine wins handily. But the process of getting there in rehearsal is far more fun and physically engaging in a way that supports the text when framed as a game. The game of wit is imbedded in the text, but layering on new games for the actors to play increases intensity and boosts confidence, making for a more interesting scene.

Games in rehearsal have the added benefit of easing tension, and shifting actors from thinking of their own choices within the text (and consequently frequently panicking about not looking stupid), to just playing a game. Shifting the actor's personal objective from doing the scene really, really well to "I want to do my best to win this stupid little game the director just gave me" removes all the self-conscious pressure and puts the emphasis on the work, not on the individual doing the work. Often, through games, the actors discover something that they can uniquely bring to the scene that another person could not – like the tall actor holding the backpack very high. What gifts does one's own personal body add to the scene when each micro-beat is seen as an opportunity to play a game? Games can shift the emphasis from a purely vocal emphasis to a total body emphasis, which includes the power of lines, but also the power of physical presence on stage.

Employing games has made difficult casts gel, has made evening rehearsal times that would otherwise be exhausted and unproductive, cheerful, and useful. Games nurture collaboration and ensemble-building simply though the act of playing. They do take time, and are best used right after lines are memorized, but they can certainly be used throughout the rehearsal process, especially in a scene that is stuck or flat. Ultimately, games elevate the work. As an acting coach or director, games in a scene are a coaching tactic to unlock acting tactics. Using games in the coaching of scenes and the development of object-ives and tactics exemplifies hands-on learning and furthers the concept Stanislavski promoted: to have theatre artists create tools to make their own system.

Even when using games without text, tactics, and objectives can be clarified. Warm-up games that circle up actors are commonly used to energize or enliven a cast or to help focus a group to collaborate. Often, they go unexplained. Is this particular game about picking up the cues, stretching, learning names, or reacting in the moment? Taking a moment to define the objective of a simple warm-up game after it is completed can make it all the more useful and rewarding. Asking students who have just played a round of "Zip Zap Zop," "Why did we play that?" sets that stage for them to name the objective of the game, and prepares them to think about the objective of games in the context of their scene work, and consequently the tactics employed to achieve success in the game.

Games are just one more tool in the toolbox, and rather than down-play their less than serious nature, theatre artists can borrow a page from educational theory and the power of well- designed games to teach. "When we think of games, we think of fun. When we think of learning we think of work" Gee says. "Games show us this is wrong. They trigger deep learning that is itself part and parcel of the fun. It is what makes good games deep."[5] In the academic discipline of theatre, games are active and engaged learning that further link our work to the father of contemporary acting theory, Stanislavski, and the high priestess of improvisation, Viola Spolin.

Notes

1 Gee, James Paul. "Learning by Design: Good Video Games as Learning Machines." *E-Learning and Digital Media*, 2.1, March 2005: 5–16. doi:10.2304/elea.2005.2.1.5.
2 Gee, James Paul. *Situated Language and Learning: A Critique of Traditional Schooling*. New York: Routledge, 2004. 65–67.
3 Auburn, David. *Proof*. New York: Dramatist Play Service, 2001.
4 Spolin, Viola. *Improvisation for the Theatre*. Evanston, IL: Northwestern University Press, 1963. 184–186.
5 Gee, "Learning By Design," accessed 22 September 2018.

AFTERWORD

TWENTY FOUR

Recording Truth

The Camera in Acting Training

Welker White

Most acting programs, if they use cameras at all, view recording actors as a bridge to an industry the actor will encounter sometime after graduation. Acting teachers may feel uneasy about utilizing a technology that they suspect may seduce the actor into focusing on external concerns, limiting the possibility for full, human expression. But bringing cameras into the acting classroom is long overdue. Screen acting is a coexisting artistic path, and well-deserving of focused attention as its own art form. But there's another, potentially more compelling reason to record the actor in training: the camera is an unparalleled diagnostic tool. It allows the actor and instructor to view, together and in real time, where and how moments in behavioral language are being missed and what story is being communicated (or not) through the actor's choices.

Because an actor can't see their own work in process, the relationship between actor and acting teacher is, by necessity, a lopsided one. It is built on the premise that the "watcher" has ultimate authority over the "doer." The teacher observes the actor performing, and then communicates to the actor whether a scene, a moment, or an interpretation worked. Critiques are offered and adjustments attempted. This institutional paradigm perpetuates the assumption – one that can follow the actor throughout their career – that the actor is the least qualified evaluator of their own work's effectiveness.

There is no other art form in which the individual artist has so little personal agency in appraising their own developmental process. The painter is taught how to see: creating detailed sketches to analyze and review before moving to the canvas (or clay, or any other endless range of media) where they will add, subtract, and adjust, stroke by stroke, in careful visual observation of their art made manifest. The dancer is trained to use the mirror as a crucial analytical tool; learning over years of practice how to make critical adjustments in line, form, and position as they gain proficiency and exactitude over their bodies in motion. The vocalist's training is built on learning to hear; hours of recording lessons for later playback, in order to learn how to evaluate modifications in tone placement that impact the resonance or quality of their vocal production. There is no equivalent in the actor's training. Communicating to the actor whether or not they are telling a clear story, how their bodies are enabling (or preventing) truthful and spontaneous behavior, and if words, thoughts, and actions are interconnected is not the same as teaching the actor how to assess for themselves whether they are doing these things.

Many acting teachers might recognize the nagging feeling that they are not empowering their students as well as they might to help them to become the ultimate arbiters of their own work. After all, it is acting teachers who know that, when all is said and done, our opinions are inextricably linked to our own training, biases, and taste. That work on a particular scene might look quite different under the tutelage of a teacher from another program, or even the one down the hall. Teachers are human beings after all, and as such can only express what we understand to be true as filtered through our own set of unique experiences.

A camera has no such biases. It is a simple machine, capable of recording human behavior exactly as it exists. It has no agenda, no point of view, no preferences.

For an acting teacher, the camera acts as a neutral intermediary. Used effectively, it offers incontrovertible documentation of an actor's work. A recording can be watched, reviewed, and individual moments isolated. Habits may be mutually identified, often without confusion, recrimination, or blame. As the actor begins to gain competence in applying theoretical ideas and putting them into practice, they soon take the lead in identifying areas that require attention. Over time, the balance begins to shift; the actor drives the evaluation and modification of their work, with the teacher in position of guide rather than judge.

My own work as a teacher is focused, for the most part, on aiding students to take technique built for the stage, and adapt it to serve the visual world of cinematic storytelling. There are unique differences in how stories are told on-stage versus on-screen. But both stage and screen demand truthful human behavior in equal measure from the actor. I've discovered that a camera, placed close to an actor's face, will immediately expose a lack of authenticity in any moment of the actor's work. This transcends medium. In an effort to aid the actor in identifying potential lapses in truthful responses, I utilize a range of simple exercises to be recorded and played back. These are designed to engage the imagination, practice living truthfully under given circumstances, and strengthen clear, moment-to-moment storytelling.

Below, please find a couple of sample exercises designed to be recorded on an actor's phone. Additionally, I've included adjustments to the exercises, as well as where you might take this tool further in order to empower your acting students to begin to accurately watch and assess their own work.

60 Second Observation Exercise, Part 1

Directions

- Ask students to find a partner.
- In pairs, students will alternate between being the *cameraperson* or the *subject*, using their phones to record one another.
- Invite partners to find a space to record each other, outside of the classroom if possible.
- Ask the *subject*(s) to locate something to observe. This should be something they can literally see (cars in parking lot, groups of friends gathering in a hallway, a couple conversing, etc.).
- Ask the *cameraperson*(s) to simply record the *subject* in the act of observing.
- After 60 seconds, the *cameraperson* stops recording.
- Partners switch, and repeat exercise.

When the Students Have Returned to the Classroom, Engage in the Following Discussion

- What did it feel like to be recorded?
- Did knowing your recording would be watched later cause you to alter your behavior?
- Did you "forget" how to simply observe something?
- Did a minute feel especially long? Short?
- Did your mind wander during the exercise? If so, how did you respond?

Allow for any other responses the students may want to share. Now, play back all recordings on a monitor or projector for the entire group.

After Watching, Begin a Discussion This Way

- What did you notice in your own recording?
- Did you see yourself indicating your experience of observing versus actually observing?
- Were you trying to make it interesting/entertaining?
- Did you find yourself concerned with being "natural"?
- Upon watching your own recording, did time feel different than it did while you were being recorded?

Allow for any other responses the students may want to share. At this stage, it is likely many of the actors won't yet be able to assess themselves beyond what felt "good" or "real." This is fine. It takes time to lay a framework whereby these are no longer descriptive terms that hold value for the actor. Many of the videos from this initial pass may have been recorded from too far away to have a detailed view of the actor's face upon re-watching. Encourage camerapersons to get closer to the actor on a second pass.

Send the students back out, with the same instructions, allowing for one major adjustment: this time the subject being recorded should work under imaginary circumstances rather than observing something they can literally see.

60-Second Observation Exercise, Part 2

Directions as Before, with the Following Adjustments

- The subject being recorded should now invent, in their imagination, something specific to observe.
- Ask actors to take a few minutes, privately, to fill out some "given circumstances" that will provide them with something to observe of their own creation.
- Ask the partner doing the recording to make any adjustments necessary to more clearly capture the subject. Shooting in landscape mode, getting closer to the subject, and facing the subject head-on instead of from the side are all adjustments that will be useful in watching the subject's behavior more clearly upon later viewing.

Upon return to the classroom, re-engage in a discussion both before and after viewing all actors' work. You might begin by adding the following to the earlier discussion questions:

- Was it easier or more difficult to observe something you created in your imagination?
- Did you give yourself strong enough given circumstances to keep yourself engaged?
- How did time feel during this pass? Any different from the previous pass?
- If your partner got even closer to you with the camera this time, how did that alter your behavior?

This basic exercise of encouraging the actor to actively observe something created in their imagination can be repeated any number of times (under new imaginary circumstances), exploring what it feels like to let go of any level of manufactured behavior for the benefit of an audience. Encourage actors to be scrupulous in observing their recordings so that they begin to see past any concerns about physical appearance, and instead recognize whether authentic behavior is present.

The next step in utilizing the camera in helping actors to self-assess truthful behavior is to add a simple story for the actor to play through. Building on the work they've done committing to imaginary circumstances, the "Storytelling" exercise that follows offers a set of events to observe and experience, in a clear, moment-to-moment progression.

Just as they did in the 60-Second Observation Exercise, students should pair up and record one another on their phones.

Storytelling Exercise: Street Scene, Part 1

Street Scene

- On a sidewalk, **A** is looking for their keys in their bag.
- After a moment or two, **A** registers a laugh among the ambient street noises. Then, another louder laugh, and **A** looks to see where it's coming from.
- After a moment, **A** notices the laughing is coming from a person across the street. It's **A**'s Ex.
- BEAT – **A**'s Ex greets someone.
- **A**'s Ex and the new person share a kiss.
- Eventually, the happy couple walk off together, out of sight.
- **A** finds their keys.

Directions

- Invite students to take a moment to read through the script, above. All actors will play the role of **A**.
- Again, each actor is acting alone; imagining the events unfolding in front of them as depicted in the short script.
- As in the 60-Second Observation Exercise, the *cameraperson* is not acting in any way opposite the *subject* (A). Their job is simply to capture their partner on their phone.
- Remind partners to shoot in landscape setting, in a "mid-shot": framing their partner from mid-chest to just above the head, and keeping the subject's eyes in frame whenever possible.
- This exercise has no time limit.
- Invite actors to record the exercise outside on a sidewalk, if feasible.

Since actors have already had a few passes at 60-Second Observation Exercise prior to doing Storytelling Exercise, just jump in to watching the entire group's work before a discussion.

After Watching, Begin a Discussion This Way with the Entire Group

- What did you see in your own recording? What didn't you see?
- Was the story told?
- Did you skip over moments in the story progression?
- Did you find you gave a lot of attention to the task of finding the keys? Is this because this was something you could tangibly do?

At this stage, some actors may be able to identify that they skipped over certain events of the story, but many will feel that they behaved "as I would in real life." Upon viewing, you may notice that some actors spent more time focusing on the task of finding the keys than on any of the other moments in the story. It's also likely that most of the recordings were rushed, and that the events of the scene had very little effect on **A**. Many of the actors will have given equal value to all moments in the scene, rather than identifying a progression; **A** did not change from the beginning of the scene to the end. At this juncture, go back and review the events as a group, writing them down on a large board if possible, for everyone to see.

It should look something like this:

- **A** looks for keys in their bag.
- **A** registers a laugh coming from the ambient street noises.
- **A** hears a louder laugh, and looks up to see where it's coming from.
- **A** sees their ex, standing across street.
- **A**'s ex greets someone new.
- **A**'s ex and person share kiss.
- **A** watches ex and person walk off down street.
- **A** finds keys.

Now that the events of the scene have been agreed upon by the group, ask the actors to gauge the value of each event. They will quickly appraise that the task of looking for the keys at the beginning and hearing a random laugh have low value in the scene. The second, louder laugh, draws their attention: "I'm curious." Seeing their ex is a huge shift in the scene, as is seeing their ex greet another person. Ask the group which event has the highest value in the scene; they will identify that it is the sharing of the kiss between their ex and the "new person." Discuss whether, in the first pass, the events built on one another, so that they increased in value, leading to the highest point: the kiss. Most importantly, remind them that all scenes represent a journey for a character, and this one is no different. **A** has gone through something that has altered them.

In an effort to encourage the actors to give each moment its due, ask them to try another pass. The following adjustments to the exercise will address rushing through events, or skipping them altogether, as well as encouraging actors to live more fully through each moment.

Storytelling Exercise: Street Scene, Part 2

Directions as Before, with the Following Adjustments

- Invite actors to repeat the exercise, twice, in two different takes.
- For the first take, the *cameraperson* will now read out loud, slowly, the events of the scene and the *subject* will follow along as instructed (see below). The *cameraperson* should verbalize the beats by counting ("1, 2, 3," etc.) after each event.

- A looks for keys in their bag. 3 BEATS
- A registers a laugh coming from the ambient street noises. 1 BEAT
- A hears a louder laugh, and looks up to see where coming from. 3 BEATS
- A sees it's a person – their ex, standing across street. 4 BEATS
- A's ex greets someone new. 6 BEATS
- A's ex and person share kiss. 5 BEATS
- A watches ex and person walk off down street. 7 BEATS
- A finds keys. 3 BEATS

- Ask the *cameraperson* to hold on **A** for four to five beats after **A** finds the keys at the end of the scene.
- On the actor's second take, the *cameraperson* should NOT read out loud. The *subject* should now move through the scene at their desired pace.
- As always, ask *cameraperson*s to shoot in "landscape" mode, in a mid-shot or close-up, keeping actor's full face in the camera's frame. (Note: It is not important for the camera to catch the looking/finding of keys.)

Upon returning to the classroom, view both takes from each actor if time allows. For the take where the events of the scene were read out loud to them, simply mute the monitor so that the group is viewing without sound.

After Watching, Discuss

- What did it feel like to be read the events out loud while playing through them? Did it enable you to "live" more fully through each moment or was it confining?

- Watching your own, as well as others' recordings: what did time look and feel like this pass?
- Was the story told more clearly?
- Did you see yourself as **A** go through a journey from the beginning of the scene to the end?
- Were there still places where you felt the need to indicate an emotional response vs. just allowing something to move through you? And if so, why?

As you continue to explore using the camera, you will begin to witness a shift; from actors attempting to "be real" or "natural" to identifying themselves as instruments through which a story moves. The camera is wonderfully beneficial in determining whether the connective tissue between thoughts and words is engaged. It's also effective in enabling students to pinpoint whether they are holding their breath, where personal habits are creeping in, where they are pushing, or simply whether they are fully present. You might record actors already doing basic acting exercises in your rotation: Hagen's Object Exercises or Meisner's Repetition Exercises come to mind. Further along, the camera can be used judiciously in taking a closer look at brief exchanges in scenes or plays where you find actors have gotten stuck in a kind of rote delivery, or where work lacks specificity.

Asking the actor to confront their image and take ownership of themselves as artists requires sensitivity. We are asking actors to embody human beings, and as such must always reinforce that each individual is wonderfully compelling and beautiful just as they are. When we allow ourselves to be seen, in all our humanity, we are all fascinating to watch.

Contributors

Conrad Alexandrowicz was born in Toronto and spent many years there and in Vancouver. He holds a BFA in Dance and an MFA in Directing. Over a decades-long career in performance he migrated from dance to theatre, and has been a dancer, choreographer, writer of texts for dance, a playwright, actor, and director. For many years, he was the artistic director of Wild Excursions Performance, the company he founded to present his work. To date he has created over 50 dance- and physical-theatre works, some of which have been presented across Canada, in New York City, France, and the UK. An associate professor in the Department of Theatre at the University of Victoria, he specializes in movement for actors and physical-theatre creation, and continues his explorations into that mysterious territory where movement and text overlap. His writing has been published in *Theatre, Dance and Performance Training*, the *Canadian Journal for Practice-Based Research in Theatre*, and *Studies in Theatre and Performance*. His first book, entitled *Acting Queer: Gender Dissidence and the Subversion of Realism*, is forthcoming from Palgrave.

Aaron Alpern is a Theatre Instructor and Program Coordinator for the Kendall Campus of Miami Dade College where he has directed *Waiting for Lefty*, *The Tempest*, *Glengarry Glen Ross*, *Fuddy Meers*, and *Lobby Hero*. He has also taught at the New World School for The Arts and Florida International University. Aaron earned his undergraduate degree from the University of Michigan and his MFA in Acting from The California Institute for The Arts. As a professional actor he has worked in the West at the Colorado Shakespeare Festival, the PCPA Theatre Festival, the Western Stage, and throughout the Midwest including Detroit, Chicago, Milwaukee, Rockford, and Pittsburgh, performing at First Folio, Chicago Shakespeare, Writers Theatre, Timeline, Next Act, Northern Stage, Jewish Ensemble Theatre,

Meadowbrook, Tipping Point and Quantum Theatre, and as the Equity Guest Artist for Hillsdale College and the Grand Valley Shakespeare festival respectively. Aaron has worked promoting diversity in higher education with the University of Michigan's Center for Research on Learning and Teaching, the University of Miami's SEEDS (Scientists and Engineers Expanding Diversity and Success) and Florida International University's Office of Advancement for Women, Equity, and Diversity.

Davida Bloom is a Professor in the Department of Theatre and Music Studies at The College at Brockport: State University of New York. As a theatre generalist in the department she engages in both scholarly and creative activity. She is the author of *Rape, Rage, and Feminism in Contemporary American Drama* (McFarland & Company, 2016) as well as numerous journal articles. She also appears regularly in theatrical productions in the Rochester, New York area, most recently in productions of *Indecent* by Paula Vogel and *Mrs. Warren's Profession* by G. B. Shaw.

Diane Bonfiglio earned a Bachelor of Science in Psychology from Ashland University, and Master of Arts and Doctor of Philosophy degrees in Clinical Psychology from The Ohio State University. She completed her clinical internship at Henry Ford Hospital in Detroit, Michigan. Dr. Bonfiglio is an Ohio-licensed psychologist with a clinical specialty in health psychology. She is an associate professor of psychology at Ashland University. Dr. Bonfiglio's research focuses on positive factors, such as optimism and social support, in health and well-being. Through her collaboration with Fabio Polanco, she has extended her work on positive factors into the study of flow. She and her collaborators and students have published papers and presented their work at national and regional conferences including the annual meetings of the Society of Behavioral Medicine, the Academy of Consultation-Liaison Psychiatry, and Midwestern Psychological Association.

Hillary Haft Bucs is an Associate Professor of Theatre at Western New England University where she teaches Acting, Improvisational Comedy, and Playwriting, and has directed over 15 productions including *Urinetown*, *Legally Blonde*, and *Beauty and the Beast*. Previously, she taught acting at Smith College and the University of Pittsburgh. Hillary's improv training and performance work began in Chicago, the home of improvisation, at the Second City Training Center; she trained and performed with iO and Annoyance Theatre, and worked with Michael Gellman's TheatreWorks. As an improviser, she has been a member of a variety of troupes in Pittsburgh, Chicago, and NYC. Hillary's TYA (Theatre for Young Audiences) play, *It's Good To Be an Ant* had its equity premiere at the John Anson Ford Theatre in 2000, and toured Los Angeles for three years before a 2015 production at Gretna Theatre in Pennsylvania. Hillary has been an active member of the Association for Theatre in Higher Education since 2007, most recently as the Acting Program co-conference planner. Her book reviews have appeared in *Theatre Topics*, the *New England Theatre Journal*, and *Methods*. She received her BS in Theatre from Northwestern and MFA in Performance from the University of Pittsburgh.

Rebecca Covey is an Equity actor, designated Linklater Voice Teacher and Associate Professor in Acting, Voice and Movement at Florida International University (FIU) in Miami. At FIU she serves as Head of Performance and as the resident Voice and Dialect Director. She also works as a professional dialect coach with Zoetic Stage, Gable Stage, and Miami New Drama. As an actor, Rebecca has performed in Equity theatres throughout the Midwest as well as in California, Scotland, Australia, and France. Professor Covey earned a BFA in Acting and a BA in French from the University of California, Santa Barbara as well as an MFA in Acting from the University of Wisconsin. She taught at the Theatre School at DePaul University, Northern Illinois University, and Columbia College, Chicago. Her scholarly research focuses on helping neurodiverse theatre artists reach their full potential. Additional interests include: the intersection of gender, culture, and voice; accents and dialects; and heightened language including Shakespeare, Moliere, and Shaw. She has presented papers and workshops at international conferences with the Voice and Speech Trainers Association and the Association of Theatre in Higher Education, as well as with the Southeastern Theatre Conference and the Kennedy Center American College Theatre Festival.

Lynn Deboeck teaches in the Theatre Department and Gender Studies Division at the University of Utah. Her scholarly research revolves around gender representation in drama, particularly that of maternity. She most recently had a chapter published in *Lifting the Mantilla: Unveiling the Mystique of Motherhood*. As a director, she focuses on works by women and she is a frequent presenter at national conferences, including the Association for Theatre in Higher Education, the American Society for Theatre Research and the Women and Theatre Program. Lynn also is an active researcher of pedagogy. Her recent grant project, "Teaching with Liveness," enabled students in both theatre and non-theatre courses to engage with live performance as not just an art form, but an engaging learning experience. Her background in actor training mainly comes from her PhD program at the University of Kansas and the multiple positions she served at that institution, including acting instructor, director, and departmental acting coach. She has directed both academically (at the University of Kansas, Ottawa University and the University of Utah) and with amateur and professional theatre companies (in South Bend, IN and the Washington, DC area) for the past 16 years.

Jean Dobie Giebel received her BA in Speech, Communications, and Theatre from Baldwin-Wallace University, and her MFA in Directing from Indiana University, Bloomington. She is currently a Professor of Drama and Associate Dean for Curriculum and Personnel for the College of Liberal Arts and Sciences at Hofstra University. She teaches all levels of acting from fundamentals classes to advanced scene study and Shakespearean verse technique, as well as directing classes and dramaturgical skills. She has directed over 50 academic productions. Professionally, Jean has served as an Associate Director for The Mint Theatre Company and Riverside Shakespeare Company in New York. She has acted off-Broadway, off-off-Broadway, in regional theater, and has appeared in numerous TV commercials. Her professional directing credits include productions at the New 42nd Street Theatre, The Mint Theatre, Pulse Ensemble Theater, Riverside Shakespeare Company, ATA Chernuchin Theater, 45th Street Theatre, Dixon Place, and the Chain Theater. Her original play, *Chasing the River*, has been optioned for TV. Jean is a member of SAG/AFTRA, SDC, and DG. She lives on Long Island with her husband, voice-over artist Tim Giebel. More information can be found at www.jeandobiegiebel.com

Caroline Good is a Lessac Certified Trainer who teaches alongside master teachers at the international Lessac Training Summer Intensive for Voice and Movement Integration and teaches a variety of performance courses at DePauw University. She has performed professionally onstage and in film, and has been a guest artist instructor at Indiana Repertory Theatre (IRT), at Wabash College, and has served as dialect and voice coach on numerous productions. She has choreographed and directed contemporary versions of *The Bacchae*, *Antigone*, and *Trojan Women* incorporating Lessac principles. She presented her "Greek Chorus in Context" for the Hellenic Studies Symposium, and her choral ode project has been incorporated into the Lessac Summer Intensive. She has presented workshops for the Lessac Institute, ATHE, NCA, MATC, WUF in Lisbon, Portugal and her work is published in *Theatre/Practice*. Founder and creator of "Shakespearience" and "Shakespeared!" Youth Theatre Workshops, Caroline has since directed her own comedic pop-culture adaptations of *Romeo and Juliet*, *Hamlet*, *Taming of the Shrew*, *Twelfth Night*, *The Tempest*, and others for high school and middle school students. She also directs the Children's Theatre Workshops program at the Putnam County Playhouse.

Janet Hayatshahi is an actor, director, and educator. Janet is currently an Assistant Professor of Theatre at Randolph-Macon College in Ashland, VA. She holds a BFA from Ithaca College and an MFA from the University of California, San Diego. Acting credits include: *The Heiress* (Arena Stage), *Launching Ships* (Tentacular Performance Group), *A Dream Play*, *Macbeth*, *nu, [sic]*, *Berzerkergäng*, *Richard III* (Sledgehammer Theatre), *Master Class* (Poway Center for Performing Arts),

Remains (Mo'olelo Performing Arts Company), *Taming of the Shrew*, *Macbeth* (Central Coast Shakespeare), *Beyond Therapy*, *Marvin's Room* (Centerpoint), *Agamemnon* (European Repertory Theatre), *Infernal Machine*, and *Knights of the Round Table* (Eclipse Theatre Company). Select directing credits: *The Hatmaker's Wife* (Moxie Theatre), *9 Parts of Desire* (Mo'olelo Performing Arts Company), *The Turn of the Screw* (Cygnet Theatre). Janet's theatrical interests lie in ensemble-driven, collaboratively created works, blending a physical approach and embodied practice with text and storytelling, particularly with new works or reinventions of classic tales. Visit www.hayat shahi.com

Kevin Hoffmann is a professional actor, teacher, and theatre artist currently teaching at Elon University. He holds a BFA in Acting from Elon University and an MFA in Acting from the Old Globe Theatre/University of San Diego Professional Actor Training Program. Kevin's area of scholarly interest lies in the connections between the Michael Chekhov Technique and the Stanislavski system and in movement and physical-based acting methodologies. He holds certifications from the Great Lakes Michael Chekhov Consortium and the Michael Chekhov Association. He is currently pursuing his teaching certification in Alexander Technique with Chesapeake Bay Alexander Studies. Kevin has also taught at Millikin University and Dickinson College. Professional acting highlights include *Twelfth Night* and *Whisper House* (world premiere of Duncan Sheik musical) at The Old Globe, *Proof* at Virginia Rep, *The Taming of the Shrew* at Delaware Shakespeare Festival, as well as performances at Theater at Monmouth, Montgomery Theatre, Revolution Shakespeare, and others. Visit him online at www.kevinhoff mann.com

David Hugo has been a Professor in the Theatre Department at Long Island University, CW Post since 2007. He teaches freshman acting and all the musical theatre acting courses. David has performed regionally, on national tours, and on Broadway. He was last seen on Broadway in *Les Misérables* where he portrayed Grantaire in the final Broadway cast. In 2005, David pursued a master's degree in theatre at LIU Post where he was introduced to the Suzuki method, which changed the course of his career. He found the Suzuki method to be an excellent technique for teaching musical theatre, and he was able to devise a way to integrate it into his musical theatre curriculum. In addition to an MA in Theatre from LIU Post, David holds a BFA in Acting from Syracuse University and an Associate Degree in Music from Onondaga Community College.

Anjalee Deshpande Hutchinson is the Chair of the Department of Theatre and Dance at Bucknell University in Lewisburg, PA. As an Associate Professor, Anjalee teaches classes in acting, directing, and devising.

She is a graduate of the MFA directing program at Northwestern University and studied under Robert Falls of the Goodman Theatre, Mary Zimmerman of The Lookingglass Theatre and Barbara Gaines of The Chicago Shakespeare Theatre. Anjalee's specialization is in devised theatre and the Michael Chekhov acting technique. Ms. Hutchinson is an accredited teacher of the Chekhov Technique through The National Michael Chekhov Association and is certified teacher of the Meisner Technique through the True Acting Institute. Anjalee recently published a book on Acting/Directing Technique entitled, *Acting Exercises for Non-Traditional Staging: Michael Chekhov Reimagined*. Ms. Hutchinson is also a freelance actor/director/devisor. Recent acting credits include acting with the Tectonic Theatre Project Workshop of *Square Peg, Round Hole* which recently went to Broadway as the show *Uncommon Sense*.

Timothy Johnson is a director, performer, flutist, playwright, and educator. For his New York City production of *On Strivers Row* he received an AUDELCO nomination for Best Direction of a Play, along with three additional nominations including Best Dramatic Production. In their review of this production *The New York Times* said that "Timothy Johnson has shaped 16 striking performances here." He is a member of the 2018 Lincoln Center Theater Directors Lab. As an actor, his performance highlights include *Legends!* starring Mary Martin and Carol Channing, *REGINA* at the Scottish Opera, *A Chorus Line* on Broadway and the National Tour, and *The Temptation of St. Anthony* directed by Robert Wilson at the Melbourne International Arts Festival. As a flutist, he was a first-place winner of Baldwin-Wallace College Conservatory Annual Concerto Competition. His play *Listening to the Tree* achieved semi-finalist status for the 2012 Eugene O'Neill National Playwrights Conference. He is a former Artistic Associate of Rosie's Theater Kids. Timothy is currently an Assistant Professor of Theatre Arts, Acting at Marymount Manhattan College. He holds an MFA in Acting from the University of Washington Professional Actor Training Program.

John Kaufmann is a theatre teacher, director, and performer focusing on experimental and interactive work. Kaufmann worked as planetarium supervisor at Pacific Science Center where he developed live shows including *Starball* and *The Sky from Scratch*. In Seattle, he worked with Seattle Children's Theatre, Jet City Improv, and was on the development team for several *Cranium* board games including *Hullabaloo*. He developed original activities and served as the Interactive Host for TEDx Seattle in 2018. At Beloit College, he directed over a dozen plays including *Rent, Macbeth*, and *Clybourne Park*, and he used forum theatre techniques to develop *Race Replays*. Kaufmann earned his MFA in theatre directing from The University of Iowa and currently teaches theatre at Evergreen Valley College in San Jose, California.

Jeanne Leep is the Producer of Edgewood College Theatre and the Chair of the Department of Theatre Arts at Edgewood College. She received her PhD in Theatre with an emphasis on directing from Wayne State University and her MA from the University of Michigan in Theatre Studies. She has also studied at the Moscow Art Theatre and the Royal Shakespeare Company. She is the author of *Theatrical Improvisation, Short Form, Long Form, and Sketch-Based Improv*, and the co-founder of River City Improv, a performance improvisational troupe based in Grand Rapids, Michigan. Some past directing credits include *Metamorphoses, Our Town, Love's Labour's Lost, The Penelopiad*, and *Body Awareness*. A longtime member of the Association of Theatre in Higher Education (ATHE), Dr. Leep recently served as the Chair for the Acting Focus Group.

Deric McNish is an Assistant Professor of Acting, Voice, and Speech at Michigan State University, where he serves as Director of the BFA in Acting. He earned a PhD from the University of Colorado Boulder and an MFA from Case Western Reserve University and the Cleveland Play House. Deric's research focuses on inclusive, accessible, and interdisciplinary approaches to teaching and learning. Recent publications include "Training Actors with Disabilities" in *New Directions in Teaching Theatre Arts* (Palgrave Macmillan, 2018), "Performance of Fluency" (*Voice and Speech Review*, 2017), and "A Moving Target: Success and the Reset Button" in *Perform: Succeeding as a Creative Professional* (Focal Press, 2017). He is the co-author of *Drama in the Language Classroom* (University of Michigan Press, 2019) and a Senior Editor of the International Dialects of English Archive.

Tom Pacio is currently the Interdisciplinary Arts Coordinator at Vassar College where he directs the Creative Arts across Disciplines Initiative. He also teaches acting, script analysis, and performing skills for the classroom at SUNY Dutchess. Prior teaching experience includes New York University, The CAP21 Musical Theatre Conservatory, Vassar College, The Stella Adler School of Acting, and the University of Pittsburgh. He served as both Education Director and Producing Director for Vassar and New York Stage and Film's Powerhouse Theater and the Industry Practicum Director for CAP21. Directing credits include *On the Town*, devised musicals *Looking for Someone*, and *Sympathetic Frequencies*, *Scapin*, and a reading of a new musical adaptation of *The Tell Tale Heart*. Other professional experience includes working for a bi-coastal talent agency, for several casting directors, and in the offices of the world-renowned Nederlander Organization. As a performer, Tom has toured with national companies of *Crazy for You*, *West Side Story*, *The Wizard of Oz*, and *White Christmas*. He has numerous regional and stock credits and has performed in *The Radio City Christmas Spectacular*. He holds an MFA in Performance

Pedagogy from the University of Pittsburgh and a BFA in Acting from NYU's Tisch School of the Arts.

Fabio Polanco is the recipient of the 2018 Kent State University Excellence in Research and Scholarship Award and Ashland University's 2013 Taylor Excellence in Teaching Award. His acting credits include the Broadway national tour of *Les Misérables*, *Missionaries* by Elizabeth Swados at Brooklyn Academy of Music, the US premiere of David Hare's adaptation of Brecht's *The Life of Galileo* at Berkeley Repertory Theatre, the world premiere of *These Mortal Hosts* at the Cleveland Play House, as well as performances at the O'Neill Theatre Center, Idaho Shakespeare Festival, Signature Theatre Company, The Repertory Theatre of St. Louis, Great Lakes Theatre Festival, Cincinnati Playhouse in the Park, Porthouse Theatre, Arden Theatre Company, and Dobama Theatre. Film credits include *The Lifeguard*, *The Next Three Days*, directed by Paul Haggis, and *The Ides of March*, directed by George Clooney. Directing credits include *Intimate Apparel*, *Macbeth*, *Night Train to Bolina*, *Sunday in the Park with George*, *Measure for Measure*, *Dead Man Walking*, *Circle Mirror Transformation*, and the Midwest premiere of *Missionaries* for which he was a finalist for Northern Ohio Live! Magazine's Award of Achievement in Theatre. Professor Polanco received his MFA from Case Western Reserve University and his BA from Temple University.

Maria Porter is an actor, director, and teacher. As an actor she has performed in New York, regionally, and internationally. Maria is a master teacher of the Suzuki method of actor training, and has integrated it with other acting techniques to create an original pedagogy. Her work demonstrations and master classes in this pedagogy have been featured in festivals and conferences in Wales, Denmark, England, Cuba, Peru, Greece, Spain, and Switzerland. She has directed and co-created several ensemble-based performances, which have been featured in festivals in Italy, Canada, Prague, New York, Colombia, and Scotland. Maria received her MFA in Acting from the University of California, San Diego, and is a member of the Magdalena Project, an international network of women in theatre. She is on the faculty of Long Island University, where she is Director of Undergraduate Theatre Studies, and has received the David Newton Award for Excellence in Teaching.

Valerie Clayman Pye is an Assistant Professor of Theatre in the School of Performing Arts at LIU Post, where she teaches acting, voice and speech, and Shakespeare in Performance. She holds a PhD in Performance Practice, Drama, and an MFA in Staging Shakespeare from the University of Exeter, where she worked with Shakespeare's Globe and the Royal Shakespeare Company. Valerie's research focuses on actor training pedagogy, facilitating performances of heightened text, and on practice-as-research (PaR). She writes about the intersection between text and performance and on the dynamics of performance at Shakespeare's Globe. She also holds an MFA in Acting from Brooklyn College. Valerie is a professional actor and director whose work has reached audiences in over 20 countries. As a voice and speech coach, Valerie has worked in theatre, film, and television, coaching Academy, BAFTA, Emmy, and Golden Globe Award nominees. Valerie's publications include articles in *Methods: A Journal of Acting Pedagogy*, *Shakespeare*, and *The Voice and Speech Review*. Her book, *Unearthing Shakespeare: Embodied Performance and the Globe* was published by Routledge in January 2017. Valerie was named a 2018–20 LabWorks Artist at the New Victory Theatre in NYC, where she is developing *Shakespeare's Stars* along with Spellbound Theatre.

Dennis Schebetta is an actor, director, and writer in film and theatre. He is currently Assistant Professor at Skidmore College and has taught at Carnegie Mellon University, University of Pittsburgh, and Bellevue College. He holds an MFA in Theatre Pedagogy from Virginia Commonwealth University and also trained in New York City with William Esper, master teacher of the Meisner technique, in the two-year studio intensive program. His professional acting credits include Ensemble Studio Theater, Vital Theater, Pulse Ensemble Theater, Saratoga Shakespeare Company, Genesius Guild Theater, Northeast Theatre Ensemble, Pittsburgh Playhouse, The Hiawatha Project, and Off the Wall Theater. As a theatre director, he has directed productions off-off Broadway at Ensemble Studio Theatre, 29th Street Rep, and Brass Tacks Theatre. As a film director and award-winning writer, his short film *My Date with Adam* has been an official selection of several international film festivals such as New Filmmakers LA, New Filmmakers NYC, Boston Sci-Fi Festival, Phoenix International Film Festival, and the London Sci-Fi Film Festival. Visit www.dennischebetta.com

Kim Shively is an Assistant Professor in the Department of Performing Arts at Elon University where she teaches acting and directs. Kim is a member of Actors' Equity Association and SAG-AFTRA and has enjoyed a professional career in theatre, television, commercials, hosting, and voice-over. Professional credits include work with Shakespeare Orange County, Laguna Playhouse, and the Asolo Rep; roles on *Guiding Light, As the World Turns, The Young and the Restless, CSI: Miami*; and appearances in over a dozen national commercials both on camera and as a voice-over artist. Shively is Assistant Faculty for Theatrical Intimacy Education, an organization dedicated to training theatre professionals and students in best practices for theatrical intimacy work. As a director, Kim has worked for various organizations, developing and producing content. After teaching and coaching actors and professionals in Los Angeles for over a decade, Kim is passionate about training working actors who live dynamic, creative lives, and know how to shape culture through generating their own work and content.

Kim earned a BFA in Theatre Performance at Chapman University and an MFA at the FSU/Asolo Conservatory.

Nathan Stith holds a PhD in Theatre from the University of Colorado, Boulder. He is currently an Assistant Professor in the Department of Human Communication and Theatre at Trinity University, in San Antonio, Texas. Nathan teaches all levels of acting, musical theatre performance, musical theatre history, and voice and speech. Nathan is a member of Actor's Equity and SAG/AFTRA. Prior to returning to academia, he spent 15 years in New York, working as a director and actor, including national tours of *Romeo and Juliet*, *Jesus Christ Superstar*, and work in regional theatres across the country. His on-screen work includes numerous independent films and a recurring role on the daytime drama *One Life to Live*. Nathan is an Artistic Associate at Oldcastle Theatre Company in Bennington, Vermont, where he regularly performs, and has directed recent productions of *The 39 Steps* and *Brighton Beach Memoirs*.

Lesley-Ann Timlick has an MFA from University of California, Davis, and completed post-graduate study at the National Theatre Conservatory/National Center for Voice and Speech. She holds certifications in the Feldenkrais Method, Michael Chekhov Technique, and Meisner Technique. Lesley-Ann studied with vocal masters Kristin Linklater, Patsy Rodenburg, Arthur Lessac, Cecily Berry, Katherine Fitzmaurice, and Andrew Wade. She interned with Bonnie Raphael at the American Repertory Theatre at Harvard. She is an award-winning teacher and has worked professionally in both the US and Canada. Lesley-Ann has coached for such companies as the Colorado Shakespeare Festival, American Repertory Theatre at Harvard, Denver Center Theatre Company, Gables Stage, and New Theatre Miami. She has held positions on the Governing Council for the Association of Theatre and Higher Education and the board of the Association of Theatre Movement Educators. During her tenure at FIU, she has served as both the Chairperson/Artistic Director and Head of Acting Training.

Welker White is on faculty at Brooklyn College's MFA Acting Program, where she teaches acting on film. Through her company The Moving Frame, Welker brings screen acting workshops and intensives to training programs and artistic communities throughout the US and abroad. Welker has brought her teaching to students at NYU Graduate Acting, Brown/Trinity MFA Acting, Bowdoin College, The Actors Center, Drew University, Montclair State University BFA Acting, FSU/Asolo Acting Conservatory, The Atlantic Conservatory, The 16th Street Studio in Melbourne, Australia, Syracuse University's Tepper Semester, and many more. Welker has a long-standing presence in New York theatre and beyond, originating roles by major playwrights such as Lisa Kron, John Patrick Shanley, Craig Lucas, Sam Shepard,

Mac Wellman, Howard Korder, David Ives, Amy Freed, and Joanna Murray Smith. Welker's credits on film and television include *Goodfellas*, *Dead Poet's Society*, *Law and Order*, *Sex and the City*, *Eat Pray Love*, *This Is My Life*, *The Irishman*, and *Bad Education*. Welker holds an MFA in Directing from Brooklyn College, and a BS in Theatre Studies from CUNY, graduating *summa cum laude*. She has received many academic grants and awards, and is a proud member of SAG-AFTRA, AEA, and The Actors Center.

Abstracts

Part I Playing Objectives

Chapter 1

Money in your Pocket: Meisner, Objectives, and the First Six Lines

Dennis Schebetta

Keywords: Meisner, William Esper, Repetition, Improvisation

Taking Meisner's famous Repetition exercise further, Schebetta connects improvisation to the first six lines of scene work. By having students approach their scene as "an improvisation with text," he takes the pressure off the student perfecting the character objective, and focuses on play, which in this case is throwing "snowballs." Schebetta explores William Esper's perspective, "a good objective is like money in your pocket," which means "objectives are not something you can act … but actions are the specific building blocks of behavior upon which you achieve (or don't achieve) your objective."

Chapter 2

Psychological Gesture: Michael Chekhov Exercises on Physicalizing the Objective

Anjalee Deshpande Hutchinson

Keywords: Psychological Gesture, Michael Chekhov, Acting Technique, Archetypal Personae

Using one of Chekhov's most useful tools, Psychological Gesture, Hutchinson's essay explores ways in which actors can move from an archetypal metaphor to specific character psychology. "Psychological

Gesture: Michael Chekhov Exercises on Physicalizing the Objective" introduces ways to access creative impulses and manifest them in performance, and to circumvent the intellect as the actor's starting point. Hutchinson offers valuable insight to explore character objective through the physical imagination.

Chapter 3

Making Sport of Objectives: Teaching through Student-Developed Physical Competition

John Kaufmann

Keywords: Tactics, Original Scene Development, Physical Investment, Measure of Success

Kaufmann guides the reader through a multi-week acting assignment called the "Real Action Scene." Students develop an original scene that culminates in a genuine physical contest between the actors; they create characters, the context that brings them together, a "pre-game ritual" and rules of a game that either player could potentially win. "Making Sport of Objectives ..." steers actors toward physical investment, clear measures of success, and high stakes.

Chapter 4

Structured Improvised Scenes

Timothy Johnson

Keywords: Foundational Acting Tools, Improvisation, Igniting Playfulness, First day of class

Johnson's exercise is a perfect exploration for the first day of acting class, from beginning to advanced levels. "Structured Improvised Scenes" has students jump into exploring objectives, obstacles, tactics, and given circumstances using an improvised scenario. Johnson's exercise can span the first several class meetings as beginning students explore playful interactions of opposing objectives, and advanced students reignite the joy in their training.

Chapter 5

Scoring the Un-scorable

Maria Porter

Keywords: Scoring, Suzuki Method, Personal Metaphor, Drama-mapping, Label, Greek Drama

"Scoring the Un-scorable" addresses the challenges of working with heightened texts that don't conform easily to the demands of Stanislavski's method(s). In this essay, Porter reveals a highly original, systematic method of scoring texts, such as the Greeks, which eventually leads to objectives and actions. Along the way, actors discover elements that help them connect personally to heightened material in a fun, accessible way.

Chapter 6

Creating a Physical Score in a Snap: Using Social Media to Appeal to the Smartphone Generation

Tom Pacio

Keywords: Smartphone Use, Physical Score, Tableau Work, Social Media, Script Analysis

Starting with the premise that smartphone use and social media has changed the way stories are now told, "Creating a Physical Score in a Snap" capitalizes on acting students' digital expertise as an entryway into creating physical scores and scene work. This essay draws the connection between curating and labeling on Instagram and Snapchat with the imaginative work of given circumstances in character development. Pacio's work is cutting edge, accessible, and fun – it challenges the way we guide students to use their imagination and connects their daily technological experiences with acting technique.

Part II Overcoming Obstacles

Chapter 7

Engaging Obstacles

Kevin Hoffmann

Keywords: Counter Action, Spontaneous Givens, Imagined Obstacles, The Magic "But"

"Engaging Obstacles" offers a thorough primer on Stanislavski's concept of obstacle, and highlights how students can use strong obstacles to connect to objectives. Hoffman's exercises explore different aspects of activating the obstacle to increase actors' physical choices and heighten their investment in both the given and the imaginary circumstances. "Engaging Obstacles" acts as a lesson plan that combines theory with physical explorations that help the student viscerally discover the difference between strong and weak obstacles, and how they affect objectives.

Chapter 8

Active Obstacle Image Scoring

David Hugo

Keywords: Musical Theatre, Archetypal Gesture, Michael Chekhov, Solo Work, Physical Score, Imagery

In this essay, Hugo challenges the common practice of starting the actor's analysis by identifying the character's objective. Instead, he asks the vital question: what if the actor begins with an active image of their obstacle, and discovers their objective by fighting to overcome what's in their way? "Active Obstacle Image Scoring" offers an innovative way for the actor to work solo and to find organic responses to their work.

Chapter 9

Resistance

Janet Hayatshahi

Keywords: Physical Action, Reaction, Opposition, Motivation, Iben Nagel, Embodied Performance

Hayatshahi's "Resistance" exercise looks at actor motivation through a physically charged perspective, focusing not only on *action* but also on *reaction* using a *push and pull* method to activate the work. Based on the use of fabric in Iben Nagel's "Green Exercise," Hayatshahi adds components of text and vocalization, shifts in tempo, use of space, and creates vignettes to further experiment with scripted scene work. "Resistance" aims to give actors options for creating an embodied character.

Chapter 10

Returning the Dress: Demonstrating Objectives, Obstacles, and Tactics

Davida Bloom

Keywords: Beginning Acting Students, Improvisation, Empathy, Neuroscience, Sonia Moore, Magic If

Bloom's exercise introduces beginning acting students to the concepts of objectives, obstacles, and tactics through an improvised scenario, which she connects "control theory" and cognitive neuroscience. Two students explore a real-life scenario filled with conflict which leads to an embodied shift in tactics. Only after the completion of the exercise do the students learn that their actions were connected to the terminology set forth by Stanislavski.

Chapter 11

Improvised Fantasies: Heightening Objectives and Obstacles in Scene Work

Hillary Haft Bucs

Keywords: Improvisation, Scene Work, Robert Barton, Viola Spolin, Keith Johnstone

Haft Bucs adapts Robert Barton's "Rehearsed Futures" exercise into an improvisational exploration of fantasized scenic outcomes. "Improvised Fantasies" is both a playful and illuminating examination whereby one actor verbalizes and then improvises their character's fantasy: first, of the perfect outcome of achieving their objective, followed by the worst possible outcome. These improvisations bring the obstacle into greater resonance.

Chapter 12

Optimizing the Obstacle: Using Indicators of Csíkszentmihályi's Flow to Help Select, Test, and Experience Stanislavski's Obstacles

Fabio Polanco and Diane Bonfiglio

Keywords: Flow, Optimal Experience, Mihaly Csíkszentmihályi, Obstacle Cards

"Optimizing the Obstacle ..." focuses on how knowledge of flow and flow indicators can be used to help actors select, test, and bolster the effectiveness of obstacles. This chapter examines how Csíkszentmihályi's nine flow indicators apply to Stanislavki's teachings. Polanco and Bonfiglio introduce the use of Obstacle Cards, which teaches actors how properly calibrating the balance between the objective/task and the obstacle can lead to more dynamic and engaging performances.

Part III Identifying Tactics

Chapter 13

The Tag-tic that Works

Lynn Deboeck

Keywords: Warm-up, Play, Freeze Tag, Viewpoints, Improvisation

Deboeck reveals the hidden potential in the simple game, tag, that can unlock student actors' inhibitions in order to help the creative process proceed, unhindered. Using psychology, evolutionary theory, and first-hand experiential data, the game of tag is shown to offer not only a simple inroad to creative work, but a system of play that can, and does, serve as a complete warm-up for the actor's instrument.

Chapter 14

Improvising Tactical Choices Based on Status or "Who's Driving the Dramatic Action Bus?"

Jean Dobie Giebel

Keywords: Beat Shifts, Johnstone's Status, Spolin's Orientation, Stanislavski's Units of Action, Dramatic Structure

Giebel takes students through a series of exercises that combine the collaborative and imaginative work of Viola Spolin with Keith Johnstone's concept of status to explore the conflict shifts within dramatic structure. The exercise's goal is to help students transition from improvisation to text analysis through the process of identifying the status shifts in beat changes. Defining beats through status explorations allows students to improvise moment-to-moment tactical choices, build collaboration and infuse improvisational play into their out-of-class rehearsal process.

Chapter 15

Transformational Tactics: Engaging Students in the Heroic Pursuit of Their Objective

Kim Shively

Keywords: Meisner, Point of View (POV), Repetition, Side-Coaching

Shively expands on the work of Sanford Meisner through Point of View (POV), the lens through which a character sees the world, which transforms them into the hero of their own story and enables the actor to respond truthfully in the moment. This chapter chronicles a methodology of side-coaching, influenced by the "Repetition" exercise, which promotes tactical shifts. "Transformational Tactics: Engaging Students in the Heroic Pursuit of Their Objective" is valuable, not only for scene study, but for auditions and on-camera acting.

Chapter 16

Hunter/Hunted: Experiential Learning and the Actor's Craft

Valerie Clayman Pye

Keywords: Play, Beat Change, Clive Barker, Rose Bonczek, Experiential Learning

Without ever mentioning Stanislavski's terms, Pye's version of "Hunter/Hunted" allows students to experience the foundation of the actor's craft in a visceral, high-stakes way. "Hunter/Hunted: Experiential Learning and the Actor's Craft" reveals the differences between beat changes and tactic changes and provides touchpoints that can be returned to when working with scripted text. Suitable for actors at all levels, this exercise will also help to reveal how emotion is released as a by-product of an actor's full commitment to their objective, especially when that objective is confronted with an obstacle.

Chapter 17

Tactics and Action Drives: Stanislavski Meets Laban

Conrad Alexandrowicz

Keywords: Rudolph Laban, Action Drives, Physical Theatre, Post-dramatic Theatre

In this essay, Alexandrowicz considers the disruptive division often found between acting, voice, and movement as separate, rather than integrated, disciplines. "Tactics and Action Drives: Stanislavski Meets Laban" demonstrates deliberate ways to integrate the work of Rudolph Laban in the acting studio. Alexandrowicz offers practical explorations that enable actors to experience space, time, and weight, and to integrate Laban's action drives into their work.

Chapter 18

Stanislavski in the Voice Studio

Deric McNish

Keywords: Voice, Speech, Holistic Actor Training, Integration, Louis Colaianni

"Stanislavski in the Voice Studio" explores the reciprocal relationship between Stanislavski's system and voice training and the benefits of their mutual connection. McNish includes innovative adaptions of the "Exaggeration Circle" and Louis Colaianni's "Phonetic Pillow" technique to playfully and actively guide students to connect sound with playable tactics in order to achieve an objective. "Stanislavski in the Voice Studio" provides instructors with simple solutions to bring objective work into vocal warm-ups and vocal intention to their work with objectives.

Chapter 19

Stimulating Embodied Tactical Actions

Lesley-Ann Timlick

Keywords: Feldenkrais, Chekhov, Laban, Voice, Speech, Movement

This chapter introduces the premise of the "six cardinal directions," and how multi-dimensional explorations of the body can lead to complex explorations of text. Timlick focuses on exercises that integrate movement, breath, sound, and text adapted from and influenced by the work of Feldenkrais, Laban, and Michael Chekhov. Featuring specific scripts for the instructor to follow, these explorations help students increase their use of tactics vocal and physical changes connected to time, space, and imagination.

Chapter 20

NRGs and the Nature of Action: The Lessac Tactic Circle

Caroline Good

Keywords: Lessac's Body NRGs, Potency, Buoyancy, Radiancy, Tactic Circle, Physical Behavior

Good presents an overview of Lessac's body NRGs (pronounced "energies") of *potency*, *buoyancy*, and *radiancy*, and demonstrates ways to apply them to pursuing an objective. Her exercise, "The Lessac Tactic Circle" incorporates Lessac's NRGs to inform and enhance a variety of tactics, to galvanize the interactive connection between scene partners, and to reactivate the actor. Instructors will discover specific tools to guide actors to play along the spectrum of the specific physical and vocal behavior possibilities that live within each tactic.

Chapter 21

Relaying Action – from Breath to Text

Aaron Alpern and Rebecca Covey

Keywords: Breath, Voice, Speech, Sound Exchange, Smartphone Integration

Alpern and Covey have created a synergy of exercises that playfully combine voice and breath work with playable tactics. This chapter features the "Tactic Verb Relay" and other exercises that incorporate partner work, to solidify the progressive connection between breath, sound, text, and playable actions. "Relaying Action – from Breath to Text" includes ready-to-go lesson plans for students with a range of experience.

Chapter 22

Using Improvisation to Identify Tactics

Nathan Stith

Keywords: Improvisation, Robert Cohen, Content-less Dialogue

Stith's chapter focuses on a series of three improvisational exercises, the final one adapted from Robert Cohen's exercise, "One Two Three Four Five Six Seven." These exercises aim to explore multiple tactics in pursuit of a single objective by improvising, picking objectives out of a hat, and ending with content-less dialogue. "Using Improvisation to Identify Tactics" is geared for beginning acting students and non-majors to help them engage playfully with their scene partner and find a variety of playable tactics.

Chapter 23

Activating the Actor with Game Theory: Using Gamification to Create Playable Tactics on Stage

Jeanne Leep

Keywords: Play, Improvisation, Game Theory, Scripted Work, Spolin, Johnstone

Leep brings game playing and game theory to the rehearsal process to invigorate scripted scene work. Through improvisation, Leep explores how matching the right exploration/game (such as Spolin's "Contact Exercise") with a particular beat in a scene reveals a myriad of tactics to play. In addition, the act of playing games with scripted work "lowers the stakes for the players, and ultimately enhances the scene."

Afterword

Chapter 24

Recording Truth: The Camera in Acting Training

Welker White

Keywords: On-camera Acting, Personal Agency, Diagnostic Tools, Observation, Smartphone Integration

"Recording Truth: The Camera in Acting Training" illuminates how the camera can be a powerful diagnostic tool for both instructors and students alike. Using just the technology in our pockets, actors can discover how an actor's choices shape our storytelling, and empowers students to assess and evaluate their own work. This chapter includes two partnered exercises: "60-Second Observation" and "Storytelling," which are recorded with an actor's cell phone and then played back along with guided discussion. In this essay, White offers a useful and innovative examination of how visual cinematic storytelling, and the camera itself, can enhance classroom methods and help the actor to practice 'living truthfully' within their given circumstances.

Index